Suzuki
GS/GSX 550
4-valve Fours
Owners
Workshop
Manual

by Pete Shoemark
with an additional Chapter on the 1986 to 1988 models
by Penny Cox

Models covered
GS550 E. US February 1983 to 1985
GSX550 E. UK March 1984 to January 1988
GS550 ES. US February 1983 to 1986
GSX550 ES. UK April 1983 to December 1988
GSX550 EF. UK March 1984 to January 1988
GS550 L. US October 1982 to 1986

All models are fitted with a 572 cc dohc engine

(1133 – 602)   ABCDE
                 FGHIJ
                 KLMNO
                 PQR

Haynes Publishing Group
Sparkford Nr Yeovil
Somerset BA22 7JJ England

Haynes Publications, Inc
861 Lawrence Drive
Newbury Park
California 91320 USA

Acknowledgements

Our thanks are due to Fran Ridewood and Co of Wells, Somerset, who supplied the GSX550 ESD model featured in this manual.

The Avon Rubber Company supplied information on tyre care and fitting, and NGK Spark Plugs (UK) Ltd provided information on plug maintenance and electrode conditions.

A book in the **Haynes Owners Workshop Manual Series**

Printed by J.H. Haynes & Co. Ltd, Sparkford, Nr Yeovil, Somerset BA22 7JJ, England

ISBN 1 85010 593 6

Library of Congress Catalog Card Number 89-80125

British Library Cataloguing in Publication Data

Shoemark, Pete, *1952–*
Suzuki GS/GSX 550 4 – valve fours owners
workshop manual
1. Motorcycles. Maintenance & repair.
Amateurs' manuals
I. Title   II. Cox, Penny, *1962–*
III. Series
629.28'775
ISBN 1-85010-593-6

Contents

Left-hand view of the UK Suzuki GSX550 ESD model

Right-hand view of the US Suzuki GS550 ESE model

About this manual

The purpose of this manual is to present the owner with a concise and graphic guide which will enable him to tackle any operation from basic routine maintenance to a major overhaul. It has been assumed that any work would be undertaken without the luxury of a well-equipped workshop and a range of manufacturer's service tools.

To this end, the machine featured in the manual was stripped and rebuilt in our own workshop, by a team comprising a mechanic, a photographer and the author. The resulting photographic sequence depicts events as they took place, the hands shown being those of the author and the mechanic.

The use of specialised, and expensive, service tools was avoided unless their use was considered to be essential due to risk of breakage or injury. There is usually some way of improvising a method of removing a stubborn component, providing that a suitable degree of care is exercised.

The author learnt his motorcycle mechanics over a number of years, faced with the same difficulties and using similar facilities to those encountered by most owners. It is hoped that this practical experience can be passed on through the pages of this manual.

Where possible, a well-used example of the machine is chosen for the workshop project, as this highlights any areas which might be particularly prone to giving rise to problems. In this way, any such difficulties are encountered and resolved before the text is written, and the techniques used to deal with them can be incorporated in the relevant section. Armed with a working knowledge of the machine, the author undertakes a considerable amount of research in order that the maximum amount of data can be included in the manual.

A comprehensive section, preceding the main part of the manual, describes procedures for carrying out the routine maintenance of the machine at intervals of time and mileage. This section is included particularly for those owners who wish to ensure the efficient day-to-day running of their motorcycle, but who choose not to undertake overhaul or renovation work.

Each Chapter is divided into numbered sections. Within these sections are numbered paragraphs. Cross reference throughout the manual is quite straightforward and logical. When reference is made 'See Section 6.10' it means Section 6, paragraph 10 in the same Chapter. If another Chapter were intended, the reference would read, for example, 'See Chapter 2, Section 6.10'. All the photographs are captioned with a section/paragraph number to which they refer and are relevant to the Chapter text adjacent.

Figures (usually line illustrations) appear in a logical but numerical order, within a given Chapter. Fig. 1.1 therefore refers to the first figure in Chapter 1.

Left-hand and right-hand descriptions of the machines and their components refer to the left and right of a given machine when the rider is seated normally.

Motorcycle manufacturers continually make changes to specifications and recommendations, and these, when notified, are incorporated into our manuals at the earliest opportunity.

Introduction to the Suzuki GS/GSX 550 models

The 550 cc four-valve Suzuki fours, known as GS models in the US and as GSX models in the UK, are developments of the earlier and successful GS/GSX 1000 and 1100 range. The engine and gearbox design is generally very similar to that of the larger models, the main departure being the adoption of a plain bearing crankshaft in place of the earlier all-roller design. In common with their predecessors, the 550 models make use of a four valve combustion chamber cylinder head design.

In the patented TSCC (Twin Swirl Combustion Chamber) arrangement Suzuki have taken advantage of the benefits of better cylinder filling conferred by a four-valve design. In addition, the combustion chamber has been carefully shaped to provoke turbulence. This in conjunction with the central placing of the spark plug and the shallow valve angle ensures rapid and even burning of the fuel/air mixture, enhancing the efficiency of the engine.

Four basic model types are produced, starting with a handlebar faired model, a half fairing model and a fully faired version. In addition, the L models provide a Custom-styled variant. In line with current styling trends, much of the frame is constructed from square section steel tubing, finished in silver to resemble the works racing frames. Front suspension is by conventional telescopic fork, some models featuring anti-dive units. Rear suspension is by Suzuki's rising-rate fully floating cantilever arrangement.

All models covered in this manual are identified by their model suffix letter, which relates to the codes issued by Suzuki for each production year. Modified versions of these models have been introduced over the years and it is therefore important that the machine is identified exactly, not only when using this manual but also when ordering spare parts. Given below is a list of all models, the initial frame number with which each version's production run commenced and the approximate dates of import. Note that the latter may not necessarily coincide with the machine's date of registration.

UK models	Initial frame no.	Dates of import	
GSX550 EE	GN71D-105088	Mar '84 – Jan '88	
GSX550 ESD	GN71D-100001	Apr '83 – 1984	
GSX550 ESE	GN71D-105088	1984 – Mar '86	
GSX550 EFE	GN71D-105088	Mar '84 – Jan '88	

US models	Initial frame no.	Dates of import	Model year
GS550 ED	JS1GN74A D2100001	Feb '83 – Dec '83	1983
GS550 EF	JS1GN74A F2100001	Jul '84 – 1985	1985
GS550 ESD	JS1GN74A D2100001	Feb '83 – Dec '83	1983
GS550 ESE	JS1GN74A F2100001	Feb '84 – Dec '84	1984
GS550 ES3	JS1GN74A D2105921	Feb '84 – Dec '84	1984
GS550 ESF	JS1GN74A F2100001	Jul '84 – 1985	1985
GS550 LD	JS1GN72L D2100001	Oct '82 – 1983	1983
GS550 LF	JS1GN72L F2100001	Jul '84 – 1985	1985

Refer to Chapter 7 for information relating to the GSX550 ESG, ESH, and the GS550 ESG, LG models.

Model dimensions and weights

UK GSX550 models

	UK ESD, ESE, EFE	UK EE model
Overall length	2120 mm (83.5 in)	2120 mm (83.5 in)
Overall width	770 mm (30.3 in)	550 mm (21.7 in)
Overall height	1175 mm (46.3 in)	1110 mm (43.7 in)
Wheelbase	1420 mm (55.9 in)	1420 mm (55.9 in)
Ground clearance	155 mm (6.1 in)	155 mm (6.1 in)
Seat height	785 mm (30.9 in)	N/Av
Dry weight .... ESE:	194 kg (427.8 lb)	192 kg (423.4 lb)
EFE:	196 kg (432.2 lb)	

US GS550 models

Overall length:
ED, ESD, ESE, ES3, EF, ESF .... 2120 mm (83.5 in)
LD, LF .... 2085 mm (82.1 in)
Overall width:
ED, EF .... 750 mm (29.5 in)
ESD, ESE, ES3, ESF .... 770 mm (30.3 in)
LD, LF .... 880 mm (34.6 in)
Overall height:
ED, EF .... 1110 mm (43.7 in)
ESD, ESE, ES3, ESF .... 1175 mm (46.3 in)
LD, LF .... 1150 mm (45.3 in)
Wheelbase:
ED, ESD, ESE, ES3, EF, ESF .... 1420 mm (55.9 in)
LD, LF .... 1445 mm (56.9 in)
Ground clearance:
ED, ESD, ESE, ES3, EF, ESF .... 155 mm (6.1 in)
LD, LF .... 145 mm (5.7 in)
Seat height:
ED, ESD, ESE, ES3, EF, ESF .... 785 mm (30.9 in)
LD, LF .... 760 mm (29.9 in)
Dry weight:
ED, EF .... 192 kg (423.4 lb)
ESD, ESE, ES3, ESF .... 194 kg (427.8 lb)
LD, LF .... 186 kg (410.1 lb)

Ordering spare parts

When ordering spare parts for any Suzuki model it is advisable to deal direct with an official Suzuki dealer who will be able to supply most items ex-stock. Where parts have to be ordered, an authorised dealer will be able to obtain them as quickly as possible. The engine and frame numbers must always be quoted in full. This avoids the risk of incorrect parts being supplied and is particularly important where detail modifications have been made in the middle of production runs. In some instances it will be necessary for the dealer to check compatibility of later parts designs with earlier models. The frame number is stamped into the steering head and the engine number on a raised boss on the crankcase.

It is recommended that genuine Suzuki parts are used. Although pattern parts are often cheaper, remember that there is no guarantee that they are of the same specification as the original, and in some instances may be positively dangerous. Note also that the use of non-standard parts may invalidate the warranty in the event of a subsequent failure.

Some of the more expendable parts such as oils, greases, spark plugs, tyres and bulbs, can safely be obtained from auto accessory shops. These are often more conveniently located and may open during weekends. It is also possible to obtain parts on a mail order basis from specialists who advertise in the motorcycle magazines.

Engine number is stamped into boss above clutch cover

Frame number is stamped on side of steering head

Safety first!

Professional motor mechanics are trained in safe working procedures. However enthusiastic you may be about getting on with the job in hand, do take the time to ensure that your safety is not put at risk. A moment's lack of attention can result in an accident, as can failure to observe certain elementary precautions.

There will always be new ways of having accidents, and the following points do not pretend to be a comprehensive list of all dangers; they are intended rather to make you aware of the risks and to encourage a safety-conscious approach to all work you carry out on your vehicle.

Essential DOs and DON'Ts

DON'T rely on a single jack when working underneath the vehicle. Always use reliable additional means of support, such as axle stands, securely placed under a part of the vehicle that you know will not give way.

DON'T attempt to loosen or tighten high-torque nuts (e.g. wheel hub nuts) while the vehicle is on a jack; it may be pulled off.

DON'T start the engine without first ascertaining that the transmission is in neutral (or 'Park' where applicable) and the parking brake applied.

DON'T suddenly remove the filler cap from a hot cooling system – cover it with a cloth and release the pressure gradually first, or you may get scalded by escaping coolant.

DON'T attempt to drain oil until you are sure it has cooled sufficiently to avoid scalding you.

DON'T grasp any part of the engine, exhaust or catalytic converter without first ascertaining that it is sufficiently cool to avoid burning you.

DON'T allow brake fluid or antifreeze to contact vehicle paintwork.

DON'T syphon toxic liquids such as fuel, brake fluid or antifreeze by mouth, or allow them to remain on your skin.

DON'T inhale dust – it may be injurious to health (see *Asbestos* below).

DON'T allow any spilt oil or grease to remain on the floor – wipe it up straight away, before someone slips on it.

DON'T use ill-fitting spanners or other tools which may slip and cause injury.

DON'T attempt to lift a heavy component which may be beyond your capability – get assistance.

DON'T rush to finish a job, or take unverified short cuts.

DON'T allow children or animals in or around an unattended vehicle.

DO wear eye protection when using power tools such as drill, sander, bench grinder etc, and when working under the vehicle.

DO use a barrier cream on your hands prior to undertaking dirty jobs – it will protect your skin from infection as well as making the dirt easier to remove afterwards; but make sure your hands aren't left slippery. Note that long-term contact with used engine oil can be a health hazard.

DO keep loose clothing (cuffs, tie etc) and long hair well out of the way of moving mechanical parts.

DO remove rings, wristwatch etc, before working on the vehicle – especially the electrical system.

DO ensure that any lifting tackle used has a safe working load rating adequate for the job.

DO keep your work area tidy – it is only too easy to fall over articles left lying around.

DO get someone to check periodically that all is well, when working alone on the vehicle.

DO carry out work in a logical sequence and check that everything is correctly assembled and tightened afterwards.

DO remember that your vehicle's safety affects that of yourself and others. If in doubt on any point, get specialist advice.

IF, in spite of following these precautions, you are unfortunate enough to injure yourself, seek medical attention as soon as possible.

Asbestos

Certain friction, insulating, sealing, and other products – such as brake linings, brake bands, clutch linings, torque converters, gaskets, etc – contain asbestos. *Extreme care must be taken to avoid inhalation of dust from such products since it is hazardous to health.* If in doubt, assume that they *do* contain asbestos.

Fire

Remember at all times that petrol (gasoline) is highly flammable. Never smoke, or have any kind of naked flame around, when working on the vehicle. But the risk does not end there – a spark caused by an electrical short-circuit, by two metal surfaces contacting each other, by careless use of tools, or even by static electricity built up in your body under certain conditions, can ignite petrol vapour, which in a confined space is highly explosive.

Always disconnect the battery earth (ground) terminal before working on any part of the fuel or electrical system, and never risk spilling fuel on to a hot engine or exhaust.

It is recommended that a fire extinguisher of a type suitable for fuel and electrical fires is kept handy in the garage or workplace at all times. Never try to extinguish a fuel or electrical fire with water.

Note: *Any reference to a 'torch' appearing in this manual should always be taken to mean a hand-held battery-operated electric lamp or flashlight. It does NOT mean a welding/gas torch or blowlamp.*

Fumes

Certain fumes are highly toxic and can quickly cause unconsciousness and even death if inhaled to any extent. Petrol (gasoline) vapour comes into this category, as do the vapours from certain solvents such as trichloroethylene. Any draining or pouring of such volatile fluids should be done in a well ventilated area.

When using cleaning fluids and solvents, read the instructions carefully. Never use materials from unmarked containers – they may give off poisonous vapours.

Never run the engine of a motor vehicle in an enclosed space such as a garage. Exhaust fumes contain carbon monoxide which is extremely poisonous; if you need to run the engine, always do so in the open air or at least have the rear of the vehicle outside the workplace.

If you are fortunate enough to have the use of an inspection pit, never drain or pour petrol, and never run the engine, while the vehicle is standing over it; the fumes, being heavier than air, will concentrate in the pit with possibly lethal results.

The battery

Never cause a spark, or allow a naked light, near the vehicle's battery. It will normally be giving off a certain amount of hydrogen gas, which is highly explosive.

Always disconnect the battery earth (ground) terminal before working on the fuel or electrical systems.

If possible, loosen the filler plugs or cover when charging the battery from an external source. Do not charge at an excessive rate or the battery may burst.

Take care when topping up and when carrying the battery. The acid electrolyte, even when diluted, is very corrosive and should not be allowed to contact the eyes or skin.

If you ever need to prepare electrolyte yourself, always add the acid slowly to the water, and never the other way round. Protect against splashes by wearing rubber gloves and goggles.

When jump starting a car using a booster battery, for negative earth (ground) vehicles, connect the jump leads in the following sequence: First connect one jump lead between the positive (+) terminals of the two batteries. Then connect the other jump lead first to the negative (−) terminal of the booster battery, and then to a good earthing (ground) point on the vehicle to be started, at least 18 in (45 cm) from the battery if possible. Ensure that hands and jump leads are clear of any moving parts, and that the two vehicles do not touch. Disconnect the leads in the reverse order.

Mains electricity

When using an electric power tool, inspection light etc, which works from the mains, always ensure that the appliance is correctly connected to its plug and that, where necessary, it is properly earthed (grounded). Do not use such appliances in damp conditions and, again, beware of creating a spark or applying excessive heat in the vicinity of fuel or fuel vapour.

Ignition HT voltage

A severe electric shock can result from touching certain parts of the ignition system, such as the HT leads, when the engine is running or being cranked, particularly if components are damp or the insulation is defective. Where an electronic ignition system is fitted, the HT voltage is much higher and could prove fatal.

Tools and working facilities

The first priority when undertaking maintenance or repair work of any sort on a motorcycle is to have a clean, dry, well-lit working area. Work carried out in peace and quiet in the well-ordered atmosphere of a good workshop will give more satisfaction and much better results than can usually be achieved in poor working conditions. A good workshop must have a clean flat workbench or a solidly constructed table of convenient working height. The workbench or table should be equipped with a vice which has a jaw opening of at least 4 in (100 mm). A set of jaw covers should be made from soft metal such as aluminium alloy or copper, or from wood. These covers will minimise the marking or damaging of soft or delicate components which may be clamped in the vice. Some clean, dry, storage space will be required for tools, lubricants and dismantled components. It will be necessary during a major overhaul to lay out engine/gearbox components for examination and to keep them where they will remain undisturbed for as long as is necessary. To this end it is recommended that a supply of metal or plastic containers of suitable size is collected. A supply of clean, lint-free, rags for cleaning purposes and some newspapers, other rags, or paper towels for mopping up spillages should also be kept. If working on a hard concrete floor note that both the floor and one's knees can be protected from oil spillages and wear by cutting open a large cardboard box and spreading it flat on the floor under the machine or workbench. This also helps to provide some warmth in winter and to prevent the loss of nuts, washers, and other tiny components which have a tendency to disappear when dropped on anything other than a perfectly clean, flat, surface.

Unfortunately, such working conditions are not always available to the home mechanic. When working in poor conditions it is essential to take extra time and care to ensure that the components being worked on are kept scrupulously clean and to ensure that no components or tools are lost or damaged.

A selection of good tools is a fundamental requirement for anyone contemplating the maintenance and repair of a motor vehicle. For the owner who does not possess any, their purchase will prove a considerable expense, offsetting some of the savings made by doing-it-yourself. However, provided that the tools purchased are of good quality, they will last for many years and prove an extremely worthwhile investment.

To help the average owner to decide which tools are needed to carry out the various tasks detailed in this manual, we have compiled three lists of tools under the following headings: *Maintenance and minor repair, Repair and overhaul,* and *Specialized.* The newcomer to practical mechanics should start off with the simpler jobs around the vehicle. Then, as his confidence and experience grow, he can undertake more difficult tasks, buying extra tools as and when they are needed. In this way, a *Maintenance and minor repair* tool kit can be built-up into a *Repair and overhaul* tool kit over a considerable period of time without any major cash outlays. The experienced home mechanic will have a tool kit good enough for most repair and overhaul procedures and will add tools from the specialized category when he feels the expense is justified by the amount of use these tools will be put to.

It is obviously not possible to cover the subject of tools fully here. For those who wish to learn more about tools and their use there is a book entitled *Motorcycle Workshop Practice Manual* available from the publishers of this manual.

As a general rule, it is better to buy the more expensive, good quality tools. Given reasonable use, such tools will last for a very long time, whereas the cheaper, poor quality, item will wear out faster and need to be renewed more often, thus nullifying the original saving. There is also the risk of a poor quality tool breaking while in use, causing personal injury or expensive damage to the component being worked on. It should be noted, however, that many car accessory shops and the large department stores sell tools of reasonable quality at competitive prices. The best example of this is found with socket sets, where a medium-priced socket set will be quite adequate for the home owner and yet prove less expensive than a selection of individual sockets and accessories. This is because individual pieces are usually only available from expensive, top quality, ranges and whilst they are undeniably good, it should be remembered that they are intended for professional use.

The basis of any toolkit is a set of spanners. While open-ended spanners with their slim jaws, are useful for working on awkwardly-positioned nuts, ring spanners have advantages in that they grip the nut far more positively. There is less risk of the spanner slipping off the nut and damaging it, for this reason alone ring spanners are to be preferred. Ideally, the home mechanic should acquire a set of each, but if expense rules this out a set of combination spanners (open-ended at one end and with a ring of the same size at the other) will provide a good compromise. Another item which is so useful it should be considered an essential requirement for any home mechanic is a set of socket spanners. These are available in a variety of drive sizes. It is recommended that the ½-inch drive type is purchased to begin with as although bulkier and more expensive than the ⅜-inch type, the larger size is far more common and will accept a greater variety of torque wrenches, extension pieces and socket sizes. The socket set should comprise sockets of sizes between 8 and 24 mm, a reversible ratchet drive, an extension bar of about 10 inches in length, a spark plug socket with a rubber insert, and a universal joint. Other attachments can be added to the set at a later date.

Maintenance and minor repair tool kit

Set of spanners 8 – 24 mm
Set of sockets and attachments
Spark plug spanner with rubber insert – 10, 12, or 14 mm as appropriate
Adjustable spanner
C-spanner/pin spanner
Torque wrench (same size drive as sockets)
Set of screwdrivers (flat blade)
Set of screwdrivers (cross-head)
Set of Allen keys 4 – 10 mm
Impact screwdriver and bits
Ball pein hammer – 2 lb
Hacksaw (junior)
Self-locking pliers – Mole grips or vice grips
Pliers – combination
Pliers – needle nose
Wire brush (small)
Soft-bristled brush
Tyre pump
Tyre pressure gauge
Tyre tread depth gauge
Oil can
Fine emery cloth
Funnel (medium size)
Drip tray
Grease gun
Set of feeler gauges
Brake bleeding kit
Strobe timing light
Continuity tester (dry battery and bulb)
Soldering iron and solder
Wire stripper or craft knife
PVC insulating tape
Assortment of split pins, nuts, bolts, and washers

Repair and overhaul toolkit

The tools in this list are virtually essential for anyone undertaking major repairs to a motorcycle and are additional to the tools listed above. Concerning Torx driver bits, Torx screws are encountered on some of the more modern machines where their use is restricted to fastening certain components inside the engine/gearbox unit. It is therefore recommended that if Torx bits cannot be borrowed from a local dealer, they are purchased individually as the need arises. They are not in regular use in the motor trade and will therefore only be available in specialist tool shops.

Plastic or rubber soft-faced mallet
Torx driver bits
Pliers – electrician's side cutters
Circlip pliers – internal (straight or right-angled tips are available)
Circlip pliers – external
Cold chisel
Centre punch
Pin punch
Scriber
Scraper (made from soft metal such as aluminium or copper)
Soft metal drift
Steel rule/straight edge

Assortment of files
Electric drill and bits
Wire brush (large)
Soft wire brush (similar to those used for cleaning suede shoes)
Sheet of plate glass
Hacksaw (large)
Valve grinding tool
Valve grinding compound (coarse and fine)
Stud extractor set (E-Z out)

Specialized tools

This is not a list of the tools made by the machine's manufacturer to carry out a specific task on a limited range of models. Occasional references are made to such tools in the text of this manual and, in general, an alternative method of carrying out the task without the manufacturer's tool is given where possible. The tools mentioned in this list are those which are not used regularly and are expensive to buy in view of their infrequent use. Where this is the case it may be possible to hire or borrow the tools against a deposit from a local dealer or tool hire shop. An alternative is for a group of friends or a motorcycle club to join in the purchase.

Valve spring compressor
Piston ring compressor
Universal bearing puller
Cylinder bore honing attachment (for electric drill)
Micrometer set
Vernier calipers
Dial gauge set
Cylinder compression gauge
Vacuum gauge set
Multimeter
Dwell meter/tachometer

Care and maintenance of tools

Whatever the quality of the tools purchased, they will last much longer if cared for. This means in practice ensuring that a tool is used for its intended purpose; for example screwdrivers should not be used as a substitute for a centre punch, or as chisels. Always remove dirt or grease and any metal particles but remember that a light film of oil will prevent rusting if the tools are infrequently used. The common tools can be kept together in a large box or tray but the more delicate, and more expensive, items should be stored separately where they cannot be damaged. When a tool is damaged or worn out, be sure to renew it immediately. It is false economy to continue to use a worn spanner or screwdriver which may slip and cause expensive damage to the component being worked on.

Fastening systems

Fasteners, basically, are nuts, bolts and screws used to hold two or more parts together. There are a few things to keep in mind when working with fasteners. Almost all of them use a locking device of some type; either a lock washer, lock nut, locking tab or thread adhesive. All threaded fasteners should be clean, straight, have undamaged threads and undamaged corners on the hexagon head where the spanner fits. Develop the habit of replacing all damaged nuts and bolts with new ones.

Rusted nuts and bolts should be treated with a rust penetrating fluid to ease removal and prevent breakage. After applying the rust penetrant, let it 'work' for a few minutes before trying to loosen the nut or bolt. Badly rusted fasteners may have to be chiseled off or removed with a special nut breaker, available at tool shops.

Flat washers and lock washers, when removed from an assembly should always be replaced exactly as removed. Replace any damaged washers with new ones. Always use a flat washer between a lock washer and any soft metal surface (such as aluminium), thin sheet metal or plastic. Special lock nuts can only be used once or twice before they lose their locking ability and must be renewed.

If a bolt or stud breaks off in an assembly, it can be drilled out and removed with a special tool called an E-Z out. Most dealer service departments and motorcycle repair shops can perform this task, as well as others (such as the repair of threaded holes that have been stripped out).

Spanner size comparison

Jaw gap (in)	Spanner size	Jaw gap (in)	Spanner size
0.250	$\frac{1}{4}$ in AF	0.945	24 mm
0.276	7 mm	1.000	1 in AF
0.313	$\frac{5}{16}$ in AF	1.010	$\frac{9}{16}$ in Whitworth; $\frac{5}{8}$ in BSF
0.315	8 mm	1.024	26 mm
0.344	$\frac{11}{32}$ in AF; $\frac{1}{8}$ in Whitworth	1.063	$1\frac{1}{16}$ in AF; 27 mm
0.354	9 mm	1.100	$\frac{5}{16}$ in Whitworth; $\frac{11}{16}$ in BSF
0.375	$\frac{3}{8}$ in AF	1.125	$1\frac{1}{8}$ in AF
0.394	10 mm	1.181	30 mm
0.433	11 mm	1.200	$\frac{11}{16}$ in Whitworth; $\frac{3}{4}$ in BSF
0.438	$\frac{7}{16}$ in AF	1.250	$1\frac{1}{4}$ in AF
0.445	$\frac{3}{8}$ in Whitworth; $\frac{1}{4}$ in BSF	1.260	32 mm
0.472	12 mm	1.300	$\frac{3}{4}$ in Whitworth; $\frac{7}{8}$ in BSF
0.500	$\frac{1}{2}$ in AF	1.313	$1\frac{5}{16}$ in AF
0.512	13 mm	1.390	$\frac{13}{16}$ in Whitworth; $\frac{15}{16}$ in BSF
0.525	$\frac{1}{4}$ in Whitworth; $\frac{5}{16}$ in BSF	1.417	36 mm
0.551	14 mm	1.438	$1\frac{7}{16}$ in AF
0.563	$\frac{9}{16}$ in AF	1.480	$\frac{7}{8}$ in Whitworth; 1 in BSF
0.591	15 mm	1.500	$1\frac{1}{2}$ in AF
0.600	$\frac{5}{16}$ in Whitworth; $\frac{3}{8}$ in BSF	1.575	40 mm; $\frac{15}{16}$ in Whitworth
0.625	$\frac{5}{8}$ in AF	1.614	41 mm
0.630	16 mm	1.625	$1\frac{5}{8}$ in AF
0.669	17 mm	1.670	1 in Whitworth; $1\frac{1}{8}$ in BSF
0.686	$\frac{11}{16}$ in AF	1.688	$1\frac{11}{16}$ in AF
0.709	18 mm	1.811	46 mm
0.710	$\frac{3}{8}$ in Whitworth; $\frac{7}{16}$ in BSF	1.813	$1\frac{13}{16}$ in AF
0.748	19 mm	1.860	$1\frac{1}{8}$ in Whitworth; $1\frac{1}{4}$ in BSF
0.750	$\frac{3}{4}$ in AF	1.875	$1\frac{7}{8}$ in AF
0.813	$\frac{13}{16}$ in AF	1.969	50 mm
0.820	$\frac{7}{16}$ in Whitworth; $\frac{1}{2}$ in BSF	2.000	2 in AF
0.866	22 mm	2.050	$1\frac{1}{4}$ in Whitworth; $1\frac{3}{8}$ in BSF
0.875	$\frac{7}{8}$ in AF	2.165	55 mm
0.920	$\frac{1}{2}$ in Whitworth; $\frac{9}{16}$ in BSF	2.362	60 mm
0.938	$\frac{15}{16}$ in AF		

Standard torque settings

Specific torque settings will be found at the end of the specifications section of each chapter. Where no figure is given, bolts should be secured according to the table below.

Fastener type (thread diameter)	kgf m	lbf ft
5mm bolt or nut	0.45 – 0.6	3.5 – 4.5
6 mm bolt or nut	0.8 – 1.2	6 – 9
8 mm bolt or nut	1.8 – 2.5	13 – 18
10 mm bolt or nut	3.0 – 4.0	22 – 29
12 mm bolt or nut	5.0 – 6.0	36 – 43
5 mm screw	0.35 – 0.5	2.5 – 3.6
6 mm screw	0.7 – 1.1	5 – 8
6 mm flange bolt	1.0 – 1.4	7 – 10
8 mm flange bolt	2.4 – 3.0	17 – 22
10 mm flange bolt	3.0 – 4.0	22 – 29

Choosing and fitting accessories

The range of accessories available to the modern motorcyclist is almost as varied and bewildering as the range of motorcycles. This Section is intended to help the owner in choosing the correct equipment for his needs and to avoid some of the mistakes made by many riders when adding accessories to their machines. It will be evident that the Section can only cover the subject in the most general terms and so it is recommended that the owner, having decided that he wants to fit, for example, a luggage rack or carrier, seeks the advice of several local dealers and the owners of similar machines. This will give a good idea of what makes of carrier are easily available, and at what price. Talking to other owners will give some insight into the drawbacks or good points of any one make. A walk round the motorcycles in car parks or outside a dealer will often reveal the same sort of information.

The first priority when choosing accessories is to assess exactly what one needs. It is, for example, pointless to buy a large heavy-duty carrier which is designed to take the weight of fully laden panniers and topbox when all you need is a place to strap on a set of waterproofs and a lunchbox when going to work. Many accessory manufacturers have ranges of equipment to cater for the individual needs of different riders and this point should be borne in mind when looking through a dealer's catalogues. Having decided exactly what is required and the use to which the accessories are going to be put, the owner will need a few hints on what to look for when making the final choice. To this end the Section is now sub-divided to cover the more popular accessories fitted. Note that it is in no way a customizing guide, but merely seeks to outline the practical considerations to be taken into account when adding aftermarket equipment to a motorcycle.

Fairings and windscreens

A fairing is possibly the single, most expensive, aftermarket item to be fitted to any motorcycle and, therefore, requires the most thought before purchase. Fairings can be divided into two main groups: front fork mounted handlebar fairings and windscreens, and frame mounted fairings.

The first group, the front fork mounted fairings, are becoming far more popular than was once the case, as they offer several advantages over the second group. Front fork mounted fairings generally are much easier and quicker to fit, involve less modification to the motorcycle, do not as a rule restrict the steering lock, permit a wider selection of handlebar styles to be used, and offer adequate protection for much less money than the frame mounted type. They are also lighter, can be swapped easily between different motorcycles, and are available in a much greater variety of styles. Their main disadvantages are that they do not offer as much weather protection as the frame mounted types, rarely offer any storage space, and, if poorly fitted or naturally incompatible, can have an adverse effect on the stability of the motorcycle.

The second group, the frame mounted fairings, are secured so rigidly to the main frame of the motorcycle that they can offer a substantial amount of protection to motorcycle and rider in the event of a crash. They offer almost complete protection from the weather and, if double-skinned in construction, can provide a great deal of useful storage space. The feeling of peace, quiet and complete relaxation encountered when riding behind a good full fairing has to be

experienced to be believed. For this reason full fairings are considered essential by most touring motorcyclists and by many people who ride all year round. The main disadvantages of this type are that fitting can take a long time, often involving removal or modification of standard motorcycle components, they restrict the steering lock and they can add up to about 40 lb to the weight of the machine. They do not usually affect the stability of the machine to any great extent once the front tyre pressure and suspension have been adjusted to compensate for the extra weight, but can be affected by sidewinds.

The first thing to look for when purchasing a fairing is the quality of the fittings. A good fairing will have strong, substantial brackets constructed from heavy-gauge tubing; the brackets must be shaped to fit the frame or forks evenly so that the minimum of stress is imposed on the assembly when it is bolted down. The brackets should be properly painted or finished – a nylon coating being the favourite of the better manufacturers – the nuts and bolts provided should be of the same thread and size standard as is used on the motorcycle and be properly plated. Look also for shakeproof locking nuts or locking washers to ensure that everything remains securely tightened down. The fairing shell is generally made from one of two materials: fibreglass or ABS plastic. Both have their advantages and disadvantages, but the main consideration for the owner is that fibreglass is much easier to repair in the event of damage occurring to the fairing. Whichever material is used, check that it is properly finished inside as well as out, that the edges are protected by beading and that the fairing shell is insulated from vibration by the use of rubber grommets at all mounting points. Also be careful to check that the windscreen is retained by plastic bolts which will snap on impact so that the windscreen will break away and not cause personal injury in the event of an accident.

Having purchased your fairing or windscreen, read the manufacturer's fitting instructions very carefully and check that you have all the necessary brackets and fittings. Ensure that the mounting brackets are located correctly and bolted down securely. Note that some manufacturers use hose clamps to retain the mounting brackets; these should be discarded as they are convenient to use but not strong enough for the task. Stronger clamps should be substituted; car exhaust pipe clamps of suitable size would be a good alternative. Ensure that the front forks can turn through the full steering lock available without fouling the fairing. With many types of frame-mounted fairing the handlebars will have to be altered or a different type fitted and the steering lock will be restricted by stops provided with the fittings. Also check that the fairing does not foul the front wheel or mudguard, in any steering position, under full fork compression. Re-route any cables, brake pipes or electrical wiring which may snag on the fairing and take great care to protect all electrical connections, using insulating tape. If the manufacturer's instructions are followed carefully at every stage no serious problems should be encountered. Remember that hydraulic pipes that have been disconnected must be carefully re-tightened and the hydraulic system purged of air bubbles by bleeding.

Two things will become immediately apparent when taking a motorcycle on the road for the first time with a fairing – the first is the tendency to underestimate the road speed because of the lack of wind pressure on the body. This must be very carefully watched until one has grown accustomed to riding behind the fairing. The second thing is the alarming increase in engine noise which is an unfortunate but inevitable by-product of fitting any type of fairing or windscreen, and is caused by normal engine noise being reflected, and in some cases amplified, by the flat surface of the fairing.

Luggage racks or carriers

Carriers are possibly the commonest item to be fitted to modern motorcycles. They vary enormously in size, carrying capacity, and durability. When selecting a carrier, always look for one which is made specifically for your machine and which is bolted on with as few separate brackets as possible. The universal-type carrier, with its mass of brackets and adaptor pieces, will generally prove too weak to be of any real use. A good carrier should bolt to the main frame, generally using the two suspension unit top mountings and a mudguard mounting bolt as attachment points, and have its luggage platform as low and as far forward as possible to minimise the effect of any load on the machine's stability. Look for good quality, heavy gauge tubing, good welding and good finish. Also ensure that the carrier does not prevent opening of the seat, sidepanels or tail compartment, as appropriate. When using a carrier, be very careful not to overload it. Excessive weight placed so high and so far to the rear of any motorcycle will have an adverse effect on the machine's steering and stability.

Luggage

Motorcycle luggage can be grouped under two headings: soft and hard. Both types are available in many sizes and styles and have advantages and disadvantages in use.

Soft luggage is now becoming very popular because of its lower cost and its versatility. Whether in the form of tankbags, panniers, or strap-on bags, soft luggage requires in general no brackets and no modification to the motorcycle. Equipment can be swapped easily from one motorcycle to another and can be fitted and removed in seconds. Awkwardly shaped loads can easily be carried. The disadvantages of soft luggage are that the contents cannot be secure against the casual thief, very little protection is afforded in the event of a crash, and waterproofing is generally poor. Also, in the case of panniers, carrying capacity is restricted to approximately 10 lb, although this amount will vary considerably depending on the manufacturer's recommendation. When purchasing soft luggage, look for good quality material, generally vinyl or nylon, with strong, well-stitched attachment points. It is always useful to have separate pockets, especially on tank bags, for items which will be needed on the journey. When purchasing a tank bag, look for one which has a separate, well-padded, base. This will protect the tank's paintwork and permit easy access to the filler cap at petrol stations.

Hard luggage is confined to two types: panniers, and top boxes or tail trunks. Most hard luggage manufacturers produce matching sets of these items, the basis of which is generally that manufacturer's own heavy-duty luggage rack. Variations on this theme occur in the form of separate frames for the better quality panniers, fixed or quickly-detachable luggage, and in size and carrying capacity. Hard luggage offers a reasonable degree of security against theft and good protection against weather and accident damage. Carrying capacity is greater than that of soft luggage, around 15 – 20 lb in the case of panniers, although top boxes should never be loaded as much as their apparent capacity might imply. A top box should only be used for lightweight items, because one that is heavily laden can have a serious effect on the stability of the machine. When purchasing hard luggage look for the same good points as mentioned under fairings and windscreens, ie good quality mounting brackets and fittings, and well-finished fibreglass or ABS plastic cases. Again as with fairings, always purchase luggage made specifically for your motorcycle, using as few separate brackets as possible, to ensure that everything remains securely bolted in place. When fitting hard luggage, be careful to check that the rear suspension and brake operation will not be impaired in any way and remember that many pannier kits require re-siting of the indicators. Remember also that a non-standard exhaust system may make fitting extremely difficult.

Handlebars

The occupation of fitting alternative types of handlebar is extremely popular with modern motorcyclists, whose motives may vary from the purely practical, wishing to improve the comfort of their machines, to the purely aesthetic, where form is more important than function. Whatever the reason, there are several considerations to be borne in mind when changing the handlebars of your machine. If fitting lower bars, check carefully that the switches and cables do not foul the petrol tank on full

lock and that the surplus length of cable, brake pipe, and electrical wiring are smoothly and tidily disposed of. Avoid tight kinks in cable or brake pipes which will produce stiff controls or the premature and disastrous failure of an overstressed component. If necessary, remove the petrol tank and re-route the cable from the engine/gearbox unit upwards, ensuring smooth gentle curves are produced. In extreme cases, it will be necessary to purchase a shorter brake pipe to overcome this problem. In the case of higher handlebars than standard it will almost certainly be necessary to purchase extended cables and brake pipes. Fortunately, many standard motorcycles have a custom version which will be equipped with higher handlebars and, therefore, factory-built extended components will be available from your local dealer. It is not usually necessary to extend electrical wiring, as switch clusters may be used on several different motorcycles, some being custom versions. This point should be borne in mind however when fitting extremely high or wide handlebars.

When fitting different types of handlebar, ensure that the mounting clamps are correctly tightened to the manufacturer's specifications and that cables and wiring, as previously mentioned, have smooth easy runs and do not snag on any part of the motorcycle throughout the full steering lock. Ensure that the fluid level in the front brake master cylinder remains level to avoid any chance of air entering the hydraulic system. Also check that the cables are adjusted correctly and that all handlebar controls operate correctly and can be easily reached when riding.

Crashbars

Crashbars, also known as engine protector bars, engine guards, or case savers, are extremely useful items of equipment which can contribute protection to the machine's structure if a crash occurs. They do not, as has been inferred in the US, prevent the rider from crashing, or necessarily prevent rider injury should a crash occur.

It is recommended that only the smaller, neater, engine protector type of crashbar is considered. This type will offer protection while restricting, as little as is possible, access to the engine and the machine's ground clearance. The crashbars should be designed for use specifically on your machine, and should be constructed of heavy-gauge tubing with strong, integral mounting brackets. Where possible, they should bolt to a strong lug on the frame, usually at the engine mounting bolts.

The alternative type of crashbar is the larger cage type. This type is not recommended in spite of their appearance which promises some protection to the rider as well as to the machine. The larger amount of leverage imposed by the size of this type of crashbar increases the risk of severe frame damage in the event of an accident. This type also decreases the machine's ground clearance and restricts access to the engine. The amount of protection afforded the rider is open to some doubt as the design is based on the premise that the rider will stay in the normally seated position during an accident, and the crash bar structure will not itself fail. Neither result can in any way be guaranteed.

As a general rule, always purchase the best, ie usually the most expensive, set of crashbars you an afford. The investment will be repaid by minimising the amount of damage incurred, should the machine be involved in an accident. Finally, avoid the universal type of crashbar. This should be regarded only as a last resort to be used if no alternative exists. With its usual multitude of separate brackets and spacers, the universal crashbar is far too weak in design and construction to be of any practical value.

Exhaust systems

The fitting of aftermarket exhaust systems is another extremely popular pastime amongst motorcyclists. The usual motive is to gain more performance from the engine but other considerations are to gain more ground clearance, to lose weight from the motorcycle, to obtain a more distinctive exhaust note or to find a cheaper alternative to the manufacturer's original equipment exhaust system. Original equipment exhaust systems often cost more and may well have a relatively short life. It should be noted that it is rare for an aftermarket exhaust system alone to give a noticeable increase in the engine's power output. Modern motorcycles are designed to give the highest power output possible allowing for factors such as quietness, fuel economy, spread of power, and long-term reliability. If there were a magic formula which allowed the exhaust system to produce more power without affecting these other considerations you can be sure that the manufacturers, with their large research and development facilities, would have found it and made use of it. Performance increases of a worthwhile and noticeable nature only come from well-tried and properly matched modifications to the entire engine, from the air filter, through the carburettors, port timing or camshaft and valve design, combustion chamber shape, compression ratio, and the exhaust system. Such modifications are well outside the scope of this manual but interested owners might refer to the 'Piper Tuning Manual' produced by the publisher of this manual; this book goes into the whole subject in great detail.

Whatever your motive for wishing to fit an alternative exhaust system, be sure to seek expert advice before doing so. Changes to the carburettor jetting will almost certainly be required for which you must consult the exhaust system manufacturer. If he cannot supply adequately specific information it is reasonable to assume that insufficient development work has been carried out, and that particular make should be avoided. Other factors to be borne in mind are whether the exhaust system allows the use of both centre and side stands, whether it allows sufficient access to permit oil and filter changing and whether modifications are necessary to the standard exhaust system. Many two-stroke expansion chamber systems require the use of the standard exhaust pipe; this is all very well if the standard exhaust pipe and silencer are separate units but can cause problems if the two, as with so many modern two-strokes, are a one-piece unit. While the exhaust pipe can be removed easily by means of a hacksaw it is not so easy to refit the original silencer should you at any time wish to return the machine to standard trim. The same applies to several four-stroke systems.

On the subject of the finish of aftermarket exhausts, avoid black-painted systems unless you enjoy painting. As any trail-bike owner will tell you, rust has a great affinity for black exhausts and re-painting or rust removal becomes a task which must be carried out with monotonous regularity. A bright chrome finish is, as a general rule, a far better proposition as it is much easier to keep clean and to prevent rusting. Although the general finish of aftermarket exhaust systems is not always up to the standard of the original equipment the lower cost of such systems does at least reflect this fact.

When fitting an alternative system always purchase a full set of new exhaust gaskets, to prevent leaks. Fit the exhaust first to the cylinder head or barrel, as appropriate, tightening the retaining nuts or bolts by hand only and then line up the exhaust rear mountings. If the new system is a one-piece unit and the rear mountings do not line up exactly, spacers must be fabricated to take up the difference. Do not force the system into place as the stress thus imposed will rapidly cause cracks and splits to appear. Once all the mountings are loosely fixed, tighten the retaining nuts or bolts securely, being careful not to overtighten them. Where the motorcycle manufacturer's torque settings are available, these should be used. Do not forget to carry out any carburation changes recommended by the exhaust system's manufacturer.

Electrical equipment

The vast range of electrical equipment available to motorcyclists is so large and so diverse that only the most general outline can be given here. Electrical accessories vary from electric ignition kits fitted to replace contact breaker points, to additional lighting at the front and rear, more powerful horns, various instruments and gauges, clocks, anti-theft systems, heated clothing, CB radios, radio-cassette players, and intercom systems, to name but a few of the more popular items of equipment.

As will be evident, it would require a separate manual to cover this subject alone and this section is therefore restricted to outlining a few basic rules which must be borne in mind when fitting electrical equipment. The first consideration is whether your machine's electrical system has enough reserve capacity to cope with the added demand of the accessories you wish to fit. The motorcycle's manufacturer or importer should be able to furnish this sort of information and may also be able to offer advice on uprating the electrical system. Failing this, a good dealer or the accessory manufacturer may be able to help. In some cases, more powerful generator components may be available, perhaps from another motorcycle in the manufacturer's range. The second consideration is the legal requirements in force in your area. The local police may be prepared to help with this point. In the UK for example, there are strict regulations governing the position and use of auxiliary riding lamps and fog lamps.

When fitting electrical equipment always disconnect the battery first to prevent the risk of a short-circuit, and be careful to ensure that all connections are properly made and that they are waterproof. Remember that many electrical accessories are designed primarily for use in cars and that they cannot easily withstand the exposure to vibration and to the weather. Delicate components must be rubber-mounted to insulate them from vibration, and sealed carefully to prevent the entry of rainwater and dirt. Be careful to follow exactly the accessory manufacturer's instructions in conjunction with the wiring diagram at the back of this manual.

Accessories – general

Accessories fitted to your motorcycle will rapidly deteriorate if not cared for. Regular washing and polishing will maintain the finish and will provide an opportunity to check that all mounting bolts and nuts are securely fastened. Any signs of chafing or wear should be watched for, and the cause cured as soon as possible before serious damage occurs.

As a general rule, do not expect the re-sale value of your motorcycle to increase by an amount proportional to the amount of money and effort put into fitting accessories. It is usually the case that an absolutely standard motorcycle will sell more easily at a better price than one that has been modified. If you are in the habit of exchanging your machine for another at frequent intervals, this factor should be borne in mind to avoid loss of money.

Fault diagnosis

Contents

1 Introduction

This Section provides an easy reference-guide to the more common ailments that are likely to afflict your machine. Obviously, the opportunities are almost limitless for faults to occur as a result of obscure failures, and to try and cover all eventualities would require a book. Indeed, a number have been written on the subject.

Successful fault diagnosis is not a mysterious 'black art' but the application of a bit of knowledge combined with a systematic and logical approach to the problem. Approach any fault diagnosis by first accurately identifying the symptom and then checking through the list of possible causes, starting with the simplest or most obvious and progressing in stages to the most complex. Take nothing for granted, but above all apply liberal quantities of common sense.

The main symptom of a fault is given in the text as a major heading below which are listed, as Section headings, the various systems or areas which may contain the fault. Details of each possible cause for a fault and the remedial action to be taken are given, in brief, in the paragraphs below each Section heading. Further information should be sought in the relevant Chapter.

Starter motor problems

2 Starter motor not rotating

Engine stop switch off.

Battery voltage low. Switching on the headlamp and operating the horn will give a good indication of the charge level. If necessary recharge the battery from an external source.

Neutral gear not selected. Where a neutral indicator switch is fitted.

Faulty neutral indicator switch or clutch interlock switch (where fitted). Check the switch wiring and switches for correct operation.

Ignition switch defective. Check switch for continuity and connections for security.

Engine stop switch defective. Check switch for continuity in 'Run' position. Fault will be caused by broken, wet or corroded switch contacts. Clean or renew as necessary.

Starter button switch faulty. Check continuity of switch. Faults as for engine stop switch.

Starter relay (solenoid) faulty. If the switch is functioning correctly a pronounced click should be heard when the starter button is depressed. This presupposes that current is flowing to the solenoid when the button is depressed.

Wiring open or shorted. Check first that the battery terminal connections are tight and corrosion free. Follow this by checking that all wiring connections are dry, tight and corrosion free. Check also for frayed or broken wiring. Occasionally a wire may become trapped between two moving components, particularly in the vicinity of the steering head, leading to breakage of the internal core but leaving the softer but more resilient outer cover intact. This can cause mysterious intermittent or total power loss.

Starter motor defective. A badly worn starter motor may cause high current drain from a battery without the motor rotating. If current is found to be reaching the motor, after checking the starter button and starter relay, suspect a damaged motor. The motor should be removed for inspection.

3 Starter motor rotates but engine does not turn over

Starter motor clutch defective. Suspect jammed or worn engagement rollers, plungers and springs.

Damaged starter motor drive train. Inspect and renew component where necessary. Failure in this area is unlikely.

4 Starter motor and clutch function but engine will not turn over

Engine seized. Seizure of the engine is always a result of damage to internal components due to lubrication failure, or component breakage resulting from abuse, neglect or old age. A seizing or partially seized component may go un-noticed until the engine has cooled down and an attempt is made to restart the engine. Suspect first seizure of the valves, valve gear and the pistons. Instantaneous seizure whilst the engine is running indicates component breakage. In either case major dismantling and inspection will be required.

Engine does not start when turned over

5 No fuel flow to carburettor

No fuel or insufficient fuel in tank.

Fuel tap lever position incorrectly selected.

Float chambers require priming after running dry (vacuum taps only).

Tank filler cap air vent obstructed. Usually caused by dirt or water. Clean the vent orifice.

Fuel tap or filter blocked. Blockage may be due to accumulation of rust or paint flakes from the tank's inner surface or of foreign matter from contaminated fuel. Remove the tap and clean it and the filter. Look also for water droplets in the fuel.

Fuel line blocked. Blockage of the fuel line is more likely to result from a kink in the line rather than the accumulation of debris.

6 Fuel not reaching cylinder

Float chamber not filling. Caused by float needle or floats sticking in up position. This may occur after the machine has been left standing for an extended length of time allowing the fuel to evaporate. When this occurs a gummy residue is often left which hardens to a varnish-like substance. This condition may be worsened by corrosion and crystaline deposits produced prior to the total evaporation of contaminated fuel. Sticking of the float needle may also be caused by wear. In any case removal of the float chamber will be necessary for inspection and cleaning.

Blockage in starting circuit, slow running circuit or jets. Blockage of these items may be attributable to debris from the fuel tank by-passing the filter system or to gumming up as described in paragraph 1. Water droplets in the fuel will also block jets and passages. The carburettor should be dismantled for cleaning.

Fuel level too low. The fuel level in the float chamber is controlled by float height. The float height may increase with wear or damage but will never reduce, thus a low float height is an inherent rather than developing condition. Check the float height and make any necessary adjustment.

7 Engine flooding

Float valve needle worn or stuck open. A piece of rust or other debris can prevent correct seating of the needle against the valve seat thereby permitting an uncontrolled flow of fuel. Similarly, a worn needle or needle seat will prevent valve closure. Dismantle the carburettor float bowl for cleaning and, if necessary, renewal of the worn components.

Fuel level too high. The fuel level is controlled by the float height which may increase due to wear of the float needle, pivot pin or operating tang. Check the float height, and make any necessary adjustment. A leaking float will cause an increase in fuel level, and thus should be renewed.

Cold starting mechanism. Check the choke (starter mechanism) for correct operation. If the mechanism jams in the 'On' position subsequent starting of a hot engine will be difficult.

Blocked air filter. A badly restricted air filter will cause flooding. Check the filter and clean or renew as required. A collapsed inlet hose will have a similar effect.

8 No spark at plug

Ignition switch not on.

Engine stop switch off.

Fuse blown. Check fuse for ignition circuit. See wiring diagram.

Battery voltage low. The current draw required by a starter motor is sufficiently high that an under-charged battery may not have enough spare capacity to provide power for the ignition circuit during starting. Use of the kickstart (where fitted) is recommended until the battery has been recharged either by the machine's generator or from an external charger.

Starter motor inefficient. A starter motor with worn brushes and a worn or dirty commutator will draw excessive amounts of current causing power starvation in the ignition system. See the preceding paragraph. Starter motor overhaul will be required.

Spark plug failure. Clean the spark plug thoroughly and reset the electrode gap. Refer to the spark plug section and the colour condition guide in Chapter 3. If the spark plug shorts internally or has sustained visible damage to the electrodes, core or ceramic insulator it should be renewed. On rare occasions a plug that appears to spark vigorously will fail to do so when refitted to the engine and subjected to the compression pressure in the cylinder.

Spark plug cap or high tension (HT) lead faulty. Check condition and security. Replace if deterioration is evident.

Spark plug cap loose. Check that the spark plug cap fits securely over the plug and, where fitted, the screwed terminal on the plug end is secure.

Shorting due to moisture. Certain parts of the ignition system are susceptible to shorting when the machine is ridden or parked in wet weather. Check particularly the area from the spark plug cap back to the ignition coil. A water dispersant spray may be used to dry out waterlogged components. Recurrence of the problem can be prevented by using an ignition sealant spray after drying out and cleaning.

Ignition or stop switch shorted. May be caused by water, corrosion or wear. Water dispersant and contact cleaning sprays may be used. If this fails to overcome the problem dismantling and visual inspection of the switches will be required.

Shorting or open circuit in wiring. Failure in any wire connecting any of the ignition components will cause ignition malfunction. Check also that all connections are clean, dry and tight.

Ignition coil failure. Check the coil, referring to Chapter 3.

9 Weak spark at plug

Feeble sparking at the plug may be caused by any of the faults mentioned in the preceding Section other than those items in paragraphs 1 to 3.

10 Compression low

Spark plug loose. This will be self-evident on inspection, and may be accompanied by a hissing noise when the engine is turned over. Remove the plug and check that the threads in the cylinder head are not damaged. Check also that the plug sealing washer is in good condition.

Cylinder head gasket leaking. This condition is often accompanied by a high pitched squeak from around the cylinder head and oil loss, and may be caused by insufficiently tightened cylinder head fasteners, a warped cylinder head or mechanical failure of the gasket material. Re-torqueing the fasteners to the correct specification may seal the leak in some instances but if damage has occurred this course of action will provide, at best, only a temporary cure.

Valve not seating correctly. The failure of a valve to seat may be caused by insufficient valve clearance, pitting of the valve seat or face, carbon deposits on the valve seat or seizure of the valve stem or valve gear components. Valve spring breakage will also prevent correct valve closure. The valve clearances should be checked first and then, if these are found to be in order, further dismantling will be required to inspect the relevant components for failure.

Cylinder, piston and ring wear. Compression pressure will be lost if any of these components are badly worn. Wear in one component is invariably accompanied by wear in another. A top end overhaul will be required.

Piston rings sticking or broken. Sticking of the piston rings may be caused by seizure due to lack of lubrication or heating as a result of poor carburation or incorrect fuel type. Gumming of the rings may

result from lack of use, or carbon deposits in the ring grooves. Broken rings result from over-revving, overheating or general wear. In either case a top-end overhaul will be required.

Engine stalls after starting

11 General causes

Improper cold start mechanism operation. Check that the operating controls function smoothly and, where applicable, are correctly adjusted. A cold engine may not require application of an enriched mixture to start initially but may baulk without choke once firing. Likewise a hot engine may start with an enriched mixture but will stop almost immediately if the choke is inadvertently in operation.

Ignition malfunction. See Section 9, 'Weak spark at plug'.

Carburettor incorrectly adjusted. Maladjustment of the mixture strength or idle speed may cause the engine to stop immediately after starting. See Chapter 2.

Fuel contamination. Check for filter blockage by debris or water which reduces, but does not completely stop, fuel flow or blockage of the slow speed circuit in the carburettor by the same agents. If water is present it can often be seen as droplets in the bottom of the float bowl. Clean the filter and, where water is in evidence, drain and flush the fuel tank and float bowl.

Intake air leak. Check for security of the carburettor mounting and hose connections, and for cracks or splits in the hoses. Check also that the carburettor top is secure and that the vacuum gauge adaptor plug (where fitted) is tight.

Air filter blocked or omitted. A blocked filter will cause an over-rich mixture; the omission of a filter will cause an excessively weak mixture. Both conditions will have a detrimental effect on carburation. Clean or renew the filter as necessary.

Fuel filler cap air vent blocked. Usually caused by dirt or water. Clean the vent orifice.

Poor running at idle and low speed

12 Weak spark at plug or erratic firing

Battery voltage low. In certain conditions low battery charge, especially when coupled with a badly sulphated battery, may result in misfiring. If the battery is in good general condition it should be recharged; an old battery suffering from sulphated plates should be renewed.

Spark plug fouled, faulty or incorrectly adjusted. See Section 8 or refer to Chapter 3.

Spark plug cap or high tension lead shorting. Check the condition of both these items ensuring that they are in good condition and dry and that the cap is fitted correctly.

Spark plug type incorrect. Fit plug of correct type and heat range as given in Specifications. In certain conditions a plug of hotter or colder type may be required for normal running.

Faulty ignition coil. Partial failure of the coil internal insulation will diminish the performance of the coil. No repair is possible, a new component must be fitted.

13 Fuel/air mixture incorrect

Intake air leak. See Section 11.

Mixture strength incorrect. Adjust slow running mixture strength using pilot adjustment screw.

Carburettor synchronisation.

Pilot jet or slow running circuit blocked. The carburettor should be removed and dismantled for thorough cleaning. Blow through all jets and air passages with compressed air to clear obstructions.

Air cleaner clogged or omitted. Clean or fit air cleaner element as necessary. Check also that the element and air filter cover are correctly seated.

Cold start mechanism in operation. Check that the choke has not been left on inadvertently and the operation is correct. Where applicable check the operating cable free play.

Fuel level too high or too low. Check the float height and adjust as necessary. See Section 7.

Fuel tank air vent obstructed. Obstruction usually caused by dirt or water. Clean vent orifice.

Valve clearance incorrect. Check, and if necessary, adjust, the clearances.

14 Compression low

See Section 10.

Acceleration poor

15 General causes

All items as for previous Section.

Sticking throttle vacuum piston.

Brakes binding. Usually caused by maladjustment or partial seizure of the operating mechanism due to poor maintenance. Check brake adjustment (where applicable). A bent wheel spindle or warped brake disc can produce similar symptoms.

Poor running or lack of power at high speeds

16 Weak spark at plug or erratic firing

All items as for Section 12.

HT lead insulation failure. Insulation failure of the HT lead and spark plug cap due to old age or damage can cause shorting when the engine is driven hard. This condition may be less noticeable, or not noticeable at all at lower engine speeds.

17 Fuel/air mixture incorrect

All items as for Section 13, with the exception of items 2 and 4.

Main jet blocked. Debris from contaminated fuel, or from the fuel tank, and water in the fuel can block the main jet. Clean the fuel filter, the float bowl area, and if water is present, flush and refill the fuel tank.

Main jet is the wrong size. The standard carburettor jetting is for sea level atmospheric pressure. For high altitudes, usually above 5000 ft, a smaller main jet will be required.

Jet needle and needle jet worn. These can be renewed individually but should be renewed as a pair. Renewal of both items requires partial dismantling of the carburettor.

Air bleed holes blocked. Dismantle carburettor and use compressed air to blow out all air passages.

Reduced fuel flow. A reduction in the maximum fuel flow from the fuel tank to the carburettor will cause fuel starvation, proportionate to the engine speed. Check for blockages through debris or a kinked fuel line.

Vacuum diaphragm split. Renew.

18 Compression low

See Section 10.

Knocking or pinking

19 General causes

Carbon build-up in combustion chamber. After a high mileage has been covered a large accumulation of carbon may occur. This may glow red hot and cause premature ignition of the fuel/air mixture, in advance of normal firing by the spark plug. Cylinder head removal will be required to allow inspection and cleaning.

Fuel incorrect. A low grade fuel, or one of poor quality may result in compression induced detonation of the fuel resulting in knocking and pinking noises. Old fuel can cause similar problems. A too highly leaded fuel will reduce detonation but will accelerate deposit formation in the combustion chamber and may lead to early pre-ignition as described in item 1.

Spark plug heat range incorrect. Uncontrolled pre-ignition can result from the use of a spark plug the heat range of which is too hot.

Weak mixture. Overheating of the engine due to a weak mixture can result in pre-ignition occurring where it would not occur when engine temperature was within normal limits. Maladjustment, blocked jets or passages and air leaks can cause this condition.

Overheating

20 Firing incorrect

Spark plug fouled, defective or maladjusted. See Section 8.

Spark plug type incorrect. Refer to the Specifications and ensure that the correct plug type is fitted.

21 Fuel/air mixture incorrect

Slow speed mixture strength incorrect. Adjust pilot air screw.

Main jet wrong size. The carburettor is jetted for sea level atmospheric conditions. For high altitudes, usually above 5000 ft, a smaller main jet will be required.

Air filter badly fitted or omitted. Check that the filter element is in place and that it and the air filter box cover are sealing correctly. Any leaks will cause a weak mixture.

Induction air leaks. Check the security of the carburettor mountings and hose connections, and for cracks and splits in the hoses. Check also that the carburettor top is secure and that the vacuum gauge adaptor plug (where fitted) is tight.

Fuel level too low. See Section 6.

Fuel tank filler cap air vent obstructed. Clear blockage.

22 Lubrication inadequate

Engine oil too low. Not only does the oil serve as a lubricant by preventing friction between moving components, but it also acts as a coolant. Check the oil level and replenish.

Engine oil overworked. The lubricating properties of oil are lost slowly during use as a result of changes resulting from heat and also contamination. Always change the oil at the recommended interval.

Engine oil of incorrect viscosity or poor quality. Always use the recommended viscosity and type of oil.

Oil filter and filter by-pass valve blocked. Renew filter and clean the by-pass valve.

23 Miscellaneous causes

Engine fins clogged. A build-up of mud in the cylinder head and cylinder barrel cooling fins will decrease the cooling capabilities of the fins. Clean the fins as required.

Clutch operating problems

24 Clutch slip

No clutch lever play. Adjust clutch lever end play according to the procedure in Routine maintenance.

Friction plates worn or warped. Overhaul clutch assembly, replacing plates out of specification (Chapter 1).

Steel plates worn or warped. Overhaul clutch assembly, replacing plates out of specification (Chapter 1).

Clutch springs broken or worn. Old or heat-damaged (from slipping clutch) springs should be replaced with new ones (Chapter 1).

Clutch release not adjusted properly. See the adjustments section of Routine maintenance.

Clutch inner cable snagging. Caused by a frayed cable or kinked outer cable. Replace the cable with a new one. Repair of a frayed cable is not advised.

Clutch release mechanism defective. Worn or damaged parts in the clutch release mechanism could include the release unit or pushrods.

Clutch centre and outer drum worn. Severe indentation by the clutch plate tangs of the channels in the centre and drum will cause snagging of the plates preventing correct engagement. If this damage occurs, renewal of the worn components is required.

Lubricant incorrect. Use of a transmission lubricant other than that specified may allow the plates to slip.

25 Clutch drag

Clutch lever play excessive. Adjust lever at bars or at cable end if necessary (Routine maintenance).

Clutch plates warped or damaged. This will cause a drag on the clutch, causing the machine to creep. Overhaul clutch assembly (Chapter 1).

Clutch spring tension uneven. Usually caused by a sagged or broken spring. Check and replace springs (Chapter 1).

Engine oil deteriorated. Badly contaminated engine oil and a heavy deposit of oil sludge and carbon on the plates will cause plate sticking. The oil recommended for this machine is of the detergent type, therefore it is unlikely that this problem will arise unless regular oil changes are neglected.

Engine oil viscosity too high. Drag in the plates will result from the use of an oil with too high a viscosity. In very cold weather clutch drag may occur until the engine has reached operating temperature.

Clutch centre and outer drum worn. Indentation by the clutch plate tangs of the channels in the centre and drum will prevent easy plate disengagement. If the damage is light the affected areas may be dressed with a fine file. More pronounced damage will necessitate renewal of the components.

Clutch drum seized to shaft. Lack of lubrication, severe wear or damage can cause the drum to seize to the shaft. Overhaul of the clutch, and perhaps the transmission, may be necessary to repair damage (Chapter 1).

Clutch release mechanism defective. Worn or damaged release mechanism parts can stick and fail to provide leverage. Overhaul clutch cover components (Chapter 1).

Loose clutch hub nut. Causes drum and hub misalignment, putting a drag on the engine. Engagement adjustment continually varies. Overhaul clutch assembly (Chapter 1).

Gear selection problems

26 Gear lever does not return

Weak or broken centraliser spring. Renew the spring.

Gearchange shaft bent or seized. Distortion of the gearchange shaft often occurs if the machine is dropped heavily on the gear lever. Provided that damage is not severe straightening of the shaft is permissible.

27 Gear selection difficult or impossible

Clutch not disengaging fully. See Section 25.

Gearchange shaft bent. This often occurs if the machine is dropped heavily on the gear lever. Straightening of the shaft is permissible if the damage is not too great.

Gearchange arms, pawls or pins worn or damaged. Wear or breakage of any of these items may cause difficulty in selecting one or more gears. Overhaul the selector mechanism.

Gearchange shaft centraliser spring broken.

Gearchange arm spring broken. Renew spring.

Gearchange drum stopper cam or detent plunger damage. Failure, rather than wear, of these items may jam the drum thereby preventing gearchanging. The damaged items must be renewed.

Selector forks bent or seized. This can be caused by dropping the machine heavily on the gearchange lever or as a result of lack of lubrication. Though rare, bending of a shaft can result from a missed gearchange or false selection at high speed.

Selector fork end and pin wear. Pronounced wear of these items and the grooves in the gearchange drum can lead to imprecise selection and, eventually, no selection. Renewal of the worn components will be required.

Structural failure. Failure of any one component of the selector rod and change mechanism will result in improper or fouled gear selection.

28 Jumping out of gear

Detent plunger assembly worn or damaged. Wear of the plunger and the cam with which it locates and breakage of the detent spring can cause imprecise gear selection resulting in jumping out of gear. Renew the damaged components.

Gear pinion dogs worn or damaged. Rounding off the dog edges and the mating recesses in adjacent pinion can lead to jumping out of gear when under load. The gears should be inspected and renewed. Attempting to reprofile the dogs is not recommended.

Selector forks, gearchange drum and pinion grooves worn. Extreme wear of these interconnected items can occur after high mileages especially when lubrication has been neglected. The worn components must be renewed.

Gear pinions, bushes and shafts worn. Renew the worn components.

Bent gearchange shaft. Often caused by dropping the machine on the gear lever.

Gear pinion tooth broken. Chipped teeth are unlikely to cause jumping out of gear once the gear has been selected fully; a tooth which is completely broken off, however, may cause problems in this respect and in any event will cause transmission noise.

29 Overselection

Pawl spring weak or broken. Renew the spring.

Detent plunger worn or broken. Renew the damaged items.

Stopper arm spring worn or broken. Renew the spring.

Gearchange arm stop pads worn. Repairs can be made by welding and reprofiling with a file.

Selector limiter claw components (where fitted) worn or damaged. Renew the damaged items.

Abnormal engine noise.

30 Knocking or pinking

See Section 19.

31 Piston slap or rattling from cylinder

Cylinder bore/piston clearance excessive. Resulting from wear, partial seizure or improper boring during overhaul. This condition can often be heard as a high, rapid tapping noise when the engine is under little or no load, particularly when power is just beginning to be applied. Reboring to the next correct oversize should be carried out and a new oversize piston fitted.

Connecting rod bent. This can be caused by over-revving, trying to start a very badly flooded engine (resulting in a hydraulic lock in the cylinder) or by earlier mechanical failure such as a dropped valve. Attempts at straightening a bent connecting rod are not recommended. Careful inspection of the crankshaft should be made before renewing the damaged connecting rod.

Gudgeon pin, piston boss bore or small-end bearing wear or seizure. Excess clearance or partial seizure between normal moving parts of these items can cause continuous or intermittent tapping noises. Rapid wear or seizure is caused by lubrication starvation resulting from an insufficient engine oil level or oilway blockage.

Piston rings worn, broken or sticking. Renew the rings after careful inspection of the piston and bore.

32 Valve noise or tapping from the cylinder head

Valve clearance incorrect. Adjust the clearances with the engine cold.

Valve spring broken or weak. Renew the spring set.

Camshaft or cylinder head worn or damaged. The camshaft lobes are the most highly stressed of all components in the engine and are subject to high wear if lubrication becomes inadequate. The bearing surfaces on the camshaft and cylinder head are also sensitive to a lack of lubrication. Lubrication failure due to blocked oilways can occur, but over-enthusiastic revving before engine warm-up is complete is the usual cause.

Rocker arm or spindle wear. Rapid wear of a rocker arm, and the resulting need for frequent valve clearance adjustment, indicates breakthrough or failure of the surface hardening on the rocker arm tips. Similar wear in the cam lobes can be expected. Renew the worn components after checking for lubrication failure.

Worn camshaft drive components. A rustling noise or light tapping which is not improved by correct re-adjustment of the cam chain tension can be emitted by a worn cam chain or worn sprockets and chain. If uncorrected, subsequent cam chain breakage may cause extensive damage. The worn components must be renewed before wear becomes too far advanced.

33 Other noises

Big-end bearing wear. A pronounced knock from within the crankcase which worsens rapidly is indicative of big-end bearing failure as a result of extreme normal wear or lubrication failure. Remedial action in the form of a bottom end overhaul should be taken; continuing to run the engine will lead to further damage including the possibility of connecting rod breakage.

Main bearing failure. Extreme normal wear or failure of the main bearings is characteristically accompanied by a rumble from the crankcase and vibration felt through the frame and footrests. Renew the worn bearings and carry out a very careful examination of the crankshaft.

Crankshaft excessively out of true. A bent crank may result from over-revving or damage from an upper cylinder component or gearbox failure. Damage can also result from dropping the machine on either crankshaft end. Straightening of the crankshaft is not possible in normal circumstances; a replacement item should be fitted.

Engine mounting loose. Tighten all the engine mounting nuts and bolts.

Cylinder head gasket leaking. The noise most often associated with a leaking head gasket is a high pitched squeaking, although any other noise consistent with gas being forced out under pressure from a small orifice can also be emitted. Gasket leakage is often accompanied by oil seepage from around the mating joint or from the cylinder head holding down bolts and nuts. Leakage into the cam chain tunnel or oil return passages will increase crankcase pressure and may cause oil leakage at joints and oil seals. Also, oil contamination will be accelerated. Leakage results from insufficient or uneven tightening of the cylinder head fasteners, or from random mechanical failure. Retightening to the correct torque figure will, at best, only provide a temporary cure. The gasket should be renewed at the earliest opportunity.

Exhaust system leakage. Popping or crackling in the exhaust system, particularly when it occurs with the engine on the overrun, indicates a poor joint either at the cylinder port or at the exhaust pipe/silencer connection. Failure of the gasket or looseness of the clamp should be looked for.

Abnormal transmission noise

34 Clutch noise

Clutch outer drum/friction plate tang clearance excessive.
Clutch outer drum/spacer clearance excessive.
Clutch outer drum/thrust washer clearance excessive.
Primary drive gear teeth worn or damaged.
Clutch shock absorber assembly worn or damaged.

35 Transmission noise

Bearing or bushes worn or damaged. Renew the affected components.

Gear pinions worn or chipped. Renew the gear pinions.

Metal chips jammed in gear teeth. This can occur when pieces of metal from any failed component are picked up by a meshing pinion. The condition will lead to rapid bearing wear or early gear failure.

Engine/transmission oil level too low. Top up immediately to prevent damage to gearbox and engine.

Gearchange mechanism worn or damaged. Wear or failure of certain items in the selection and change components can induce mis-selection of gears (see Section 27) where incipient engagement of more than one gear set is promoted. Remedial action, by the overhaul of the gearbox, should be taken without delay.

Loose gearbox chain sprocket. Remove the sprocket and check for impact damage to the splines of the sprocket and shaft. Excessive slack between the splines will promote loosening of the securing nut; renewal of the worn components is required. When retightening the nut ensure that it is tightened fully and that, where fitted, the lock washer is bent up against one flat of the nut.

Chain snagging on cases or cycle parts. A badly worn chain or one that is excessively loose may snag or smack against adjacent components.

Exhaust smokes excessively

36 White/blue smoke (caused by oil burning)

Piston rings worn or broken. Breakage or wear of any ring, but particularly the oil control ring, will allow engine oil past the piston into the combustion chamber. Overhaul the cylinder barrel and piston.

Cylinder cracked, worn or scored. These conditions may be caused by overheating, lack of lubrication, component failure or advanced normal wear. The cylinder barrel should be renewed or rebored and the next oversize piston fitted.

Valve oil seal damaged or worn. This can occur as a result of valve guide failure or old age. The emission of smoke is likely to occur when the throttle is closed rapidly after acceleration, for instance, when changing gear. Renew the valve oil seals and, if necessary, the valve guides.

Valve guides worn. See the preceding paragraph.

Engine oil level too high. This increases the crankcase pressure and allows oil to be forced past the piston rings. Often accompanied by seepage of oil at joints and oil seals.

Cylinder head gasket blown between cam chain tunnel or oil return passage. Renew the cylinder head gasket.

Abnormal crankcase pressure. This may be caused by blocked breather passages or hoses causing back-pressure at high engine revolutions.

37 Black smoke (caused by over-rich mixture)

Air filter element clogged. Clean or renew the element.

Main jet loose or too large. Remove the float chamber to check for tightness of the jet. If the machine is used at high altitudes rejetting will be required to compensate for the lower atmospheric pressure.

Cold start mechanism jammed on. Check that the mechanism works smoothly and correctly and that, where fitted, the operating cable is lubricated and not snagged.

Fuel level too high. The fuel level is controlled by the float height which can increase as a result of wear or damage. Remove the float bowl and check the float height. Check also that floats have not punctured; a punctured float will loose buoyancy and allow an increased fuel level.

Float valve needle stuck open. Caused by dirt or a worn valve. Clean the float chamber or renew the needle and, if necessary, the valve seat.

Oil pressure indicator lamp goes on

38 Engine lubrication system failure

Engine oil defective. Oil pump shaft or locating pin sheared off from ingesting debris or seizing from lack of lubrication (low oil level) (Routine maintenance).

Engine oil screen clogged. Change oil and filter and service pickup screen (Routine maintenance).

Engine oil level too low. Inspect for leak or other problem causing low oil level and add recommended lubricant.

Engine oil viscosity too low. Very old, thin oil, or an improper weight of oil used in engine. Change to correct lubricant (Chapter 2).

Camshaft or journals worn. High wear causing drop in oil pressure. Replace cam and/or head. Abnormal wear could be caused by oil starvation at high rpm from low oil level, improper oil weight or type, or loose oil fitting on upper cylinder oil line.

Crankshaft and/or bearings worn. Same problems as paragraph 5. Overhaul lower end (Chapter 1).

Relief valve stuck open. This causes the oil to be dumped back into the sump. Repair or replace.

39 Electrical system failure

Oil pressure switch defective. Check switch according to the procedures in Chapter . Replace if defective.

Oil pressure indicator lamp wiring system defective. Check for pinched, shorted, disconnected or damaged wiring.

Poor handling or roadholding

40 Directional instability

Steering head bearing adjustment too tight. This will cause rolling or weaving at low speeds. Re-adjust the bearings.

Steering head bearings worn or damaged. Correct adjustment of the bearing will prove impossible to achieve if wear or damage has occurred. Inconsistent handling will occur including rolling or weaving at low speed and poor directional control at indeterminate higher speeds. The steering head bearing should be dismantled for inspection and renewed if required. Lubrication should also be carried out.

Bearing races pitted or dented. Impact damage caused, perhaps, by an accident or riding over a pot-hole can cause indentation of the bearing, usually in one position. This should be noted as notchiness when the handlebars are turned. Renew and lubricate the bearings.

Steering stem bent. This will occur only if the machine is subjected to a high impact such as hitting a curb or a pot-hole. The lower yoke/stem should be renewed; do not attempt to straighten the stem.

Front or rear tyre pressures too low.

Front or rear tyre worn. General instability, high speed wobbles and skipping over white lines indicates that tyre renewal may be required. Tyre induced problems, in some machine/tyre combinations, can occur even when the tyre in question is by no means fully worn.

Swinging arm bearings worn. Difficulty in holding line, particularly when cornering or when changing power settings indicates wear in the swinging arm bearings. The swinging arm should be removed from the machine and the bearings renewed.

Swinging arm flexing. The symptoms given in the preceding paragraph will also occur if the swinging arm fork flexes badly. This can be caused by structural weakness as a result of corrosion, fatigue or impact damage, or because the rear wheel spindle is slack.

Wheel bearings worn. Renew the worn bearings.

Tyres unsuitable for machine. Not all available tyres will suit the characteristics of the frame and suspension, indeed, some tyres or tyre combinations may cause a transformation in the handling characteristics. If handling problems occur immediately after changing to a new tyre type or make, revert to the original tyres to see whether an improvement can be noted. In some instances a change to what are, in fact, suitable tyres may give rise to handling deficiencies. In this case a thorough check should be made of all frame and suspension items which affect stability.

41 Steering bias to left or right

Rear wheel out of alignment. Caused by uneven adjustment of chain tensioner adjusters allowing the wheel to be askew in the fork ends. A bent rear wheel spindle will also misalign the wheel in the swinging arm.

Wheels out of alignment. This can be caused by impact damage to the frame, swinging arm, wheel spindles or front forks. Although occasionally a result of material failure or corrosion it is usually as a result of a crash.

Front forks twisted in the steering yokes. A light impact, for instance with a pot-hole or low curb, can twist the fork legs in the steering yokes without causing structural damage to the fork legs or the yokes themselves. Re-alignment can be made by loosening the yoke pinch bolts, wheel spindle and mudguard bolts. Re-align the wheel with the handlebars and tighten the bolts working upwards from the wheel spindle. This action should be carried out only when there is no chance that structural damage has occurred.

42 Handlebar vibrates or oscillates

Tyres worn or out of balance. Either condition, particularly in the front tyre, will promote shaking of the fork assembly and thus the handlebars. A sudden onset of shaking can result if a balance weight is displaced during use.

Tyres badly positioned on the wheel rims. A moulded line on each wall of a tyre is provided to allow visual verification that the tyre is correctly positioned on the rim. A check can be made by rotating the tyre; any misalignment will be immediately obvious.

Wheel rims warped or damaged. Inspect the wheels for runout as described in Chapter 5.

Swinging arm bearings worn. Renew the bearings.

Wheel bearings worn. Renew the bearings.

Steering head bearings incorrectly adjusted. Vibration is more likely to result from bearings which are too loose rather than too tight. Re-adjust the bearings.

Loose fork component fasteners. Loose nuts and bolts holding the fork legs, wheel spindle, mudguards or steering stem can promote shaking at the handlebars. Fasteners on running gear such as the forks and suspension should be check tightened occasionally to prevent dangerous looseness of components occurring.

Engine mounting bolts loose. Tighten all fasteners.

43 Poor front fork performance

Damping fluid level incorrect. If the fluid level is too low poor suspension control will occur resulting in a general impairment of roadholding and early loss of tyre adhesion when cornering and braking. Too much oil is unlikely to change the fork characteristics unless severe overfilling occurs when the fork action will become stiffer and oil seal failure may occur.

Damping oil viscosity incorrect. The damping action of the fork is directly related to the viscosity of the damping oil. The lighter the oil used, the less will be the damping action imparted. For general use, use the recommended viscosity of oil, changing to a slightly higher or heavier oil only when a change in damping characteristic is required. Overworked oil, or oil contaminated with water which has found its way past the seals, should be renewed to restore the correct damping performance and to prevent bottoming of the forks.

Damping components worn or corroded. Advanced normal wear of the fork internals is unlikely to occur until a very high mileage has been covered. Continual use of the machine with damaged oil seals which allows the ingress of water, or neglect, will lead to rapid corrosion and wear. Dismantle the forks for inspection and overhaul. See Chapter 4.

Weak fork springs. Progressive fatigue of the fork springs, resulting in a reduced spring free length, will occur after extensive use. This condition will promote excessive fork dive under braking, and in its advanced form will reduce the at-rest extended length of the forks and thus the fork geometry. Renewal of the springs as a pair is the only satisfactory course of action.

Bent stanchions or corroded stanchions. Both conditions will prevent correct telescoping of the fork legs, and in an advanced state can cause sticking of the fork in one position. In a mild form corrosion will cause stiction of the fork thereby increasing the time the suspension takes to react to an uneven road surface. Bent fork stanchions should be attended to immediately because they indicate that impact damage has occurred, and there is a danger that the forks will fail with disastrous consequences.

44 Front fork judder when braking (see also Section 56)

Wear between the fork stanchions and the fork legs. Renewal of the affected components is required.

Slack steering head bearings. Re-adjust the bearings.

Warped brake disc or drum. If irregular braking action occurs fork judder can be induced in what are normally serviceable forks. Renew the damaged brake components.

45 Poor rear suspension performance

Rear suspension unit damper worn out or leaking. The damping performance of most rear suspension units falls off with age. This is a gradual process, and thus may not be immediately obvious. Indications of poor damping include hopping of the rear end when cornering or braking, and a general loss of positive stability. See Chapter 4.

Weak rear spring. If the suspension unit spring fatigues it will promote excessive pitching of the machine and reduce the ground clearance when cornering. Although replacement springs are available separately from the rear suspension damper unit it is probable that if spring fatigue has occurred the damper unit will also require renewal.

Swinging arm flexing or bearings worn. See Sections 40 and 41.

Bent suspension unit damper rod. This is likely to occur only if the machine is dropped or if seizure of the piston occurs. If either happens the suspension unit should be renewed.

Abnormal frame and suspension noise

46 Front end noise

Oil level low or too thin. This can cause a 'spurting' sound and is usually accompanied by irregular fork action.

Spring weak or broken. Makes a clicking or scraping sound. Fork oil will have a lot of metal particles in it.

Steering head bearings loose or damaged. Clicks when braking. Check, adjust or replace.

Fork clamps loose. Make sure all fork clamp pinch bolts are tight.

Fork stanchion bent. Good possibility if machine has been dropped. Repair or replace stanchion.

47 Rear suspension noise

Fluid level too low. Leakage of the suspension unit, usually evident by oil on the outer surfaces, can cause a spurting noise. The suspension unit should be renewed.

Defective rear suspension unit with internal damage. Renew the suspension unit.

Brake problems

48 Brakes are spongy or ineffective – disc brakes

Air in brake circuit. This is only likely to happen in service due to neglect in checking the fluid level or because a leak has developed. The problem should be identified and the brake system bled of air.

Pads worn. Check the pad wear against the wear lines provided and renew the pads if necessary.

Contaminated pads. Cleaning pads which have been contaminated with oil, grease or brake fluid is unlikely to prove successful; the pads should be renewed.

Pads glazed. This is usually caused by overheating. The surface of the pads may be roughened using glass-paper or a fine file.

Brake fluid deterioration. A brake which on initial operation is firm but rapidly becomes spongy in use may be failing due to water contamination of the fluid. The fluid should be drained and then the system refilled and bled.

Master cylinder seal failure. Wear or damage of master cylinder internal parts will prevent pressurisation of the brake fluid. Overhaul the master cylinder unit.

Caliper seal failure. This will almost certainly be obvious by loss of fluid, a lowering of fluid in the master cylinder reservoir and contamination of the brake pads and caliper. Overhaul the caliper assembly.

Brake lever or pedal improperly adjusted. Adjust the clearance between the lever end and master cylinder plunger to take up lost motion, as recommended in Routine maintenance.

49 Brakes drag – disc brakes

Disc warped. The disc must be renewed.

Caliper piston, caliper or pads corroded. The brake caliper assembly is vulnerable to corrosion due to water and dirt, and unless cleaned at regular intervals and lubricated in the recommended manner, will become sticky in operation.

Piston seal deteriorated. The seal is designed to return the piston in the caliper to the retracted position when the brake is released. Wear or old age can affect this function. The caliper should be overhauled if this occurs.

Brake pad damaged. Pad material separating from the backing plate due to wear or faulty manufacture. Renew the pads. Faulty installation of a pad also will cause dragging.

Wheel spindle bent. The spindle may be straightened if no structural damage has occurred.

Brake lever or pedal not returning. Check that the lever or pedal works smoothly throughout its operating range and does not snag on any adjacent cycle parts. Lubricate the pivot if necessary.

Twisted caliper support bracket. This is likely to occur only after impact in an accident. No attempt should be made to re-align the caliper; the bracket should be renewed.

50 Brake lever or pedal pulsates in operation – disc brakes

Disc warped or irregularly worn. The disc must be renewed.

Wheel spindle bent. The spindle may be straightened provided no structural damage has occurred.

51 Disc brake noise

Brake squeal. This can be caused by the omission or incorrect installation of the anti-squeal shim fitted to the rear of one pad. The arrow on the shim should face the direction of wheel normal rotation. Squealing can also be caused by dust on the pads, usually in combination with glazed pads, or other contamination from oil, grease, brake fluid or corrosion. Persistent squealing which cannot be traced to any of the normal causes can often be cured by applying a thin layer of high temperature silicone grease to the rear of the pads. Make absolutely certain that no grease is allowed to contaminate the braking surface of the pads.

Glazed pads. This is usually caused by high temperatures or contamination. The pad surfaces may be roughened using glass-paper or a fine file. If this approach does not effect a cure the pads should be renewed.

Disc warped. This can cause a chattering, clicking or intermittent squeal and is usually accompanied by a pulsating brake lever or pedal or uneven braking. The disc must be renewed.

Brake pads fitted incorrectly or undersize. Longitudinal play in the pads due to omission of the locating springs (where fitted) or because pads of the wrong size have been fitted will cause a single tapping noise every time the brake is operated. Inspect the pads for correct installation and security.

52 Brakes are spongy or ineffective – drum brakes

Brake cable deterioration. Damage to the outer cable by stretching or being trapped will give a spongy feel to the brake lever. The cable should be renewed. A cable which has become corroded due to old age or neglect of lubrication will partially seize making operation very heavy. Lubrication at this stage may overcome the problem but the fitting of a new cable is recommended.

Worn brake linings. Determine lining wear using the external brake wear indicator on the brake backplate, or by removing the wheel and withdrawing the brake backplate. Renew the shoe/lining units as a pair if the linings are worn below the recommended limit.

Worn brake camshaft. Wear between the camshaft and the bearing surface will reduce brake feel and reduce operating efficiency. Renewal of one or both items will be required to rectify the fault.

Worn brake cam and shoe ends. Renew the worn components.

Linings contaminated with dust or grease. Any accumulations of dust should be cleaned from the brake assembly and drum using a petrol dampened cloth. Do not blow or brush off the dust because it is asbestos based and thus harmful if inhaled. Light contamination from grease can be removed from the surface of the brake linings using a solvent; attempts at removing heavier contamination are less likely to be successful because some of the lubricant will have been absorbed by the lining material which will severely reduce the braking performance.

53 Brake drag – drum brakes

Incorrect adjustment. Re-adjust the brake operating mechanism.

Drum warped or oval. This can result from overheating, impact or uneven tension of the wheel spokes. The condition is difficult to correct, although if slight ovality only occurs, skimming the surface of the brake drum can provide a cure. This is work for a specialist engineer. Renewal of the complete wheel hub is normally the only satisfactory solution.

Weak brake shoe return springs. This will prevent the brake lining/shoe units from pulling away from the drum surface once the brake is released. The springs should be renewed.

Brake camshaft, lever pivot or cable poorly lubricated. Failure to attend to regular lubrication of these areas will increase operating resistance which, when compounded, may cause tardy operation and poor release movement.

54 Brake lever or pedal pulsates in operation – drum brakes

Drums warped or oval. This can result from overheating, impact or uneven spoke tension. This condition is difficult to correct, although if slight ovality only occurs skimming the surface of the drum can provide a cure. This is work for a specialist engineer. Renewal of the hub is normally the only satisfactory solution.

55 Drum brake noise

Drum warped or oval. This can cause intermittent rubbing of the brake linings against the drum. See the preceding Section.

Brake linings glazed. This condition, usually accompanied by heavy lining dust contamination, often induces brake squeal. The surface of the linings may be roughened using glass-paper or a fine file.

56 Brake induced fork judder

Worn front fork stanchions and legs, or worn or badly adjusted steering head bearings. These conditions, combined with uneven or pulsating braking as described in Sections 50 and 54 will induce more or less judder when the brakes are applied, dependent on the degree of wear and poor brake operation. Attention should be given to both areas of malfunction. See the relevant Sections.

Electrical problems

57 Battery dead or weak

Battery faulty. Battery life should not be expected to exceed 3 to 4 years, particularly where a starter motor is used regularly. Gradual sulphation of the plates and sediment deposits will reduce the battery performance. Plate and insulator damage can often occur as a result of vibration. Complete power failure, or intermittent failure, may be due to a broken battery terminal. Lack of electrolyte will prevent the battery maintaining charge.

Battery leads making poor contact. Remove the battery leads and clean them and the terminals, removing all traces of corrosion and tarnish. Reconnect the leads and apply a coating of petroleum jelly to the terminals.

Load excessive. If additional items such as spot lamps, are fitted, which increase the total electrical load above the maximum alternator output, the battery will fail to maintain full charge. Reduce the electrical load to suit the electrical capacity.

Regulator/rectifier failure.

Alternator generating coils open-circuit or shorted.

Charging circuit shorting or open circuit. This may be caused by frayed or broken wiring, dirty connectors or a faulty ignition switch. The system should be tested in a logical manner. See Section 60.

58 Battery overcharged

Rectifier/regulator faulty. Overcharging is indicated if the battery becomes hot or it is noticed that the electrolyte level falls repeatedly between checks. In extreme cases the battery will boil causing corrosive gases and electrolyte to be emitted through the vent pipes.

Battery wrongly matched to the electrical circuit. Ensure that the specified battery is fitted to the machine.

59 Total electrical failure

Fuse blown. Check the main fuse. If a fault has occurred, it must be rectified before a new fuse is fitted.

Battery faulty. See Section 57.

Earth failure. Check that the frame main earth strap from the battery is securely affixed to the frame and is making a good contact.

Ignition switch or power circuit failure. Check for current flow through the battery positive lead (red) to the ignition switch. Check the ignition switch for continuity.

60 Circuit failure

Cable failure. Refer to the machine's wiring diagram and check the circuit for continuity. Open circuits are a result of loose or corroded connections, either at terminals or in-line connectors, or because of broken wires. Occasionally, the core of a wire will break without there being any apparent damage to the outer plastic cover.

Switch failure. All switches may be checked for continuity in each switch position, after referring to the switch position boxes incorporated in the wiring diagram for the machine. Switch failure may be a result of mechanical breakage, corrosion or water.

Fuse blown. Refer to the wiring diagram to check whether or not a circuit fuse is fitted. Replace the fuse, if blown, only after the fault has been identified and rectified.

61 Bulbs blowing repeatedly

Vibration failure. This is often an inherent fault related to the natural vibration characteristics of the engine and frame and is, thus, difficult to resolve. Modifications of the lamp mounting, to change the damping characteristics may help.

Intermittent earth. Repeated failure of one bulb, particularly where the bulb is fed directly from the generator, indicates that a poor earth exists somewhere in the circuit. Check that a good contact is available at each earthing point in the circuit.

Reduced voltage. Where a quartz-halogen bulb is fitted the voltage to the bulb should be maintained or early failure of the bulb will occur. Do not overload the system with additional electrical equipment in excess of the system's power capacity and ensure that all circuit connections are maintained clean and tight.

SUZUKI GS/GSX 550 4-VALVE FOURS

Check list

Refer to relevant service interval before performing the following:

1. Check the battery electrolyte level
2. Check the tightness of all engine fasteners
3. Check the tightness of cylinder head nuts and exhaust pipe bolts
4. Clean the air filter
5. Renew the air filter
6. Check the valve clearances
7. Examine and clean the spark plugs
8. Renew the spark plugs
9. Check the engine idle speed
10. Check carburettor adjustment and synchronisation
11. Renew the fuel pipes
12. Renew the engine oil and filter
13. Check clutch adjustment
14. Clean, adjust and lubricate the final drive chain
15. Check the engine oil pressure
16. Check brake pad wear/shoe condition and check the fluid level
17. Renew the brake hoses
18. Adjust the steering head bearings
19. Check the front fork air pressure
20. Renew the front fork oil
21. Check the tightness of all chassis fasteners
22. Check the tyre pressures and check tyre condition
23. Check the engine compression
24. Clean the sump oil strainer
25. Lubricate the throttle cable and clutch cable
26. Lubricate the choke cable
27. Lubricate the handlebar lever pivots
28. Grease the throttle twistgrip
29. Lubricate the instrument drive cable(s)
30. Grease the brake pedal pivot
31. Grease the steering head bearings
32. Grease the swinging arm bushes
33. Grease the clutch release mechanism
34. Lubricate the stand pivots
35. Renew the brake fluid

Service intervals – US

Every 600 miles (1000 km) – 14

Every 2000 miles (3000 km) – 4

Every six months – 19

Every year or 4000 miles (6000 km) – 1, 3, 6, 7, 9, 12, 13, 14, 16, 22, 18, 21, 27, 25, 30, 34

Every two years or 7500 miles (12 000 km) – 1, 3, 6, 8, 9, 12, 13, 14, 16, 22, 18, 20, 21, 28, 33, 29

Every 7500 miles (12 000 km) – 5

Every two years or 15 000 miles (24 000 km) – 31, 32

Every two years – 11

Every three years or 11 000 miles (18 000 km) – 1, 3, 6, 7, 9, 12, 13, 14, 16, 22, 18, 21

Every four years or 15 000 miles (24 000 km) – 1, 3, 6, 8, 9, 12, 13, 14, 16, 22, 18, 20, 21

Every four years – 17

Service intervals – UK

Every 600 miles (1000 km) – 14

Every 2000 miles (3000 km) – 4

Every 3000 miles (5000 km) – 1, 2, 6, 23, 7, 10, 12, 15, 13, 16, 22, 18, 25, 26, 30

Every 6000 miles (10 000 km) – 8, 24, 20, 28, 29

Every 8000 miles (12 000 km) – 5

Every two years – 35

Every two years or 12 000 miles (20 000 km) – 31, 32

Every four years – 17, 11

Adjustment data

Valve clearances (cold) 0.08 – 0.13 mm (0.003 – 0.005 in)

Engine idle speed 1100 ± 100 rpm

Spark plug type
UK models NGK DR8ES or ND X27ESR-U
US models NGK D9EA or ND X27ES-U

Spark plug gap 0.6 – 0.7 mm (0.024 – 0.028 in)

Front fork air pressure
US LD, LF, EF and ESF models 0.3 kg/cm² (4.2 psi)

Tyre pressures	Front	Rear
Solo – all models	28 psi	32 psi
Dual – L models	28 psi	36 psi
Dual – E models	28 psi	40 psi

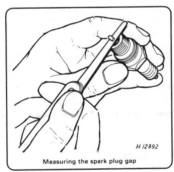

Measuring the spark plug gap

H.12392

Recommended lubricants

	Component	Quantity	Type/viscosity
①	Engine/transmission:- GS550 L model:		SAE 10W/40 SE or SF motor oil
	At oil change	2.6 lit (5.5 US pt)	
	At oil and filter change	3.1 lit (6.5 US pt)	
	All other models: At oil change	2.4 lit (5.1/4.2 US/Imp pt)	
	At oil and filter change	2.9 lit (6.1/5.1 US/Imp pt)	
②	Front forks – see manual for oil capacity, level and grade		
③	Final drive chain	As required	Gear oil or aerosol lubricant suitable for O-ring chains
④	Hydraulic brake	As required	SAE J1703, DOT 3 or DOT 4 brake fluid
⑤	Drum brake camshaft	As required	High melting point grease
⑥	Wheel bearings	As required	High melting point grease
⑦	Steering head bearings	As required	General purpose grease
⑧	Rear suspension pivots	As required	Molybdenum disulphide grease
⑨	Instrument drive cables	As required	General purpose grease
⑩	Control cables	As required	Engine oil or WD40
⑪	Throttle twistgrip	As required	General purpose grease
⑫	Pivot points	As required	Engine oil or WD40

ROUTINE MAINTENANCE GUIDE

Refer to Chapter 7 for information relating to the 1986 to 1988 GS/GSX550 ES and GS550 L models

Routine Maintenance Schedule – UK models

Operation	Initial 600 mi (1000 km)	Every 3000 mi (5000 km)	Every 6000 mi (10 000 km)	See Section No.
Engine				
Battery	Check	Check	–	2
Engine fasteners	Check	Check	–	3, 12
Air filter	Clean every 2000 miles (3000 km) and renew every 8000 miles (12 000 km)			1
Valve clearances	Check	Check	–	4
Compression	Check	Check	–	5
Spark plug	Check	Check	Renew	6
Carburettor	Check	Check	–	7
Fuel pipes	Check	Check	–	7
	Renew every four years			
Engine oil	Change	Change	–	8
Engine oil filter	Renew	Renew	–	8
Sump strainer	–	–	Clean	9
Oil pressure	–	Check	–	10
Clutch	Check	Check	–	11
Chassis				
Drive chain	Clean & adjust every 600 miles (1000 km)			13
Brakes	Check	Check	–	14
Brake hoses	Check	Check	–	15
	Renew every four years			
Brake fluid	Renew every two years			16
Tyres	Check	Check	–	17
Steering	Check	Check	–	18
Front fork oil	Change	–	Change	19
Chassis fasteners	Check	Check	–	20

Lubrication (see Section 21)

Operation	Initial and every 3000 miles (5000 km)	Every 6000 miles (10 000 km)
Throttle cable	Motor oil	–
Throttle twistgrip	–	Grease
Clutch cable	Motor oil	–
Choke cable	Motor oil	–
Speedometer cable	–	Grease
Tachometer cable	–	Motor oil
Drive chain	Motor oil every 600 miles (1000 km)	
Brake pedal pivot	Grease or oil	
Steering bearings	Grease every 2 years or 12 000 miles (20 000 km)	
Swinging arm bushes	Grease every 2 years or 12 000 miles (20 000 km)	

Routine Maintenance Schedule – US models

*Interval: :mile Operation: :km :month	600 1000 2	4000 6000 12	7500 12 000 24	11 000 18 000 36	15 000 24 000 48	See Sec No.
Battery	–	I	I	I	I	2
Engine fasteners	T	T	T	T	T	3, 12
Air filter	Clean every 2000 mi (3000 km). Renew every 7500 mi (12 000 km)					1
Valve clearances	I	I	I	I	I	4
Spark plugs	–	C	R	C	R	6
Idle speed	I	I	I	I	I	7
Fuel pipes	I	I	I	I	I	7
	Renew every 4 years					
Evaporative emission control hoses – California models	I	I	I	I	I	7
	Renew every 4 years					
Engine oil and filter	R	R	R	R	R	8
Clutch	I	I	I	I	I	11
Drive chain	I	I	I	I	I	13
	Clean & lubricate every 600 mi (1000 km)					
Brakes	I	I	I	I	I	14
Brake hoses	I	I	I	I	I	15
	Renew every 4 years					
Brake fluid	Renew every 2 years					16
Tyres	I	I	I	I	I	17
Steering	I	I	I	I	I	18
Front fork	–	–	I	–	I	19
Front fork air pressure	Check every 6 months					19
Chassis fasteners	T	T	T	T	T	20

*Based on calendar or odometer readings, whichever comes first

Note: T = Tighten
I = Inspect
R = Renew
C = Clean

Lubrication (see Section 21)

	Initial and every 4000 mi (6000 km)	Every 7500 mi (12 000 km)
Clutch/brake levers	Motor oil	–
Throttle cable	Motor oil	–
Throttle twistgrip	–	Grease
Clutch cable	Motor oil	–
Clutch release	–	Grease
Speedometer cable	–	Grease
Tachometer cable	–	Grease
Drive chain	Motor oil every 600 mi (1000 km)	
Brake pedal/linkage	Grease or oil	–
Stand pivots	Motor oil	–
Steering head bearings	Grease every 2 years/15 000 mi (24 000 km)	
Swinging arm bushes	Grease every 2 years/15 000 mi (24 000 km)	

Routine maintenance

Regular users of Haynes Owners Workshop Manuals may notice that the Routine Maintenance details do not follow our normal practice where the various operations are given under calendar and mileage headings. This is because the schedules for the UK and US models vary considerably, so to avoid confusion two separate schedules are shown on pages 26 and 27, together with reference to the appropriate section number.

Periodical routine maintenance is essential to keep the motorcycle in a peak and safe condition. Routine maintenance also saves money because it provides the opportunity to detect and remedy a fault before it develops further and causes more damage. Maintenance should be undertaken on either a calendar or mileage basis depending on whichever comes sooner. The period between maintenance tasks serves only as a guide since there are many variables eg: age of machine, riding technique and adverse conditions.

The maintenance instructions are generally those recommended by the manufacturer but are supplemented by additional tasks which, through practical experience, the author recommends should be carried out at intervals suggested. The additional tasks are primarily of a preventative nature, which will assist in eliminating unexpected failure of a component or system, due to wear and tear, and increase safety margins when riding.

All the maintenance tasks are described together with the procedures required for accomplishing them. If necessary, more general information on each topic can be found in the relevant Chapter within the main text.

Although no special tools are required for routine maintenance, a good selection of general workshop tools is essential. Included in the tools must be a range of metric ring or combustion spanners, a selection of crosshead screwdrivers, and two pairs of circlip pliers, one external opening and the other internal opening. Additionally, owing to the extreme tightness of most casing screws on Japanese machines, an impact screwdriver, together with a choice of large or small crosshead screws bits, is absolutely indispensable. This is particularly so if the engine has not been dismantled since leaving the factory.

1 Cleaning the air filter

Pull off the right-hand side panel to reveal the lid of the air filter casing. The lid is clipped into position and can be removed by pulling the two tabs at the rear edge. To free the element, remove the single retaining screw. It can now be manoeuvred out of the casing.

The pleated paper element can be cleaned by blowing compressed air through from the INSIDE face to dislodge the accumulated dust. On no account blow air through from the outside because this will force the dust deeper into the pores. Do not attempt to clean the element with solvents.

The element must be renewed at the specified intervals. If this is ignored, the increased resistance to airflow will upset the carburation, causing poor performance and fuel economy. If the machine is used in unusually dusty conditions, it is advisable to halve the cleaning and renewal intervals. The element should be renewed at once if it becomes contaminated with oil or is holed or torn. Remember that unfiltered air entering the engine will cause rapid and expensive wear to take place.

Refit the cleaned or new element by reversing the removal sequence, ensuring that it is located correctly in the casing. Refit the retaining screw, then fit the cover, ensuring that it seals properly.

2 Checking the battery

Access to the battery is gained after the seat has been unlocked and lifted away. The battery casing is translucent, making it easy to check the level of the electrolyte. Make sure that the electrolyte lies between the upper and lower level lines in each cell, and that the vent pipe has not become blocked or kinked.

Unless acid has been spilt, as may occur if the machine has fallen over, top up with distilled water only; tap water must never be used. If a spillage has occurred, wash off the acid with a solution of washing soda in water. This will neutralise the acid which should then be rinsed with plenty of water. Failure to neutralise spilt acid will result in serious corrosion. The spilt acid should be replenished with dilute sulphuric acid having a specific gravity of 1.280 at 20°C (68°F). This can be obtained from most motorcycle dealers. Remember that acid is dangerous, and protective clothing, gloves and goggles should be worn when handling it.

3 Checking and tightening the engine fasteners

This operation is particularly important on new machines or where the engine has recently been removed and reconditioned. In addition, it provides a valuable general check, often highlighting problems which might otherwise go unnoticed. Refer to Chapter 1 for details of the appropriate tightening sequence and torque settings.

4 Checking the valve clearances

The valve clearances must be checked with the engine cold, preferably after it has been left overnight. Remove the seat and fuel tank to gain access to the cylinder head cover. Remove the cover retaining bolts, then lift the cover away. If it is stuck to the gasket, try tapping around the joint face with a soft-faced mallet to break the seal. Remove the inspection cover at the right-hand end of the crankshaft.

The clearances are checked by measuring the gap between the adjuster and the end of the valve stem. To avoid any risk of inaccuracy due to movement between the rocker arm and shaft it is best to measure each pair of clearances simultaneously, using two sets of feeler gauges. It is important that the rocker is positioned on the base circle of the cam and not the cam lobe when the measurement is taken, and to simplify the process the following procedure should be followed.

Using the large hexagon on the crankshaft end, turn it until the "T" mark is aligned with the index mark and the notches on the right-hand ends of the camshafts face outwards. With the crankshaft set in this position, check and adjust the following valves:

Cylinder No.1 Inlet and exhaust
Cylinder No.2 Exhaust only
Cylinder No.3 Inlet only

The clearance for both inlet and exhaust valves is 0.08 – 1.13 mm (0.003 – 0.005 in). If any valve is outside this range, slacken the locknut using a ring spanner, then turn the adjuster head to obtain the correct clearance. Hold the adjuster firmly and secure the locknut, then recheck the clearance before moving on to the next valve. If required, a Suzuki adjuster tool, Part Number 09917-14910, can be obtained through dealers, though a small open-ended spanner will suffice.

When the above valves have been dealt with, turn the crankshaft through one complete rotation until the "T" mark is again aligned, but this time with the camshaft notches facing inwards. The following valves can now be checked and adjusted:

Cylinder No.2 Inlet only
Cylinder No.3 Exhaust only
Cylinder No.4 Inlet and exhaust

After adjustment is complete, clean the joint face of the cylinder head and cover and place a new gasket in position. Note that a thin film of RTV sealant should be applied to both sides of the gasket to ensure an oil-tight seal. The O-rings fitted to the holding bolts should also be renewed. Refit the crankcase inspection cover, then refit the tank and seat.

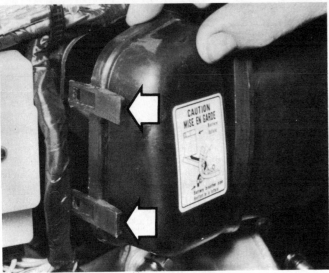

Depress tabs (arrowed) to release air filter cover

Filter element is retained by a single screw ...

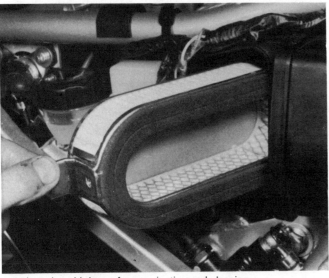

... and can be withdrawn for examination and cleaning

Battery is located in plastic tray below seat

Use two feeler gauges as shown to avoid any error due to twisting of the rocker arm

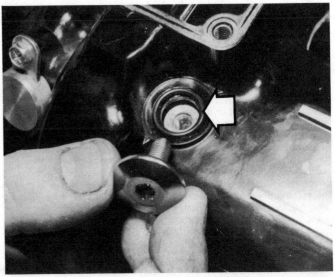

Fit new O-rings to prevent leakage around cylinder head cover screws

5 Checking the compression

The following check requires the use of a Suzuki compression gauge, Part Number 09915-64510, and an adaptor, Part Number 09915-63210, or an equivalent gauge arrangement. In view of the limited use that this equipment will get it may be considered preferable to have the check carried out by a Suzuki Service Agent.

Before making the test the cylinder head nuts should be tightened to the specified torque (see Chapter 1). Run the engine until normal operating temperature is reached, then remove the seat and fuel tank.

Disconnect the plug caps and remove the plugs. Connect the gauge assembly to one of the cylinders via the spark plug thread. Set the engine kill switch to the 'off' position, hold the throttle fully open, then crank the engine for a few seconds, noting the maximum reading for that cylinder. Repeat this process on the remaining cylinders, then compare the readings obtained with the following:

Standard compression:	10-14 kg cm² (142-199 psi)
Service limit:	8 kg cm² (114 psi)
Max. difference between cylinders	2 kg cm² (28.4 psi)

If the readings obtained are lower than those specified, one of the following faults is indicated.

a) Broken or leaking cylinder head gasket
b) Sticking or burnt valves
c) Gummed or broken piston rings
d) Badly worn piston rings or bores

In the case of c or d, this can be confirmed by pouring a small quantity of oil into the bore(s) and repeating the test. If the reading improves, the fault is likely to be related to a defect in the rings or bores, whilst if no difference is found the fault can probably be traced to the head gasket or valves.

6 Checking the spark plugs

Remove the spark plugs for examination and cleaning, noting that comparing the appearance of the electrode area with that shown in the colour section of Chapter 3 will give a good indication of engine condition and mixture strength. The plugs are best cleaned using an abrasive blasting process. Many garages offer a cleaning service, or one of the inexpensive home units can be used. Be careful to ensure that all traces of abrasive are removed after cleaning to avoid bore damage. In the absence of blasting facilities, accumulated carbon can be removed by judicious scraping, using a knife or a small screwdriver. Care must be taken to avoid damage to the electrodes or insulator nose.

Examine the plug electrodes for wear. In time, the outer earth (ground) electrode will become eroded. If it is thin or badly stepped at the end, the plug should be renewed. If the centre electrode has worn until it is nearly flush with the insulator nose, renewal will again be required. Lesser degrees of wear can be corrected by careful dressing, using a fine file or abrasive paper.

Measure the electrode gap using feeler gauges, noting that the correct clearance is 0.6 – 0.7 mm (0.024 – 0.028 in). If adjustment is required, bend the outer electrode only. Any attempt to bend the centre electrode will almost invariably crack the porcelain insulator.

The recommended plug grades are shown in the Specifications at the beginning of Chapter 3. It should not normally be necessary to depart from the standard type, but in some circumstances a change to a hotter or colder grade may be indicated. If there have been persistent problems of fouling, the plugs being prone to becoming wet due to very short journeys in cold climates, select a hotter grade. If on the other hand the machine is ridden hard in a hot climate, the plugs may become overheated, taking on a white, blistered appearance. In this case a colder type may be required. Before making any change to the plug grade it is advisable to consult a Suzuki Service Agent.

7 Checking and adjusting the carburettors

Throttle cable free play

Check the amount of free play in the throttle cable and adjust it if necessary using the adjuster at the lower end. The correct free play is 0.5 – 1.0 mm (0.02 – 0.04 in).

Fuel level check

Check the fuel level in each carburettor using the Suzuki gauge, Part Number 09913-14540, or a home-made equivalent. The check is described in Chapter 2, Section 8.

Carburettor synchronisation

Accurate carburettor synchronisation is important if the engine is to run smoothly and deliver full performance and fuel economy. In addition, poor synchronisation will often produce serious-sounding noises in the primary drive due to uneven idling. The synchronisation operation requires the use of vacuum gauge equipment and is described in detail in Chapter 2, Section 9. In the absence of the above equipment, take the machine to a Suzuki Service Agent to have the synchronisation checked.

Idle speed adjustment

The idle speed should be checked after synchronisation and with the engine at normal operating temperature. Using the large knurled knob at the centre underside of the carburettor bank, set the idle speed to 1000 – 1200 rpm. Note that on no account should the small pilot screws, located next to the intake hoses, be disturbed. These are pre-set during manufacture and no setting data is available if adjustment is lost.

Fuel hose

Check the condition of the fuel and vacuum hoses, renewing them if there is any indication of splitting or leakage. Use only synthetic rubber hose as a replacement. The hoses should be renewed every four years as a precautionary measure.

8 Changing the engine oil and filter

It is vital that the engine oil and filter are changed at the recommended intervals. Apart from the risk of damage due to the degraded oil being unable to cope with the loads imposed on it, it should be remembered that if the filter becomes badly obstructed and the bypass valve opens, any contaminants in the oil will be carried around the engine, causing severe wear or damage if left for long. There is also some risk of overheating if the oil cooler radiator becomes choked internally.

Place the machine on its centre stand and run the engine until it reaches normal operating temperature. Alternatively, and for obvious

Oil drain plug can be reached between exhaust pipes

reasons, it is preferable to carry out the oil change immediately after a run. Place a drain tray or bowl of at least 1 gallon (5 litres) capacity beneath the drain plug, which can now be removed.

While the oil is draining, slacken and remove the three domed nuts which retain the filter cover at the front of the crankcase. Where the oil pressure switch is fitted in the cover, its lead should be disconnected. Lift away the cover and remove the old filter. Clean out any residual oil from the housing, then fit the new filter element. Clean the filter cover and renew the O-ring if it is damaged. Offer up the cover and fit the retaining nuts, using a thread locking compound on their threads.

Clean and refit the drain plug, tightening it securely. Remove the filler cap at the top of the clutch housing and add an API classification SD or SE type motor oil of SAE 10W/40 viscosity. Oil should be added until it reaches the upper limit line in the sight glass. This will require about 2.9 litres (6.1/5.1 US/Imp pint). Start the engine and allow it to idle for a few minutes while checking for leaks, then stop the engine and allow the oil to settle. The level will probably have fallen now that the filter chamber has filled, and should be topped up to the correct level.

9 Cleaning the sump strainer

In addition to the normal oil change, the oil pickup strainer in the sump should be removed and cleaned at the specified interval. Drain the engine oil, then remove the exhaust system to gain access to the sump (oil pan). For more information refer to Chapter 1, Section 4. Slacken evenly and progressively the sump retaining bolts, noting the position of the wiring clips, then lift the sump away.

Clean out the inside of the sump and place it to one side to await reassembly. Remove the three bolts which retain the sump strainer to the underside of the strainer body and lift it away. Clean the strainer in a degreasing solvent and check that it is undamaged. When refitting the strainer, note that the oil inlet arrow must face forward.

Place the new element into recess, having first removed any residual oil or sludge

Check condition of O-ring seal on cover, renew if damaged

Fit cover with spring positioned as shown

Top up via filler hole to the correct level

Sump strainer is retained by three bolts. Note FRONT marking

10 Checking the oil pressure

The engine oil pressure should be checked with the engine at normal operating temperature, using a Suzuki oil pressure gauge, Part Number 09915-74510, 09915-77330 or equivalent. Remove the plug (or pressure switch) from the oil filter cover and attach the gauge. Run the engine at 3000 rpm and note the indicated pressure. The minimum pressure is 2.5 kg cm² (35.6 psi), maximum pressure being 5.5 kg cm² (78.3 psi). If pressure is below the minimum figure, the oil pump or engine components may be badly worn. Excessively high pressure may be due to a build-up of sludge deposits in the engine, usually due to neglected oil and filter changes. In either case the engine should be stripped and the fault rectified.

11 Adjusting the clutch

Slacken the adjuster locknut at the clutch lever and screw the adjuster fully inwards. Remove the clutch adjuster inspection cover from the side of the sprocket cover. Slacken the adjuster locknut and back off the adjuster screw by two or three turns. Turn the screw slowly inwards (clockwise) until slight resistance is felt. From this setting, back the screw off by 1/4 to 1/2 a turn and secure the locknut. Moving to the lower cable adjuster, slacken the locknut and set the adjuster to give about 4 mm (0.16 in) free play measured between the lever stock and blade. Tighten the locknut and slide the rubber boot back into place. Subsequent fine adjustment can be carried out at the lever adjuster.

12 Checking the exhaust system fasteners

Check the security of the nuts and bolts which retain the exhaust system to the cylinder head and the frame. If tightening is required, start with the exhaust port fasteners, then the silencer mountings. Take the opportunity to examine the system for corrosion; if it is beginning to rust now is the time to remove it and apply a suitable aerosol coating to prevent further damage.

13 Checking, adjusting and lubricating and drive chain

The final drive chain should be examined, cleaned and adjusted as described in Chapter 5, Section 17.

14 Checking the braking system

It is important that the hydraulic fluid level is monitored regularly. Although the change in level due to pad wear will be very gradual, any sudden level change can be indicative of a leak or seal failure in the system. The front reservoir level can be checked via the sight window in its side. The rear reservoir is hidden behind the right-hand side panel, but do not be tempted to ignore it; the side panel should be removed periodically and the level checked physically. If topping up is necessary use only fresh hydraulic fluid conforming to DOT 3 or SAE J1703 specification.

Check the condition of the brake pads, noting that they should be renewed as pairs if worn to the limit line. For further information see Chapter 5, Section 8.

In the case of the 'L' models check the rear drum brake for adjustment and lining wear. If necessary, remove the rear wheel to permit inspection of the shoes. See Chapter 5 for further details.

15 Checking the brake hoses

Inspect the brake hoses, looking for signs of cracking or splitting of the outer casing. If deterioration or leakage is suspected, the hose must be renewed without delay. It is recommended that the hoses are renewed as a matter of course every four years, in conjunction with the annual fluid change. For further details, refer to Chapter 5.

16 Changing the hydraulic fluid

The hydraulic fluid in the front and rear braking systems should be changed as a precautionary measure on a two-yearly basis. This is necessary because the fluid is hygroscopic, absorbing moisture from the surrounding air. As this occurs, the boiling point of the fluid is gradually lowered, and if left for long enough this may fall to the point where heat generated under hard braking may cause the formation of bubbles in the fluid. In addition, regular fluid changes will flush the system which in turn will prolong the life of the brake components. For details of the fluid changing operation, refer to Chapter 5.

17 Checking the tyre pressures

The tyre pressures should always be checked when the tyres are cold, preferably after the machine has been standing overnight. This ensures the reading is not affected by the significant pressure rise which takes place when the machine is ridden and the tyres warm up.

It is recommended that a pressure gauge is kept with the machine's toolkit and used in preference to the sometimes unreliable gauges found at filling stations.

Check the tyre treads and sidewalls for cuts or other damage. Remove any small stones which may have become trapped between the tread blocks. If left in place these can work into the tyre and may eventually cause a puncture.

Tyre pressures – cold	Front		Rear	
	psi	kg cm²	psi	kg cm²
All models – solo	28	2.00	32	2.25
All models except LD, LF – dual	28	2.00	40	2.80
LD and LF – dual	28	2.00	36	2.50

18 Checking and adjusting the steering head bearings

The machines covered by this manual are equipped with tapered roller steering head bearings. These can be expected to last for a very long time if correct adjustment is maintained. The procedure is complicated by the need to remove the fairing, where fitted, and is described in Chapter 4.

Hold clutch adjuster screw whilst locknut is secured

Set cable free play at the lower adjuster

Take care to avoid spillage when removing lid and diaphragm

Rear reservoir level can be checked via translucent window

19 Changing the front fork oil

The front fork oil will gradually deteriorate in use, allowing the damping performance to fall off. To prevent this, the damping oil should be changed at the recommended interval. To carry out the work properly it is necessary to remove the fork legs from the machine. This allows the forks to be held vertical so that the precise level in each leg can be measured during topping up. For further information, refer to Chapter 4.

20 Checking and tightening the chassis fasteners

Proceed methodically around the machine checking that all fittings and retaining fasteners are secure, particularly items susceptible to vibration. Where given, tighten fasteners to the recommended torque settings.

21 General lubrication

Regular cleaning of the controls, cables and stand pivots will prolong the life of these components and will help to draw attention to loose or damaged fasteners. It is recommended that general lubrication should be carried out immediately after the machine has been cleaned. This will make the task more pleasant and will help prevent corrosion where degreasing solvents have been used.

Control levers, pedals and gearchange linkage

Lubricate the moving parts using engine oil applied with an oil can or one of the popular aerosol maintenance sprays such as WD 40. Check that pivot and retaining bolts are secure and that the control operates smoothly.

Throttle, choke and clutch cables

Disconnect the cable at its upper end and lubricate it by introducing engine oil and allowing it to work through the cable overnight. This can be accomplished using the improvised funnel arrangement shown in the accompanying line drawing. A faster alternative is to use one of the proprietary cable lubricators available from most motorcycle dealers.

While the cables are disconnected, check the ends of the inner cable for signs of fraying, renewing the cable complete if damage is noted. Before the throttle cable is refitted, grease the throttle twistgrip as described below. Remember to adjust the cables after refitting.

Throttle twistgrip

The throttle twistgrip housing halves can be separated after the retaining screws have been removed, allowing access for throttle cable

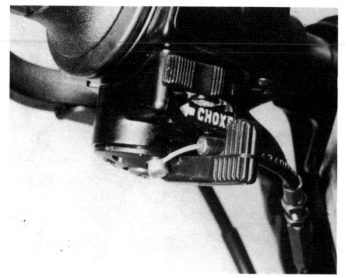

Choke cable can be unhooked for lubrication

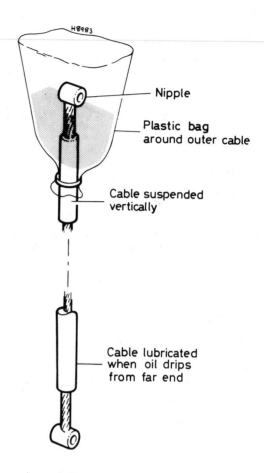

Oiling a control cable

maintenance and twistgrip lubrication. Remove all traces of old grease, then apply a film of grease to the sliding surfaces and to the cable groove.

Speedometer and tachometer drive cables

Disconnect the upper end of the speedometer cable from the underside of the instrument panel and withdraw the inner cable. Wipe off any old grease, then apply a film of fresh grease along its length. Slide the inner cable back into place, noting that it is advisable to wipe off the grease from the uppermost six inches or so to prevent the instrument head from becoming contaminated. On those machines fitted with a mechanical tachometer, the cable can be lubricated in the same way. Note that Suzuki recommend the use of engine oil, rather than grease.

Final drive chain

The procedure for lubricating the final drive chain is given in Chapter 5, Section 17. It should be noted that a sealed O-ring chain is fitted as standard. This can be expected to provide good service if properly maintained, but it is emphasised that many of the proprietary aerosol chain lubricants contain solvents which will destroy the O-rings and thus the chain. It follows that these must be avoided, but there are now one or two lubricants designed specifically for use on O-ring chains, notably PJ1 Blue Label. If the can is not clearly marked as being suitable for use on O-ring chains, stick to a heavy motor oil such as gear oil.

Stand pivots

Clean and lubricate the pivots using motor oil or an aerosol lubricant. Check that the pivot bolts and springs are secure and in good condition.

Steering head and swinging arm

This operation requires the dismantling of the respective assemblies so that a full examination can be made prior to lubrication. Refer to Chapter 4 for details.

Chapter 1 Engine, clutch and gearbox

Refer to Chapter 7 for information relating to the 1986 to 1988 GS/GSX550 ES and GS550 L models

Contents

Specifications

UK GSX550 ESD, EE, ESE and EFE models

Engine

Type	Four cylinder, dohc 16-valve, air-cooled four-stroke
Bore	60.0 mm (2.362 in)
Stroke	50.6 mm (1.992 in)
Capacity	572 cc (34.9 cu in)
Compression ratio	9.8 : 1
Max power	N/Av
Max torque	N/Av

Cylinder head

Max warpage	0.2 mm (0.008 in)

Camshafts and rockers

Cam height (inlet)	34.940 – 34.980 mm (1.3756 – 1.3772 in)
Service limit	34.640 mm (1.3638 in)
Cam height (exhaust)	34.360 – 34.400 mm (1.3528 – 1.3543 in)
Service limit	34.060 mm (1.3409 in)
Camshaft/journal oil clearance (inlet and exhaust):	
Centre journals	0.050 – 0.084 mm (0.0020 – 0.0033 in)

Service limit	0.150 mm (0.0059 in)
Outer journals	0.032 – 0.066 mm (0.0013 – 0.0026 in)
Service limit	0.150 mm (0.0059 in)
Camshaft bearing cap ID:	
Centre journals	22.030 – 22.043 mm (0.8673 – 0.8678 in)
Service limit	Not available
Outer journals	22.012 – 22.025 mm (0.8666 – 0.8671 in)
Service limit	Not available
Camshaft journal OD	21.959 – 21.980 mm (0.8645 – 0.8654 in)
Service limit	Not available
Camshaft runout – service limit	0.10 mm (0.004 in)
Cam chain length – service limit (20 links)	128.9 mm (5.075 in)
Rocker arm ID	12.000 – 12.018 mm (0.4724 – 0.4731 in)
Service limit	Not available
Rocker shaft OD	11.973 – 11.984 mm (0.4714 – 0.4718 in)
Service limit	Not available

Valves and guides

Valve head diameter:	
Inlet	21.0 mm (0.827 in)
Exhaust	18.0 mm (0.709 in)
Valve lift:	
Inlet	7.5 mm (0.295 in)
Exhaust	6.5 mm (0.256 in)
Valve clearance (cold) – inlet and exhaust	0.08 – 0.13 mm (0.003 – 0.005 in)
Guide to stem clearance:	
Inlet	0.025 – 0.052 mm (0.0010 – 0.0020 in)
Service limit	0.35 mm (0.014 in)
Exhaust	0.040 – 0.067 mm (0.0016 – 0.0026 in)
Service limit	0.35 mm (0.014 in)
Valve guide ID	5.000 – 5.012 mm (0.1969 – 0.1973 in)
Valve stem OD:	
Inlet	4.960 – 4.975 mm (0.1953 – 0.1959 in)
Exhaust	4.945 – 4.960 mm (0.1947 – 0.1953 in)
Valve stem runout (in/ex) – service limit	0.05 mm (0.002 in)
Valve head thickness (in/ex) – service limit	0.5 mm (0.02 in)
Valve stem end length (in/ex) – service limit	2.9 mm (0.114 in)
Valve seat width (in/ex)	0.9 – 1.1 mm (0.035 – 0.043 in)
Valve head radial runout	0.03 mm (0.001 in)
Valve spring free length:	
Inner (service limit)	31.6 mm (1.24 in)
Outer (service limit)	35.1 mm (1.38 in)
Valve spring pressure:	
Inner	5.0 – 5.9 kg (11 – 13 lb) @ 28.0 mm (1.10 in)
Outer	8.4 – 9.8 kg (18.5 – 21.6 lb) @ 31.5 mm (1.24 in)

Cylinder bores

Compression pressure	10 – 14 kg cm² (142 – 199 psi)
Service limit	8 kg cm² (114 psi)
Pressure difference between cylinders – service limit ...	2 kg cm² (28.4 psi)
Bore size (Std)	60.000 – 60.015 mm (2.3622 – 2.3628 in)
Service limit	60.100 mm (2.3661 in)
Bore ovality – service limit	0.2 mm (0.008 in)

Pistons

Piston/cylinder clearance	0.030 – 0.040 mm (0.0012 – 0.0016 in)
Service limit	0.120 mm (0.0047 in)
Piston diameter (Std)	59.965 – 59.980 mm (2.3608 – 2.3614 in)
Service limit	59.880 mm (2.3575 in)
Ring end gap (free):	
Top	About 8.0 mm (0.31 in)
Service limit	6.4 mm (0.25 in)
2nd	About 8.5 mm (0.33 in)
Service limit	6.8 mm (0.27 in)
Ring end gap (installed):	
Top	0.10 – 0.25 mm (0.004 – 0.010 in)
2nd	0.10 – 0.30 mm (0.004 – 0.012 in)
Service limit (top & 2nd)	0.7 mm (0.03 in)
Ring to groove clearance:	
Top (service limit)	0.180 mm (0.0071 in)
2nd (service limit)	0.150 mm (0.0059 in)
Ring groove width:	
Top	1.01 – 1.03 mm (0.040 – 0.041 in)
2nd	1.21 – 1.23 mm (0.047 – 0.048 in)
Oil	2.51 – 2.53 mm (0.099 – 0.100 in)

Gudgeon pin bore ID	16.000 – 16.006 mm (0.6299 – 0.6302 in)
Service limit	16.030 mm (0.6311 in)
Gudgeon pin OD	15.995 – 16.000 mm (0.6297 – 0.6299 in)
Service limit	15.980 mm (0.6291 in)

Crankshaft and connecting rods

Crankshaft runout – service limit	0.05 mm (0.002 in)
Small-end ID	16.010 – 16.018 mm (0.6303 – 0.6306 in)
Service limit	16.040 mm (0.6315 in)
Big-end side clearance	0.10 – 0.20 mm (0.004 – 0.008 in)
Service limit	0.30 mm (0.012 in)
Connecting rod big-end width	19.95 – 20.00 mm (0.7854 – 0.7874 in)
Crank pin width	20.10 – 20.15 mm (0.7913 – 0.7933 in)
Big-end oil clearance	0.024 – 0.048 mm (0.0009 – 0.0019 in)
Service limit	0.080 mm (0.0032 in)
Crank pin OD	31.976 – 32.000 mm (1.2589 – 1.2598 in)
Main bearing journal oil clearance	0.020 – 0.044 mm (0.0008 – 0.0017 in)
Service limit	0.080 mm (0.0032 in)
Main bearing journal OD	31.976 – 32.000 mm (1.2589 – 1.2598 in)
Crankshaft thrust bearing thickness:	
Left-hand	2.350 – 2.500 mm (0.0925 – 0.0984 in)
Right-hand	2.425 – 2.450 mm (0.0955 – 0.0965 in)
Crankshaft thrust clearance	0.045 – 0.100 mm (0.0018 – 0.0039 in)

Clutch

Type	Wet, multiplate
Number of plain plates	7
Number of friction plates	7
Friction plate thickness	3.05 – 3.20 mm (0.120 – 0.126 in)
Service limit	2.75 mm (0.108 in)
Friction plate tang width	11.8 – 12.0 mm (0.465 – 0.472 in)
Service limit	11.0 mm (0.43 in)
Plain plate thickness:	
Innermost plate	2.00 ± 0.06 mm (0.079 ± 0.002 in)
All other plates (6 off)	1.60 ± 0.06 mm (0.063 ± 0.002 in)
Plain plate warpage – service limit	0.1 mm (0.004 in)
Clutch spring free length – service limit	36.5 mm (1.44 in)
Clutch cable free play	4.0 mm (0.157 in)

Transmission

Primary reduction	1.977 : 1 (89/45 T)
Final reduction	3.285 : 1 (46/14 T)
Final drive chain:	
Type	D.I.D. 50HDL or TAKASAGO RK50SMO
Length	112 links
20-pin length (max):	
ESD model	323.0 mm (12.72 in)
Other models	323.9 mm (12.75 in)
Free play	20 – 30 mm (0.8 – 1.2 in)
Gearbox type	6-speed constant mesh
Gearbox ratios:	
1st	2.666 : 1 (32/12 T)
2nd	1.777 : 1 (32/18 T)
3rd	1.380 : 1 (29/21 T)
4th	1.173 : 1 (27/23 T)
5th	1.045 : 1 (23/22 T)
Top	0.956 : 1 (22/23 T)
Selector fork to groove clearance	0.1 – 0.3 mm (0.004 – 0.012 in)
Service limit	0.5 mm (0.020 in)
Fork groove width	5.5 – 5.6 mm (0.217 – 0.220 in)
Fork thickness	5.3 – 5.4 mm (0.209 – 0.213 in)

Torque wrench settings

Component	kgf m	lbf ft
Cylinder head cover bolt	1.3 – 1.5	9.4 – 10.9
Cylinder head nut	2.3 – 2.8	16.6 – 20.3
Cylinder head bolt	0.7 – 1.1	5.1 – 8.0
Valve clearance adjuster locknut	0.9 – 1.1	6.5 – 8.0
Camshaft cap bolt	0.8 – 1.2	5.8 – 8.7
Camshaft sprocket bolt	2.4 – 2.6	17.4 – 18.8
Cylinder head oil pipe clamp bolt	1.0 – 1.4	7.2 – 10.1
Cylinder head oil pipe union bolt:		
Inlet valve side	0.8 – 1.2	5.8 – 8.7
Exhaust valve side	0.8 – 1.2	5.8 – 8.7
Rocker shaft stopper bolt	0.8 – 1.0	5.8 – 7.2

Oil hose union bolt:

Cylinder head side	0.8 – 1.2	5.8 – 8.7
Crankcase side	2.0 – 2.4	14.5 – 17.4
Cam chain tensioner mounting bolt	0.6 – 0.8	4.3 – 5.8
Cam chain tensioner locknut	0.9 – 1.4	6.5 – 10.1
Big-end bearing cap nut	3.3 – 3.7	23.9 – 26.7
Alternator rotor bolt	14.0 – 16.0	101.3 – 115.7
Starter clutch Allen bolt	2.3 – 2.8	16.6 – 20.3
Ignition pickup rotor bolt	2.5 – 3.5	18.1 – 25.3

Crankcase bolt:

6 mm	0.9 – 1.3	6.5 – 9.4
8 mm	2.0 – 2.4	14.5 – 17.5
Oil pump mounting bolt	0.7 – 0.9	5.1 – 6.5
Neutral cam stopper bolt	1.8 – 2.8	13.0 – 20.3
Gear selector arm stopper bolt	1.5 – 2.3	10.9 – 16.6
Clutch centre bolt	5.0 – 7.0	36.2 – 50.6
Clutch spring bolt	1.1 – 1.3	8.0 – 9.4
Gearbox sprocket nut	10.0 – 15.0	72.3 – 108.5

Engine mounting bolt:

35 mm and 165 mm length	6.0 – 7.2	43.4 – 52.1
160 mm and 195 mm length	6.7 – 8.0	48.5 – 57.9

US GS550 ED, ESD, LD, ESE, ES3, EF, ESF and LF

Engine

Type	Four cylinder, dohc 16-valve, air-cooled four-stroke
Bore	60.0 mm (2.362 in)
Stroke	50.6 mm (1.992 in)
Capacity	572 cc (34.9 cu in)
Compression ratio	9.8 : 1
Max power	N/Av
Max torque	N/Av

Cylinder head

Max warpage	0.2 mm (0.008 in)

Camshafts and rockers

Cam height (inlet)	34.940 – 34.980 mm (1.3756 – 1.3772 in)
Service limit	34.640 mm (1.3638 in)
Cam height (exhaust)	34.360 – 34.400 mm (1.3528 – 1.3543 in)
Service limit	34.060 mm (1.3409 in)
Camshaft/journal oil clearance (inlet and exhaust):	
Centre journals	0.050 – 0.084 mm (0.0020 – 0.0033 in)
Service limit	0.150 mm (0.0059 in)
Outer journals	0.032 – 0.066 mm (0.0013 – 0.0026 in)
Service limit	0.150 mm (0.0059 in)
Camshaft bearing cap ID:	
Centre journals	22.030 – 22.043 mm (0.8673 – 0.8678 in)
Service limit	Not available
Outer journals	22.012 – 22.025 mm (0.8666 – 0.8671 in)
Service limit	Not available
Camshaft journal OD	21.959 – 21.980 mm (0.8645 – 0.8654 in)
Service limit	Not available
Camshaft runout – service limit	0.10 mm (0.004 in)
Cam chain length – service limit (20 links)	128.9 mm (5.075 in)
Rocker arm ID	12.000 – 12.018 mm (0.4724 – 0.4731 in)
Service limit	Not available
Rocker shaft OD	11.973 – 11.984 mm (0.4714 – 0.4718 in)
Service limit	Not available

Valves and guides

Valve head diameter:	
Inlet	21.0 mm (0.827 in)
Exhaust	18.0 mm (0.709 in)
Valve lift:	
Inlet	7.5 mm (0.295 in)
Exhaust	6.5 mm (0.256 in)
Valve clearance (cold) – inlet and exhaust	0.08 – 0.13 mm (0.003 – 0.005 in)
Guide to stem clearance:	
Inlet	0.025 – 0.052 mm (0.0010 – 0.0020 in)
Service limit	0.35 mm (0.014 in)
Exhaust	0.040 – 0.067 mm (0.0016 – 0.0026 in)
Service limit	0.35 mm (0.014 in)
Valve guide ID	5.000 – 5.012 mm (0.1969 – 0.1973 in)
Valve stem OD:	
Inlet	4.960 – 4.975 mm (0.1953 – 0.1959 in)
Exhaust	4.945 – 4.960 mm (0.1947 – 0.1953 in)

Valve stem runout (in/ex) – service limit	0.05 mm (0.002 in)
Valve head thickness (in/ex) – service limit	0.5 mm (0.02 in)
Valve stem end length (in/ex) – service limit	2.9 mm (0.114 in)
Valve seat width (in/ex)	0.9 – 1.1 mm (0.035 – 0.043 in)
Valve head radial runout	0.03 mm (0.001 in)

Valve spring free length:

Inner (service limit)	31.6 mm (1.24 in)
Outer (service limit)	35.1 mm (1.38 in)

Valve spring pressure:

Inner	5.0 – 5.9 kg (11 – 13 lb) @ 28.0 mm (1.10 in)
Outer	8.4 – 9.8 kg (18.5 – 21.6 lb) @ 31.5 mm (1.24 in)

Cylinder bores

Compression pressure:

ED, ESD, LD, ESE, ES3	10 – 14 kg cm² (142 – 199 psi)
EF, ESF, LF	10 – 15 kg cm² (142 – 214 psi)
Service limit	8 kg cm² (114 psi)
Pressure difference between cylinders – service limit	2 kg cm² (28.4 psi)
Bore size (Std)	60.000 – 60.015 mm (2.3622 – 2.3628 in)
Service limit	60.100 mm (2.3661 in)
Bore ovality – service limit	0.2 mm (0.008 in)

Pistons

Piston/cylinder clearance	0.030 – 0.040 mm (0.0012 – 0.0016 in)
Service limit	0.120 mm (0.0047 in)
Piston diameter (Std)	59.965 – 59.980 mm (2.3608 – 2.3614 in)
Service limit	59.880 mm (2.3575 in)

Ring end gap [free] (ED, ESD, ESE, ES3 and LD):

Top	About 8.0 mm (0.31 in)
Service limit	6.4 mm (0.25 in)
2nd	About 8.5 mm (0.33 in)
Service limit	6.8 mm (0.27 in)

Ring end gap [free] (EF, ESF and LF):

Top	About 7.6 mm (0.30 in)
Service limit	6.1 mm (0.24 in)
2nd	About 7.3 mm (0.29 in)
Service limit	5.8 mm (0.23 in)

Ring end gap [installed] (ED, ESD, ESE, ES3 and LD):

Top	0.10 – 0.25 mm (0.004 – 0.010 in)
2nd	0.10 – 0.30 mm (0.004 – 0.012 in)
Service limit (top & 2nd)	0.7 mm (0.03 in)

Ring end gap [installed] (EF, ESF and LF):

Top	0.10 – 0.30 mm (0.004 – 0.012 in)
2nd	0.10 – 0.30 mm (0.004 – 0.012 in)
Service limit (top & 2nd)	0.7 mm (0.03 in)

Ring to groove clearance:

Top (service limit)	0.180 mm (0.0071 in)
2nd (service limit)	0.150 mm (0.0059 in)

Ring groove width:

Top	1.01 – 1.03 mm (0.040 – 0.041 in)
2nd	1.21 – 1.23 mm (0.047 – 0.048 in)
Oil	2.51 – 2.53 mm (0.099 – 0.100 in)
Gudgeon pin bore ID	16.000 – 16.006 mm (0.6299 – 0.6302 in)
Service limit	16.030 mm (0.6311 in)
Gudgeon pin OD	15.995 – 16.000 mm (0.6297 – 0.6299 in)
Service limit	15.980 mm (0.6291 in)

Crankshaft and connecting rods

Crankshaft runout – service limit	0.05 mm (0.002 in)
Small-end ID	16.010 – 16.018 mm (0.6303 – 0.6306 in)
Service limit	16.040 mm (0.6315 in)
Big-end side clearance	0.10 – 0.20 mm (0.004 – 0.008 in)
Service limit	0.30 mm (0.012 in)
Connecting rod big-end width	19.95 – 20.00 mm (0.7854 – 0.7874 in)
Crank pin width	20.10 – 20.15 mm (0.7913 – 0.7933 in)
Big-end oil clearance	0.024 – 0.048 mm (0.0009 – 0.0019 in)
Service limit	0.080 mm (0.0032 in)
Crank pin OD	31.976 – 32.000 mm (1.2589 – 1.2598 in)
Main bearing journal oil clearance	0.020 – 0.044 mm (0.0008 – 0.0017 in)
Service limit	0.080 mm (0.0032 in)
Main bearing journal OD	31.976 – 32.000 mm (1.2589 – 1.2598 in)

Crankshaft thrust bearing thickness:

Left-hand	2.350 – 2.500 mm (0.0925 – 0.0984 in)
Right-hand	2.425 – 2.450 mm (0.0955 – 0.0965 in)
Crankshaft thrust clearance	0.045 – 0.100 mm (0.0018 – 0.0039 in)

Clutch

Type	Wet, multiplate
Number of plain plates	7
Number of friction plates	7
Friction plate thickness	3.05 – 3.20 mm (0.120 – 0.126 in)
Service limit	2.75 mm (0.108 in)
Friction plate tang width	11.8 – 12.0 mm (0.465 – 0.472 in)
Service limit	11.0 mm (0.43 in)
Plain plate thickness:	
Innermost plate	2.00 ± 0.06 mm (0.079 ± 0.002 in)
All other plates (6 off)	1.60 ± 0.06 mm (0.063 ± 0.002 in)
Plain plate warpage – service limit	0.1 mm (0.004 in)
Clutch spring free length – service limit	36.5 mm (1.44 in)
Clutch cable free play	4.0 mm (0.157 in)

Transmission

Primary reduction	1.977 : 1 (89/45 T)
Final reduction:	
ED, ESD, ESE, ES3, EF, ESF	3.428 : 1 (48/14 T)
LD, LF	3.357 : 1 (47/14 T)
Final drive chain:	
Type	D.I.D. 50HDL or TAKASAGO RK50SMO
Length	112 links
20-pin length (max):	
ESD model	323.0 mm (12.72 in)
Other models	323.9 mm (12.75 in)
Free play	20 – 30 mm (0.8 – 1.2 in)
Gearbox type	6-speed constant mesh
Gearbox ratios:	
1st	2.666 : 1 (32/12 T)
2nd	1.777 : 1 (32/18 T)
3rd	1.380 : 1 (29/21 T)
4th	1.173 : 1 (27/23 T)
5th	1.045 : 1 (23/22 T)
Top	0.956 : 1 (22/23 T)
Selector fork to groove clearance	0.1 – 0.3 mm (0.004 – 0.012 in)
Service limit	0.5 mm (0.020 in)
Fork groove width	5.5 – 5.6 mm (0.217 – 0.220 in)
Fork thickness	5.3 – 5.4 mm (0.209 – 0.213 in)

Torque wrench settings

Component	kgf m	lbf ft
Cylinder head cover bolt	1.3 – 1.5	9.4 – 10.9
Cylinder head nut	2.3 – 2.8	16.6 – 20.3
Cylinder head bolt	0.7 – 1.1	5.1 – 8.0
Valve clearance adjuster locknut	0.9 – 1.1	6.5 – 8.0
Camshaft cap bolt	0.8 – 1.2	5.8 – 8.7
Camshaft sprocket bolt	2.4 – 2.6	17.4 – 18.8
Cylinder head oil pipe clamp bolt	1.0 – 1.4	7.2 – 10.1
Cylinder head oil pipe union bolt:		
Inlet valve side	0.8 – 1.2	5.8 – 8.7
Exhaust valve side	0.8 – 1.2	5.8 – 8.7
Rocker shaft stopper bolt	0.8 – 1.0	5.8 – 7.2
Oil hose union bolt:		
Cylinder head side	0.8 – 1.2	5.8 – 8.7
Crankcase side	2.0 – 2.4	14.5 – 17.4
Cam chain tensioner mounting bolt	0.6 – 0.8	4.3 – 5.8
Cam chain tensioner locknut	0.9 – 1.4	6.5 – 10.1
Big-end bearing cap nut	3.3 – 3.7	23.9 – 26.7
Alternator rotor bolt	14.0 – 16.0	101.3 – 115.7
Starter clutch Allen bolt	2.3 – 2.8	16.6 – 20.3
Ignition pickup rotor bolt	2.5 – 3.5	18.1 – 25.3
Crankcase bolt:		
6 mm	0.9 – 1.3	6.5 – 9.4
8 mm	2.0 – 2.4	14.5 – 17.5
Oil pump mounting bolt	0.7 – 0.9	5.1 – 6.5
Neutral cam stopper bolt	1.8 – 2.8	13.0 – 20.3
Gear selector arm stopper bolt	1.5 – 2.3	10.9 – 16.6
Clutch centre bolt	5.0 – 7.0	36.2 – 50.6
Clutch spring bolt	1.1 – 1.3	8.0 – 9.4
Gearbox sprocket nut	10.0 – 15.0	72.3 – 108.5
Engine mounting bolt:		
35 mm and 165 mm length	6.0 – 7.2	43.4 – 52.1
160 mm and 195 mm length	6.7 – 8.0	48.5 – 57.9

Note: *At the time of writing no torque settings were available for the GS550 ESE and ES3 models.*

1 General description and engine modifications

The engine/gearbox unit is of the four-cylinder, air cooled, in-line type mounted transversely across the frame, the general engine and gearbox layout having many similarities with the larger capacity GS/GSX models. The cylinder head is a 16 valve design, designated TSCC (Twin Swirl Combustion Chamber) by Suzuki. The valves are arranged in pairs and are driven via short rockers by the double overhead camshafts. The camshafts are driven by a central chain from the crankshaft, chain tension being controlled by a self-adjusting tensioner unit.

The horizontally separated crankcases incorporate the crankshaft, primary drive, clutch and the 6-speed constant mesh gearbox in a common casing. The underside of the crankcase assembly is closed by a finned alloy sump (oil pan) which contains the shared lubrication supply.

In the course of its development, a number of modifications were introduced, either as improvements to the original design or due to general uprating on the later models. Brief details of the major changes are given below, but it should be noted that it is essential to quote the engine number in full when ordering replacement parts. This will ensure that the new parts will fit correctly. Note that the details below are based on those models for which information was available at the time of writing. In the case of the UK machines, the basic engine/gearbox unit has remained virtually unchanged apart from minor specification changes and cosmetic alterations.

GS550 LD: Similar in most respects to the GS550 ED and ESD models, the oil pressure switch is located in the front of the oil filter housing, rather than on the top of the crankcase. The remaining models have a blanking plug fitted in the oil filter cover.

GS550 EF, ESF and LF: The main and big-end bearing shell part numbers were changed. For details refer to the tables shown later in this Chapter.

Modified piston assemblies were fitted on later models, the main difference being smaller diameter ring grooves and a modified oil feed groove below the oil ring. Different piston rings were fitted, and it is important to avoid fitting the early type rings to late pistons or vice-versa. The early pattern rings are manufactured by NIPPON and are marked "N" on their upper faces. The later rings are made by RIKEN and are marked "R" on the upper surface. Complete piston/ring assemblies are interchangeable. Note that this modification affects some of the piston and ring measurements as shown in the Specifications. If later pattern parts are fitted to an early engine, refer to the appropriate clearances when checking engine wear.

The valve timing has been changed on all 1985 models, and thus a different inlet camshaft is fitted. This part can be identified by a "C" mark stamped into the right-hand end.

2 Operations with the engine/gearbox unit in the frame

1 The following components or assemblies can be removed or dismantled without taking the engine unit out of the frame. Whilst this

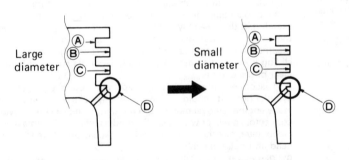

Large diameter

Small diameter

Early model piston
Part number 12111-43408

Later model piston
Part number 12111-43420

Piston: later models featured a modified piston with smaller diameter ring grooves (A, B and C) and a modified oil feed groove (D)

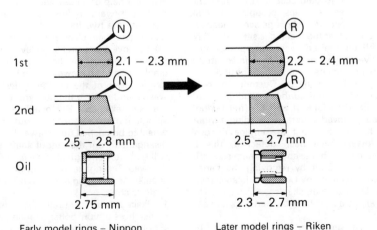

1st   2.1 – 2.3 mm   2.2 – 2.4 mm

2nd   2.5 – 2.8 mm   2.5 – 2.7 mm

Oil   2.75 mm   2.3 – 2.7 mm

Early model rings – Nippon
Part number 12140-43422

Later model rings – Riken
Part number 12140-43410

Fig. 1.1 Piston and piston rings modification

will often be advantageous, where a number of operations are to be undertaken simultaneously it may prove better to remove the engine and carry out the work on the bench.

(a) Gearchange lever and sprocket cover
(b) Gearbox sprocket, chain and gear position switch
(c) Alternator stator and rotor
(d) Starter clutch and idler gear
(e) Oil filter
(f) Sump (oil pan) and sump strainer
(g) Tachometer drive (where fitted)
(h) Cylinder head breather cover
(i) Cam chain tensioner mechanism
(j) Cylinder head cover
(k) Camshafts
(l) Cylinder head
(m) Cylinder block and pistons
(n) Starter motor
(o) Oil pressure/temperature switch
(p) Ignition pickup assembly
(q) Clutch cover
(r) Clutch assembly
(s) Oil pump assembly
(t) Gearchange components (except drum and forks)

3 Operations requiring engine/gearbox removal

1   To gain access to any of the crankcase internal components or assemblies it will be necessary to remove the engine unit from the frame to permit crankcase separation. As a guide, engine removal must precede the following operations:

(a) Removal of the crankshaft assembly, including access to the main and big-end bearings
(b) Removal of the gearbox shafts, or the gear selector drum and forks

4 Removing the engine/gearbox unit

1   Place the machine securely on its centre stand. With the engine at normal operating temperature, place a bowl or drain tray of at least 1 gall/5 litres capacity below the sump drain plug. Remove the plug and allow the oil to drain. Once the oil has drained fully, refit the plug and then clean the engine unit thoroughly with degreaser, or by steam or pressure cleaning, to remove all road dirt and oil.
2   Unlock and remove the seat, then carefully pull off the side panels. Remove the two bolts and rubber bushes which secure the rear of the fuel tank. Lift the tank up at the rear to gain access to the fuel and vacuum hoses and the fuel gauge sender leads, propping the tank against the frame. Trace and disconnect the fuel gauge sender leads at the rear underside of the tank. Check that the fuel tap is set to the 'ON' or 'RES' position, then prise off the fuel and vacuum pipes using a small screwdriver. Once the above connections have been freed, lift the tank and pull it rearwards to free it from its front mounting rubbers.
3   In the case of the basic E models and the US Custom L models, engine removal can now proceed without further attention to the bodywork. In the case of the ES (half fairing) and EF (full fairing) models, the fairings should be removed before proceeding further. Although it may seem possible to carry out the engine removal operation once the fairing lowers have been detached, this is inadvisable; the engine is a tight fit in the frame and maximum access is needed if damage is to be avoided. Start by removing the fairing lowers. On the EF model these are retained by two cross-head screws at the upper edge and by three Dzus-type quick release fasteners. The short lowers on the ES version are held by rubber-bushed pegs and can be pulled away carefully.
4   The top section of the fairing is similar on both models. Start by removing the two screws which retain each turn signal lamp to the fairing subframe; these are accessible through holes in the underside of the fairing. Lift the lamps clear and disconnect the wiring. The fairing is retained by two screws which pass through the underside of the fairing into the subframe, just to the rear of the headlamp. A single screw is fitted on each side of the fairing, near to the mounting lugs for the

lowers. Lift the fairing away and place it and the lowers in a safe place.
5   Disconnect the battery leads and remove the battery from its tray, noting the routing of the breather pipe. This varies according to model and it is worth making a quick sketch as a reminder during assembly. Moving to the left-hand side of the machine, pull off the two igniter unit connectors. Remove the two screws which secure the igniter unit to the battery tray and remove it. Free the turn signal relay from the battery tray by disengaging its rubber mounting. Disconnect the fuse box from the right-hand side of the battery tray in a similar manner. Slacken the two screws which locate the bottom edge of the battery tray and lift it clear of the frame.
6   Trace the alternator output leads back from the engine and disconnect them at the bullet connectors (three yellow leads). Disconnect the battery negative lead at the single pin connector. Free the starter relay negative lead at the relay terminal. Disconnect the oil pressure switch lead and the side stand switch lead at their respective bullet connectors. Note that the latter are well hidden between the two carburettor to air filter hoses; if necessary this can be left until access is easier, but do not forget them. Finally, disconnect the gear position indicator wiring (multi-pin connector near the coils) and the single neutral switch lead next to it. Before proceeding further, ensure that all wiring attached to the engine is freed from the frame and any cable clips.
7   Remove the two bolts which retain the air filter casing to the frame lugs just below the fuel tank rear mounting. Slacken the clips which hold the carburettors to their mounting stubs and to the air filter stubs. Disengage the air filter casing and pull it fully rearwards. Grasp the carburettor assembly and pull it back to clear the inlet stubs. Unscrew the two cold start plungers to free the cables, then disengage the throttle cable outer from its bracket. Turn the assembly slightly and unhook the throttle cable inner from the pulley. Before removing the carburettors completely, note the routing of the drain hoses, making a sketch. Lift the assembly out to the right and place it to one side. Free the large diameter engine breather hose from the cylinder head breather cover by squeezing the ears of the clip together with pliers and sliding it down the hose. Work the hose off its stub and lodge it well clear of the engine.
8   Disconnect the spark plug caps and lodge them clear of the cylinder head. It should be noted that any obstruction in this area will make engine removal much more difficult, so make sure all wiring and connectors are kept well clear. On models equipped with a mechanical tachometer, free the single bolt which secures the drive to the cylinder head and pull the cable clear.
9   Remove the two Allen bolts which retain each of the four exhaust pipe clamps to the cylinder head and slide the clamps clear. On the underside of the machine, slacken the clamps on the two inner pipes and the single clamp which secures the balance pipe. If the pipes are corroded, soak them in WD40 or similar to make separation easier. It is not necessary to disturb the heat shield clamps on the outer pipes. Remove the silencer mounting bolts from the footrest support plate. With the help of an assistant, lower the rear of the system slightly and push it forward to free the exhaust pipes from the cylinder head. Separate the two halves of the system at the balance pipe joint and manoeuvre them clear of the frame.
10 Remove the gearchange lever pinch bolt and slide the lever off its splines. Remove the bolts which retain the sprocket cover to the crankcase and lift it away; it can be left attached to the clutch cable and lodged clear of the engine if desired. Flatten the sprocket nut tab washer and remove the nut whilst holding the sprocket by depressing the rear brake pedal. Remove the split pin which secures the rear wheel spindle nut, then slacken the nut and the chain adjusters to allow the wheel to be pushed fully forward. The chain and sprocket can now be disengaged from the output shaft. Note that with a new chain there will be barely enough clearance, in which case the rear wheel must be removed. Disengage the chain from the shaft end and leave it to hang against the swinging arm. Remove the brake pedal pinch bolt and slide it off its shaft.
11 Place a drain tray under the front of the engine and remove the oil cooler hose union bolts, allowing the oil to drain. The union bolts should be left off to provide a little extra clearance during engine removal. It will be found helpful to remove the cylinder head breather cover for the same reason; it is retained by four bolts. Before proceeding further, check carefully that all leads and hoses have been disconnected.
12 The engine unit is mounted at four points by a combination of mounting brackets, each of which is retained by bolts to the frame. The

brackets, bracket retaining bolts and engine mounting bolts must be removed to obtain sufficient clearance to permit engine removal.

13 When removing the bolts it will be necessary to support the weight of the engine unit as they are withdrawn by using a jack and a wooden block on the underside of the unit, or by judicious use of a bar as a lever between the frame and crankcase. If adopting the latter method, protect the painted finish of the frame and engine unit with rag. Note that the front lower mounting bolts have shaped captive nuts which will drop clear as the bolts are removed, and that the rear upper bolt also retains the hydraulic adjuster for the rear suspension unit; this should be lodged clear of the engine unit. Once all the bolts have been displaced, the engine can be left to sit in the frame cradle.

14 The complete engine/gearbox unit is both heavy and bulky, and will prove difficult to extract from the confines of the frame cradle. A minimum of two persons will be necessary to ensure safe removal, and extra assistance would be desirable. To attempt single-handed removal of the unit is to invite damage to the engine and the operator if it slips during removal. An engine hoist or jack is a distinct advantage but not essential.

15 Arrange a strong wooden crate or a similar support to the right of the engine and at the same level. Lift the engine slightly, then rotate it by a few degrees so that the various projections will clear the frame. The unit is removed by tipping it and then manoeuvring it out from the right-hand side of the frame, and onto the near-by support.

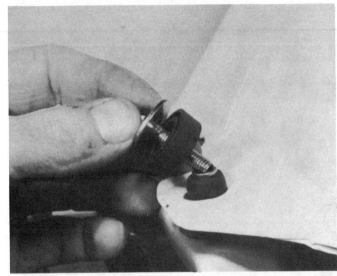

4.2 The rear of the fuel tank is secured by two rubber-bushed bolts

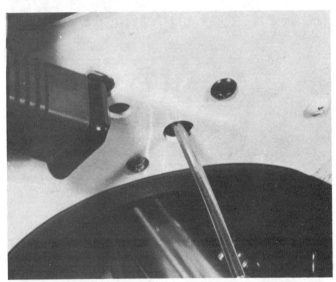

4.4a Turn signal lamp mounting screws are reached through holes in fairing

4.4b Lift the fairing away, leaving subframe in place

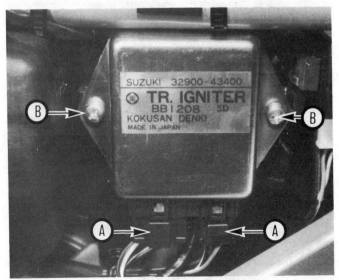

4.5a Unplug wiring connectors (A) and remove screws (B) to release igniter unit

4.5b Slacken mounting bolts at lower edge of battery tray ...

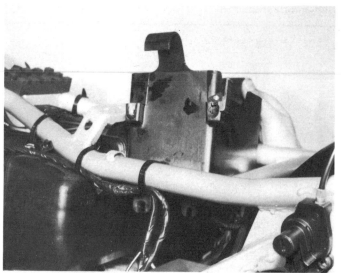
4.5c ... and lift it clear of the frame

4.6a Disconnect leads at starter relay terminals

4.6b Disconnect oil pressure sender lead

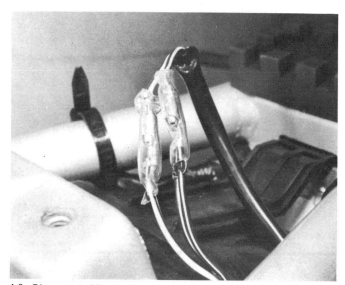
4.6c Disconnect side stand switch wiring connectors

4.7a Slacken clips holding carburettors to air filter and inlet hoses

4.7b Unscrew cold-start plungers to free cables

4.7c Free throttle cable adjuster from support bracket ...

4.7d ... then disengage at carburettor end

4.7e Slide clip away from stub and pull off the breather hose

4.10a Unscrew pinch bolt and remove the gearchange pedal

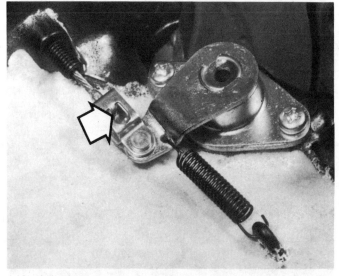

4.10b If clutch cable is to be removed, bend back the tang (arrowed) which retains it

4.10c Straighten locking tab, apply rear brake and unscrew nut

4.11a Free the oil cooler pipes and allow oil to drain

4.11b Cylinder head breather cover is best removed to provide maximum clearance

5 Dismantling the engine/gearbox unit: general

1   Before commencing any dismantling work the external surfaces of the engine unit should be cleaned thoroughly. Plug the inlet and exhaust ports with rag and refit the cylinder head breather cover to keep out the cleaning solution. Apply a proprietary degreaser, working it into the casting recesses with a stiff brush. Once all dirt has been loosened, wash off with water and allow to dry. Steam or hot pressure wash equipment may also be used to good effect.
2   Never use excessive force to remove a stubborn component; if a part proves difficult to remove, this is often due to corrosion or because the operation has been tackled in the wrong sequence. Where problems are likely to be encountered this will be mentioned in the text.
3   To facilitate dismantling, an improvised engine stand will prove invaluable. Failing this, collect an assortment of wooden blocks for use as props for the unit on the workbench.

6 Dismantling the engine/gearbox unit: removing the cylinder head cover and camshafts

1   Free the oil feed hoses at their unions on the cylinder head and at the shared crankcase union. Place both hoses, the sealing washers and the union bolts to one side as an assembly. On machines fitted with a mechanically driven tachometer, remove the driven gear assembly from the cylinder head cover, if this is still in position. Slacken the cylinder head cover bolts evenly and progressively and lift the cover away. If it proves stubborn, tap around the joint face with a hide mallet to help break the seal. Slacken the cam chain tensioner locknut and screw the lockscrew home to hold the tensioner pushrod. Release the tensioner mounting bolts and lift the assembly away.
2   Before the camshafts can be removed it will be necessary to release the internal oil pipes. Note that the two pipes are not symmetrical, and that the union bolts which retain them are of differing lengths. It is worth placing the assembly on a sheet of card and pushing the bolts through to hold the various parts in the correct relative positions. The camshaft caps are marked to indicate their position as a guide during reassembly, and should be removed in a diagonal sequence so that the shafts are kept square to the head. To aid this, slacken each bolt by about half a turn at a time until the shafts are no longer under pressure from the valve springs. Lift away the caps, taking care to retain the locating dowels.
3   Lift one of the camshafts clear of the head and disengage it from the cam chain. Place a screwdriver or a bar through the chain loop to prevent it from falling into the crankcase, then disengage the remaining shaft. The cam chain guide can now be lifted out of the tunnel.

6.1 External oil hoses are retained by banjo unions

6.2 Camshaft bearing caps are each secured by two bolts

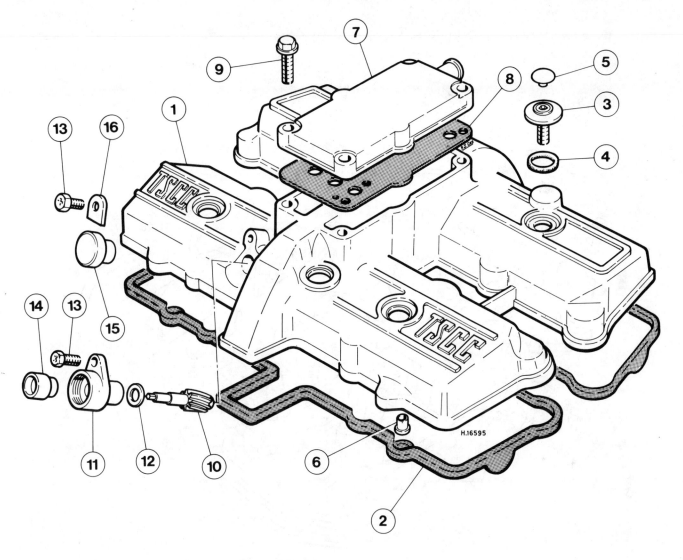

Fig. 1.2 Cylinder head cover

1 Cylinder head cover	6 Locating dowel	10 Tachometer driven gear	13 Screw
2 Cover seal	7 Breather cover	11 Tachometer driven gear	14 Oil seal
3 Bolt – 5 off	8 Gasket	housing	15 Plug
4 O-ring – 5 off	9 Bolt – 4 off	12 Seal	16 Retaining plate
5 Cap – 5 off			

Note: *items 10, 11, 12 and 14 apply to models with a mechanical tachometer; items 15 and 16 apply to models with an electronic tachometer*

7 Dismantling the engine/gearbox unit: removing the cylinder head

1   The cylinder head can be removed after the camshafts have been withdrawn as described in Section 6 above. To release the cylinder head nuts, Suzuki recommend the use of a special deep socket (Part number 09911-74520) in conjunction with a T-handle (Part number 09914-24510). In practice, a standard $^3/_8$ in drive 12 mm socket worked well as a substitute, but check first that there is adequate clearance in the nut recesses.

2   Release the single 6 mm bolt, this being located at the centre of the joint face, between the centre exhaust ports. Slacken progressively the twelve cylinder head nuts, turning each one about a half turn at a time in the reverse of the tightening sequence which is marked in the head casting.

3   Remove the nuts, followed by the flat sealing washers. It is worth noting that, despite appearances, these are non-ferrous; do not waste time attempting to fish them out with a magnet. If necessary they can be left in place until the head is removed and then tipped out. The head should now lift away. If it is stuck to the gasket, try jarring it free by placing a hardwood block against an exhaust port and tapping it upwards, having first tapped around the joint with a hide mallet or similar. **Do not** lever against the fins. Once the seal has been broken, remove the head and place to one side.

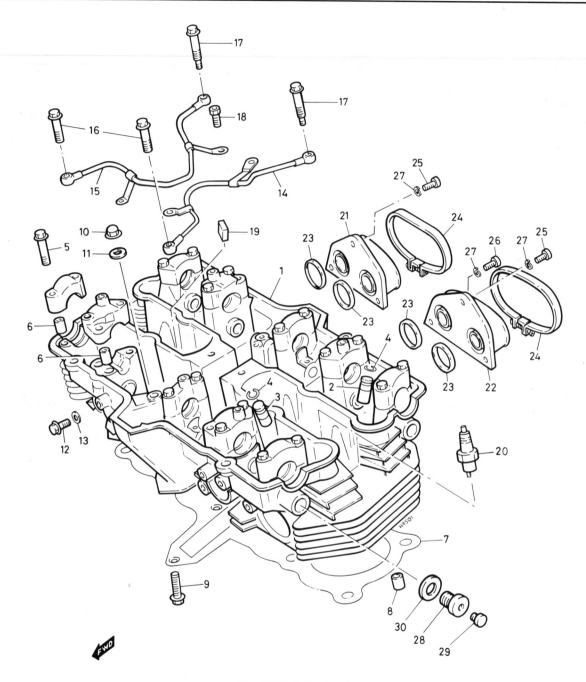

Fig. 1.3 Cylinder head

1	Cylinder head	9	Bolt
2	Inlet valve guide – 8 off	10	Nut – 12 off
3	Exhaust valve guide – 8 off	11	Sealing washer – 12 off
4	Clip – 16 off	12	Bolt – 2 off
5	Bolt – 20 off	13	Sealing washer – 2 off
6	Locating dowel – 20 off	14	Left-hand internal oil pipe
7	Cylinder head gasket	15	Right-hand internal oil pipe
8	Locating dowel – 2 off	16	Union bolt – 2 off

17	Union bolt – 2 off	24	Clamp – 2 off
18	Bolt – 2 off	25	Screw – 5 off
19	Damping blocks	26	Screw
20	Spark plug – 4 off	27	Spring washer – 6 off
21	Right-hand intake stub	28	End cap – 4 off
22	Left-hand intake stub	29	Plug – 4 off
23	O-ring – 4 off	30	Sealing washer – 4 off

8 Dismantling the engine/gearbox unit: removing the cylinder block and pistons

1   Once the cylinder head has been removed the cylinder block can be lifted off the holding studs and pistons. It is not uncommon, however, for the casting to be firmly stuck to the base gasket. If this is the case, tapping around the joint face with a hide mallet will often break the seal, but take great care not to damage the rather brittle fins. A 'cylinder disassembling tool', Part number 09912-34510 is available from Suzuki Service Agents if required, and can be used to jack the block away from the crankcase. Alternatively, the "pry point" just above the front engine mounting boss in which the above tool engages can be used as a levering point if reasonable care is taken. Do not use excessive force; if the block is firmly stuck, the locating dowels may have corroded. It is best to play safe and beg, borrow or hire the correct tool.

2   Lift the block by about an inch or so, then pack clean rag into the crankcase mouths. This will catch any debris from the pistons when they emerge and must not be omitted. Continue lifting the block and support the pistons as they drop clear of the bores.

3   Prise out the gudgeon (piston) pin circlips. These can be retained as patterns but should not be reused. Small slots in the pistons are provided to allow the clips to be dislodged using a small screwdriver. Mark each piston to indicate the bore from which it came. It is normal practice to mark the piston crowns by scribing 1 to 4 working from the left-hand end.

4   The pistons can usually be freed by pushing out the gudgeon pins by hand or with a long bar. If a pin is exceptionally tight it may prove necessary to employ a drawbolt arrangement such as that shown in the accompanying line drawing. Warming the piston with a rag soaked in very hot water will expand the alloy, making removal much easier.

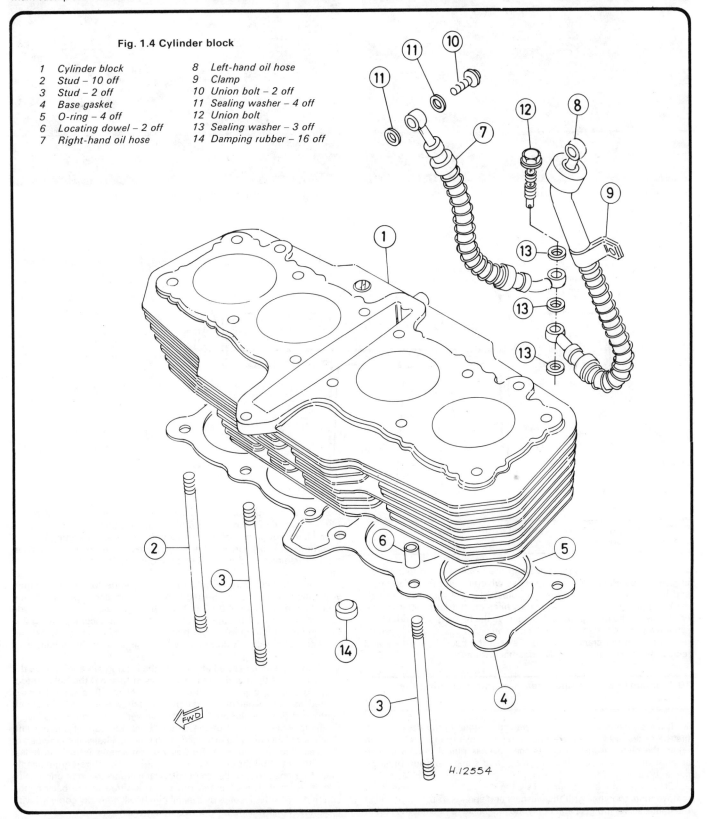

Fig. 1.4 Cylinder block

1   Cylinder block
2   Stud – 10 off
3   Stud – 2 off
4   Base gasket
5   O-ring – 4 off
6   Locating dowel – 2 off
7   Right-hand oil hose
8   Left-hand oil hose
9   Clamp
10 Union bolt – 2 off
11 Sealing washer – 4 off
12 Union bolt
13 Sealing washer – 3 off
14 Damping rubber – 16 off

H.12554

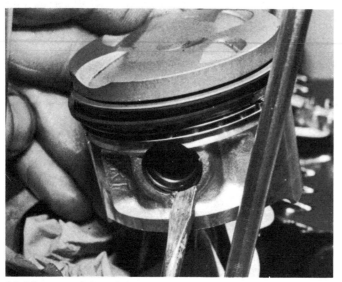

8.3 Prise out and discard the piston circlips

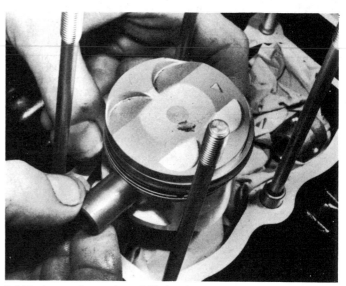

8.4 Displace gudgeon pin and lift the piston away

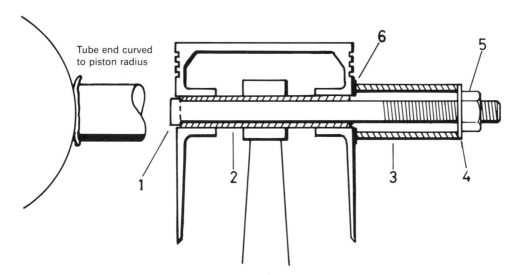

Tube end curved to piston radius

Fig. 1.5 Fabricated gudgeon pin removal tool

1   Extractor bolt
2   Gudgeon pin
3   Tube
4   Washer
5   Nut
6   Rubber washer

9 Dismantling the engine/gearbox unit: removing the ignition pickup assembly

1   Trace the pickup wiring back along the crankcase and free it from its guide clips. Remove the four screws which retain the pickup cover and lift it away. The pickup is not adjustable, and thus need not be marked prior to removal. Place a spanner on the larger of the two hexagons on the pickup rotor, then remove the holding bolt and lift the rotor away. Note the small pin which locates it; if this is loose it can be removed from the crankshaft end. Release the backplate screws and remove the backplate assembly, together with its wiring.

10 Dismantling the engine/gearbox unit: removing the clutch

1   If the clutch is to be removed with the engine in the frame, it will first be necessary to drain the engine oil. Remove the ten bolts which retain the clutch outer cover. As the cover is pulled clear a certain amount of residual oil will be released, and some provision must be made to catch this.
2   Slacken evenly and progressively the six clutch spring bolts, then remove them together with the washers and springs. If the engine is in the frame, select top gear and apply the rear brake to prevent the clutch

from turning as the bolts are unscrewed. If the engine is out of the frame, hold the clutch drum with a strap wrench, or pass a smooth round bar through one of the connecting rod eyes, supporting its ends on wooden blocks. Lift out the clutch plates, noting that the last plain plate is retained by a wire clip and should be left in position at this stage.
3   It will be necessary to hold the clutch centre to prevent rotation while the nut is removed. Suzuki Service Agents can supply a holding tool, Part number 09920-53710 for this purpose, or a home-made equivalent can be fabricated. This is shown in the accompanying line drawing and photograph. Note that there is a reinforcing ring around the edge of the clutch drum into which the jaws of the holding tool must fit.
4   With the clutch centre held, flatten the locking tab and remove the nut. The nut is tight and care must be taken to avoid the holding tool slipping and damaging the clutch centre splines. It is safer if this is treated as a two-person operation. The tab washer and the clutch centre can now be slid off the shaft, followed by the thrust washer.
5   To facilitate removal of the clutch drum, the central bearing and sleeve assembly must be extracted. Two threaded holes are provided in the sleeve for this purpose. Run two 4 mm screws into these holes, using them to pull the sleeve out of the drum. The clutch drum needle roller bearings can now be removed and the drum moved to one side to permit removal. The oil pump drive gear is fitted to the back of the clutch drum and is located by a small pin. It will normally come off with the drum. Finally, slide off the two thrust washers.

9.1 Remove ignition rotor, then remove the pickup assembly

10.2 Free the clutch cover and remove plain and friction plates

10.3 Lock clutch centre securely and remove centre nut

10.5a Use screw to draw out the bearing sleeve, then remove bearing

10.5b Clutch drum can now be moved to one side and lifted out of the casing recess

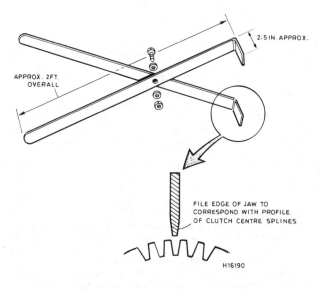

2.5 IN. APPROX.

APPROX. 2 FT. OVERALL

FILE EDGE OF JAW TO CORRESPOND WITH PROFILE OF CLUTCH CENTRE SPLINES

H16190

Fig. 1.6 Fabricated clutch holding tool

11 Dismantling the engine/gearbox unit: removing the oil pump, bearing retainers and gear indicator switch

1   With the clutch removed as described in Section 10, access to the oil pump is possible. Remove the circlip which retains the oil pump driven gear, then slide off the gear to reveal the pump body. Displace and keep safe the small driving pin. Remove the three securing screws and pull the pump clear of the casing recess.
2   If the crankcase halves are to be separated, proceed as follows. Inside the clutch recess is a bearing retainer at the end of the gearbox input shaft. This spans the crankshaft joint and must therefore be removed. Using an impact driver, remove the screws and lift the retainer away. Moving to the opposite side of the unit, flatten the locking tabs of the output shaft oil seal retainer, slacken the bolts and remove it.
4   Release the two screws which retain the gear indicator switch to the end of the selector drum. Remove the switch, taking care not to lose the small contact and spring which will be freed as it is lifted clear.

12 Dismantling the engine/gearbox unit: removing the external gearchange components

1   Note that it is not essential that the following operations are carried out prior to crankcase separation. If, however, the crankcase components are to be removed, it is better to remove the gearchange external components now.
2   Prise off the wire retaining clip from the left-hand end of the gearchange shaft. The shaft and its claw assembly can now be displaced to the right and removed, taking care not to damage the oil seal on the shaft splines. As the shaft is displaced, the ends of the centralising spring will drop clear of their locating pin.
3   Remove the two screws which hold the selector drum bearing retainer and lift it away. The selector pawl guide can be removed in a similar manner, but take care to hold the pawls in place as they are removed; they are under spring pressure and are inclined to escape.

13 Dismantling the engine/gearbox unit: removing the starter motor

1   Remove the two screws which retain the starter motor cover and lift it away. Remove the two bolts which retain the motor to the crankcase. Lever the motor body back in the recess until the drive end comes free from the casing hole, then lift the motor up and clear of the crankcase.
2   Note that access to the motor is restricted by the cam chain tensioner body, and if this is still in position it will not be possible to remove the motor from its recess. The tensioner body is retained by two bolts. Refer to Section 39 of this Chapter for details of installation.

14 Dismantling the engine/gearbox unit: removing the alternator and starter drive

1   Remove the alternator cover and lift it away, together with the alternator stator. The rotor forms an assembly with the starter clutch, this being retained on the tapered crankshaft end by a central bolt. To facilitate removal, it will be necessary to prevent the crankshaft from turning, and a number of methods for achieving this are described below.
2   Suzuki Service Agents can obtain a rotor holding tool, Part number 09930-44911. This has a crescent-shaped end with two locating bolts which engage in the large holes in the rotor edge. In the absence of this tool, a strong chain wrench can be used instead. If the cylinder block and pistons have been removed, a further alternative is to pass a smooth round bar through the left-hand connecting rod small-end eye, supporting the bar ends on small hardwood blocks. The rotor bolt is often so tight that there is risk of damage using the last method. Of the two alternatives given, the chain wrench is likely to be the safest. With the crankshaft suitably restrained, slacken and remove the rotor bolt.
3   Problems may be encountered when attempting to draw the rotor off the crankshaft taper, and it is difficult to devise a method which will avoid the use of the appropriate Suzuki Special Tools; a slide hammer

(09930-30102) and the correct attachment (09930-30180). Even when using the correct tools the rotor often proves impossible to remove; repeated use of the slide hammer making no impression. As a last resort, a suitably sized bolt can be inserted into the rotor bolt thread (such as a metric thread car wheel stud, or even a bolt with the head filed down). The slide hammer attachment should then be fitted, and a bolt screwed into it to bear upon the head of the stud (see accompanying photographs). By tightening the extractor bolt firmly and then striking repeatedly its head, the rotor can be jarred free. Although this may not be a common problem, which was probably caused by excess thread locking compound finding its way onto the crankshaft taper during initial assembly, some difficulty may be expected in this area. If similar problems are encountered it may be better to entrust the job to a reputable Suzuki Service Agent who will have the facilities to get the rotor off without damage.
4   The starter idler gear can be removed with the rotor in position, if necessary. Remove the alternator cover assembly as described above, then withdraw the idler gear shaft. The idler gear is now freed and can be manoeuvred out from behind the rotor.

13.1a Starter motor is retained by two mounting bolts

13.1b Motor can be pulled out of recess – note that cam chain tensioner must be removed to provide clearance

14.3a Using Suzuki slide hammer and adaptor to remove rotor

14.3b We had to fit stud into shaft end, then fit adaptor ...

14.3c ... followed by an extractor bolt to apply sufficient pressure to shift the rotor

Fig. 1.7 Starter clutch

1	Starter idler gear	6	Spring – 3 off
2	Idler gear shaft	7	Pin – 3 off
3	Starter clutch pinion	8	Allen bolt – 3 off
4	Starter clutch body	9	Backing plate
5	Roller – 3 off		

15 Dismantling the engine/gearbox unit: removing the sump and oil strainer and separating the crankcase halves

1   Remove the upper crankcase bolts, noting that it is a good idea to draw the outline of the crankcase on a piece of card and to push each bolt through in its correct position as it is removed. This will save a great deal of time during reassembly. Turn the unit over, placing blocks beneath the rear of the crankcase to support it horizontally. Remove the sump (oil pan) bolts and lift it away, noting the position of the wiring clips. Remove the oil gallery O-ring. Remove the three nuts which retain the oil strainer cover, then the two bolts which secure the strainer body. Lift away the body and remove its O-ring. If it is still in position, remove the three domed nuts which retain the oil filter cover and remove the cover, spring and filter element.

2   Slacken evenly and progressively the remaining crankcase bolts, and make sure that the single nut near the end of the selector drum has been removed. Note that two of the crankcase bolts are Allen-headed and hidden in the oil filter chamber. Holes in the casting allow them to be reached with a long Allen key; a 6 mm T-handled type should be used if possible, a suitable type of which may be obtained through Suzuki Service Agents as Part number 09914-25811. The crankcase

halves can now be separated by lifting the lower crankcase off the inverted upper crankcase half.

3   There will usually be a certain amount of resistance caused by the joint sealant and the various locating dowels and rings. To help separate the crankcase halves, leverage points are provided. It was found that a 6 mm nut and bolt can be used to 'jack' the cases apart, the arrangement being self-explanatory if the jacking points are identified. Note also that it will help to tap around the joint using a hide mallet.

16 Dismantling the engine/gearbox unit: removing the crankcase components

Upper crankcase half

1   Lift out the input and output shafts, placing them on a clean surface to await further attention. Be careful not to lose the C-rings (input shaft right-hand end and output shaft left-hand end), bearing location pins (on opposite ends of gearbox shafts) and the tiny oil jets (at each end of the input shaft). Remove the oil gallery O-ring and backing washer (between input shaft and crankshaft). Displace and remove the cam chain guide, taking care not to lose the small damper blocks which locate it. Check that all of the above have been accounted for before moving on.

2   Remove the crankshaft assembly, noting that it is quite likely that it will prove somewhat reluctant to come free. Hitting the crankshaft ends upwards with the palm of the hand will usually dislodge it. As the crankshaft comes free, note that the thrust bearings on either side of main bearing journal No. 2 (2nd from left) will be freed; do not lose them. Once the crankshaft has been lifted clear, disengage the cam chain and place it and the crankshaft to one side.

Lower crankcase half

3   If still in position, remove the selector drum retainer and the pawl retainer. Slacken and remove the selector drum detent plunger assembly from the underside of the casing. Slide the gear selector fork shafts out of the casing and lift away the forks, placing them on their respective shafts for safekeeping. If necessary, the shafts can be gripped with pliers to assist removal. Unhook the stopper arm spring from the lower crankcase half.

4   Slide the selector drum part way out of the casing and slide off the stopper cam components. Remove the drum completely and refit the stopper cam components in the correct order. If the stopper arm is to be removed, prise off its circlip and slide it off its locating peg. Do not disturb the selector drum needle roller bearing unless it is to be renewed.

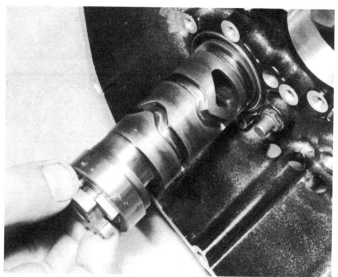

16.4 Selector drum can be withdrawn through side of casing

17 Examination and renovation: general

1   Before examining the parts of the dismantled engine unit for wear it is essential that they should be cleaned thoroughly. Use a petrol/paraffin mix or a high flash-point solvent to remove all traces of old oil and sludge which may have accumulated within the engine. Where petrol is included in the cleaning agent normal fire precautions should be taken and cleaning should be carried out in a well ventilated place.

2   Examine the crankcase castings for cracks or other signs of damage. If a crack is discovered it will require a specialist repair.

3   Examine carefully each part to determine the extent of wear, checking with the tolerance figures listed in the Specifications section of this Chapter or in the main text. If there is any doubt about the condition of a particular component, play safe and renew.

4   Use a clean lint-free rag for cleaning and drying the various components. This will obviate the risk of small particles obstructing the internal oilways, and causing the lubrication system to fail.

18 Crankshaft assembly: examination and renovation

1   Unlike the larger GS/GSX models, the 550 range utilises a plain bearing engine; the big-end and main bearings comprising renewable shells, or inserts, upon which the crankshaft and its connecting rods are supported. The main bearing shells are easily inspected after the crankcase halves have been separated. If there are any signs of scoring or wear the main bearing shells must be renewed. Under normal circumstances the crankshaft journals will not themselves have worn or suffered damage, unless the engine had been badly abused. Should the crankshaft be found to be so damaged it will be necessary to fit a new one; no provision is made for re-grinding, and undersized shells are not supplied by Suzuki.

2   Check the connecting rod end float, using metric feeler gauges. This should not exceed 0.3 mm (0.01 in), and if excessive clearance is discovered it is likely that the connecting rod thrust faces will have worn, necessitating renewal. If an accurate vernier caliper or internal and external micrometers are available, the connecting rod width and journal width can be checked after the connecting rods have been removed as described below. The correct figures are as follows:

Connecting rod big-end width: 19.95 – 20.00 mm (0.785 – 0.787 in)
Crankpin journal width: 20.10 – 20.15 mm (0.791 – 0.793 in)

3   To remove the connecting rods, slacken evenly and progressively the cap nuts. Tap the cap to dislodge it, then lift it away and remove the rod. **Do not** remove the bolts from the connecting rod; the assembly will not align correctly if this is done. Mark each rod and cap to indicate the journal to which it belongs. Examine the big-end bearing shells for signs of wear or damage as described above for the main bearing shells. If there are no signs of excessive wear or damage, the big-end and main bearing oil clearances should be checked using Plastigage. This is a compressible plastic material used to measure clearances in assembled plain bearings. It is easily obtained from most motorcycle dealers in the US, but is less common in the UK. It is suggested that a large Suzuki Service Agent or engine reconditioning specialist is tried, or alternatively, the clearances are checked by a Suzuki Service Agent.

4   To measure the oil clearances using Plastigage, place a strip of the material across the journal to be measured, avoiding the oil hole. Assemble the connecting rod and cap, then tighten the nuts initially to 1.6 – 2.2 kgf m (11.5 – 16.0 lbf ft) and finally to 3.3 – 3.7 kgf m (24.0 – 27.0 lbf ft). Take care not to turn the rod on the journal. Dismantle the rod and measure the width of the compressed Plastigage at its widest point, using the scale on the Plastigage pack. The standard clearance is 0.024 – 0.048 mm (0.0009 – 0.0019 in). If the clearance obtained exceeds the service limit of 0.080 mm (0.0031 in) a new bearing shell must be fitted. Repeat the measuring operation on the remaining connecting rods, making a written note of the clearances found.

5   If the oil clearance(s) are outside the service limit it will be necessary to select new shells according to the accompanying table. These are determined according to the size codes of the connecting rod ID and the crankpin OD. The former is etched onto the connecting rod and cap as shown in Fig. 1.9. The crankpin OD is stamped on the crankshaft near its left-hand end (see photograph 18.9). The letter "L", denoting the left-hand crankpin, is followed by the four crankpin codes, and then the letter "R" to indicate the right-hand end. The position of the code markings and their respective sizes are given in Fig. 1.10. From the above, a new bearing shell can be selected. These are colour-coded with a paint mark on one edge to indicate their thickness. Note that the entire set of shells should be renewed. Refer to Fig. 1.11 to select the correct bearing shells.

6   The main bearing oil clearances are checked, and new shells selected, in a similar manner to that described above. To measure the clearances, place a strip of Plastigage on each of the six journals, keeping it well clear of the oil holes. Carefully place the crankshaft in position, offer up the lower crankcase half, and run into position the

twelve 8 mm holding bolts (ten hexagon-headed bolts, plus the two Allen-headed bolts). Tighten the bolts in the sequence indicated by the numbers cast into the crankcase. Initial tightening should be to 1.3 kgf m (9.5 lbf ft) and final tightening should be to 2.0 – 2.4 kgf m (14.5 – 17.5 lbf ft). Separate the crankcase halves and measure the oil clearance, making a written note of each one. The standard oil clearance figure is 0.020 – 0.044 mm (0.0008 – 0.0017 in). If any one

oil clearance figure exceeds the 0.080 mm (0.0031 in) service limit, renew the complete set.
7 The crankcase ID code ("A" or "B") is stamped into the rear of the upper crankcase half as shown in Fig. 1.12. The main bearing journal codes ("A", "B" or "C") are stamped on the left-hand end of the crankshaft (see Fig. 1.13).
8 The bearing shells are colour-coded in the same way as the big-end

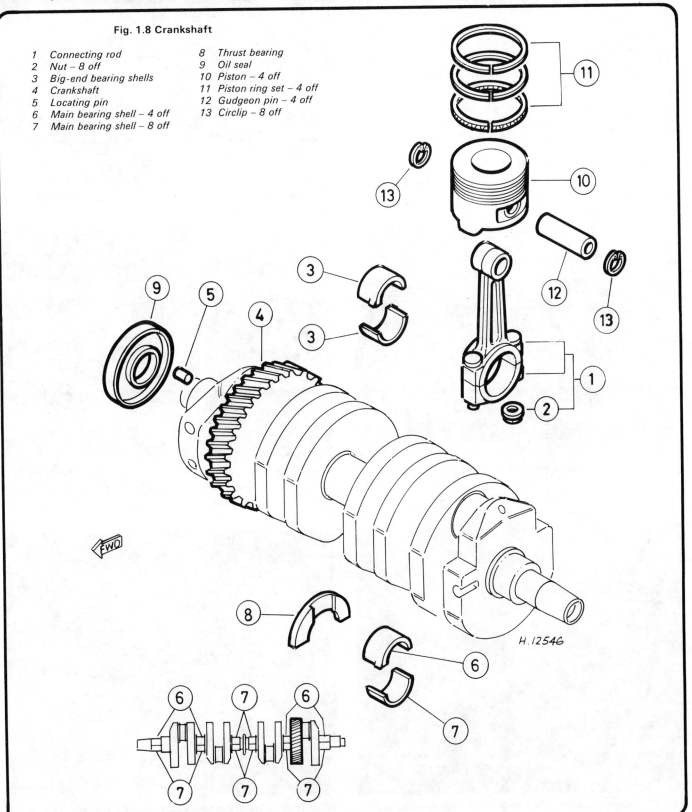

Fig. 1.8 Crankshaft

1   Connecting rod
2   Nut – 8 off
3   Big-end bearing shells
4   Crankshaft
5   Locating pin
6   Main bearing shell – 4 off
7   Main bearing shell – 8 off
8   Thrust bearing
9   Oil seal
10 Piston – 4 off
11 Piston ring set – 4 off
12 Gudgeon pin – 4 off
13 Circlip – 8 off

H.12546

bearing shells, and new shells are selected accordingly, see Fig. 1.14. Note that either plain or grooved shells are fitted (see Fig. 1.15) and that the part number codes of the latter begin "12229 – 43410 –".

9   With the crankcase installed in the inverted upper crankcase half and the thrust bearings in place, measure with feeler gauges the thrust clearance (end float) between the crankshaft and the left-hand bearing face. The crankshaft should be pushed hard across to the left during measurement. If the reading obtained exceeds the standard figure of 0.045 – 0.100mm (0.0018 – 0.0039 in), remove the right-hand thrust bearing and measure its thickness with a micrometer. If this is below the standard thickness of 2.425 – 2.450 mm (0.0955 – 0.0965 in) fit a new bearing and repeat the above clearance check.

10 If the thrust clearance is still excessive, select a new left-hand bearing according to the table shown in Fig. 1.16. Fit the new bearing and repeat the clearance check to confirm that it is now within limits.

11 Before the crankshaft is fitted it is advisable to check that the runout is within limits. Support the end journals on V-blocks and position the needle of a dial gauge against one of the centre journals. Zero the gauge, then slowly turn the crankshaft, noting the reading obtained. If runout exceeds 0.05 mm (0.0002 in) the crankshaft must be renewed.

18.3a Remove nuts and separate big-end caps – DO NOT DISTURB THE BIG-END BOLTS

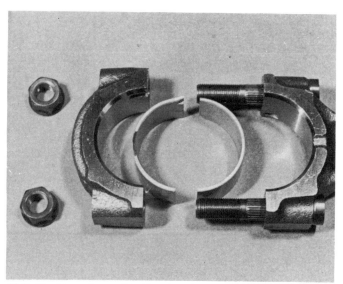

18.3b The big-end assembly. Note locating tabs on bearing shells

18.7 Main bearing journal codes are stamped into rear of crankcase

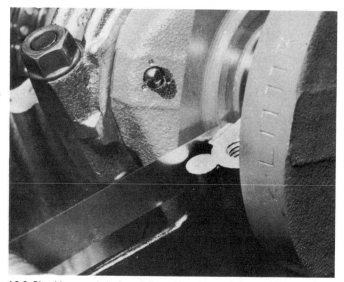

18.9 Checking crankshaft end float. Note big-end journal codes at right of picture

18.10 Thrust bearings can be checked using a micrometer

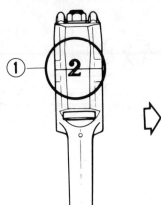

Bearing selection table

		Crank pin O.D. ②		
	Code	1	2	3
Conrod I.D. ①	1	Green	Black	Brown
	2	Black	Brown	Yellow

Connecting rod ID specification

Code	I.D. specification
1	35.000 – 35.008 mm (1.3780 – 1.3783 in)
2	35.008 – 35.016 mm (1.3783 – 1.3786 in)

Fig. 1.9 Big-end bearing size codes

Code	O.D. specification
1	31.992 – 32.000 mm (1.2595 – 1.2598 in)
2	31.984 – 31.992 mm (1.2592 – 1.2595 in)
3	31.976 – 31.984 mm (1.2589 – 1.2592 in)

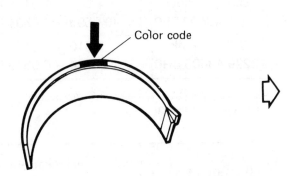

Fig. 1.10 Crankpin code markings and sizes

Color code

Color (Part No.)	Thickness
Green (12164-43400-0A0)	1.484 – 1.488 mm (0.0584 – 0.0586 in)
Black (12164-43400-0B0)	1.488 – 1.492 mm (0.0586 – 0.0587 in)
Brown (12164-43400-0C0)	1.492 – 1.496 mm (0.0587 – 0.0589 in)
Yellow (12164-43400-0D0)	1.496 – 1.500 mm (0.0589 – 0.0591 in)

Fig. 1.11 Big-end bearing shell selection table

Code	I.D. specification
A	35.000 – 35.008 mm (1.3780 – 1.3783 in)
B	35.008 – 35.016 mm (1.3783 – 1.3786 in)

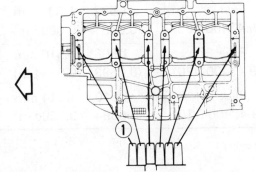

Fig. 1.12 Crankcase journal inside diameter codes

Code	O.D. specification
A	31.992 – 32.000 mm (1.2595 – 1.2598 in)
B	31.984 – 31.992 mm (1.2592 – 1.2595 in)
C	31.976 – 31.984 mm (1.2589 – 1.2592 in)

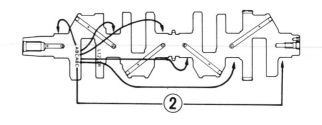

Fig. 1.13 Main bearing journal codes and locations

Crankshaft O.D. ②			
Code	A	B	C
Crankcase I.D. ① A	Green	Black	Brown
Crankcase I.D. ① B	Black	Brown	Yellow

Color (Part No.)	Specification
Green (12229-43400-010)	1.486 – 1.490 mm (0.0585 – 0.0587 in)
Black (12229-43400-020)	1.490 – 1.494 mm (0.0587 – 0.0588 in)
Brown (12229-43400-030)	1.494 – 1.498 mm (0.0588 – 0.0590 in)
Yellow (12229-43400-040)	1.498 – 1.502 mm (0.0590 – 0.0591 in)

Bearing thickness specification – 1983/84 models (grooved bearings with oil holes)

Color (Part number)	Specification
Green (12229-43400-0A0)	1.486 – 1.490 mm (0.0585 – 0.0587 in)
Black (12229-43400-0B0)	1.490 – 1.494 mm (0.0587 – 0.0588 in)
Brown (12229-43400-0C0)	1.494 – 1.498 mm (0.0588 – 0.0590 in)
Yellow (12229-43400-0D0)	1.498 – 1.502 mm (0.0590 – 0.0591 in)
U.S. Red (12229-43400-0E0)	1.502 – 1.506 mm (0.0591 – 0.0593 in)
U.S. Blue (12229-43400-0F0)	1.506 – 1.510 mm (0.0593 – 0.0594 in)
U.S. Pink (12229-43400-0G0)	1.510 – 1.514 mm (0.0594 – 0.0596 in)

Journal bearing thickness specification – 1985 models (journal bearing with oil groove)

Color (Part No.)	Specification
Red (12229-43400-0E0)	1.502 – 1.506 mm (0.0591 – 0.0593 in)
Blue (12229-43400-0F0)	1.506 – 1.510 mm (0.0593 – 0.0594 in)
Pink (12229-43400-0G0)	1.510 – 1.514 mm (0.0594 – 0.0596 in)

Optional bearing – 1983/84 models

Color (Part number)	Specification
Green (12164-43400-0A0)	1.484 – 1.488 mm (0.0584 – 0.0586 in)
Black (12164-43400-0B0)	1.488 – 1.492 mm (0.0586 – 0.0587 in)
Brown (12164-43400-0C0)	1.492 – 1.496 mm (0.0587 – 0.0589 in)
Yellow (12164-43400-0D0)	1.496 – 1.500 mm (0.0589 – 0.0591 in)

Crankpin bearing specification – 1985 models

Fig. 1.14 Main bearing shell selection table

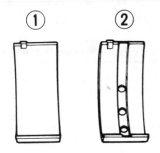

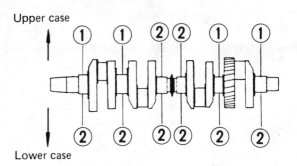

① Non-Grooved bearings
② Grooved bearings with oil holes

Fig. 1.15 Main bearing shell locations

Clearance before inserting of left-side thrust bearing	Color (Part No.)	Thrust bearing thickness	Thrust clearance
2.420 – 2.445 mm (0.0953 – 0.0963 in)	Red (12228-43411)	2.350 – 2.375 mm (0.0925 – 0.0935 in)	0.045 – 0.095 mm (0.0018 – 0.0037 in)
2.445 – 2.470 mm (0.0963 – 0.0972 in)	Black (12228-43412)	2.375 – 2.400 mm (0.0935 – 0.0945 in)	
2.470 – 2.495 mm (0.0972 – 0.0982 in)	Blue (12228-43413)	2.400 – 2.425 mm (0.0945 – 0.0955 in)	
2.495 – 2.520 mm (0.0982 – 0.0992 in)	Green (12228-43414)	2.425 – 2.450 mm (0.0955 – 0.0965 in)	
2.520 – 2.545 mm (0.0992 – 0.1002 in)	Yellow (12228-43415)	2.450 – 2.475 mm (0.0965 – 0.0974 in)	
2.545 – 2.575 mm (0.1002 – 0.1014 in)	White (12228-43416)	2.475 – 2.500 mm (0.0974 – 0.0984 in)	0.045 – 0.100 mm (0.0018 – 0.0039 in)

Fig. 1.16 Crankshaft left-hand thrust bearing selection table

19 Connecting rods: examination and renovation

1 The connecting rods are unlikely to require attention, other than as a result of catastrophic engine damage such as seizure or a dropped valve. If any of the rods are visibly damaged, have the crankshaft checked by a Suzuki Service Agent; it too may be damaged. Remember that a stressed connecting rod which breaks in use is extremely dangerous to the rider and other road users, and will probably damage the engine unit beyond repair.

2 Examine the rod for indications of cracking, particularly where other mechanical damage has been discovered. Renew any connecting rod which shows signs of damage of this type.

3 The diameter of the small-end eye can be checked using a bore micrometer, and should not exceed the 16.040 mm (0.6315 in) service limit.

19.1 Assemble big-end bearings using torque wrench. Note size number stamped across the cap and con-rod

20 Cylinder block: examination and renovation

1 An excessively worn cylinder block is usually indicated by smoking from the exhausts and by piston slap, a metallic rattle which occurs with little or no load on the engine. If the top of each bore is examined, a wear ridge will be found on the thrust side, the depth of which will vary according to the degree of wear present. The ridge denotes the upper limit of travel of the top ring.

2 Bore wear is measured using an internal or bore micrometer. Two measurements are made at right angles, just below the wear ridge. This is repeated about half way down the bore and again near the bottom of the bore, a total of six measurements. If any one measurement exceeds the service limit shown in the specifications, the cylinder block must be rebored and oversized pistons fitted.

3 In the absence of a bore micrometer, and if a decision cannot be made from a visual check of the bores, the block should be taken to a Suzuki Service Agent for checking. Needless to say, scoring or other damage to the bore surfaces will necessitate reboring, irrespective of the amount of wear.

4 Two piston oversizes are available; 0.50 mm (0.020 in) and 1.0 mm (0.040 in). It is recommended that the reboring work is entrusted to a Suzuki Service Agent, who will also be able to supply the correct oversize pistons.

21 Pistons and piston rings: examination and renovation

1 Attention to the pistons and rings can be overlooked if a rebore is required, since new components will be fitted as a matter of course.
2 Examine each piston closely, rejecting it if serious scoring or discolouration due to exhaust gas 'blow-by' is evident. Using a blunt scraper, remove carbon deposits from the piston crown, noting that the better the surface finish, the slower the subsequent build-up of carbon will be. If desired, a good surface finish can be achieved using metal polish.
3 Using a micrometer, measure the piston diameter at right angles to the gudgeon pin bore and about 15 mm (0.6 in) up from the bottom of the skirt. If the diameter is less than the service limit, the pistons must be renewed. Note that if this degree of wear is found it is likely that the piston/cylinder clearance will have exceeded the service limit. If this is so, reboring and new pistons will be required.
4 Measure the ring/groove clearances of the top and 2nd rings using feeler gauges. If either exceeds the service limit, renew the piston and rings.
5 With some experience, the rings can be removed for examination and measurement by spreading the ends slightly and sliding them off the piston. It should be noted, however, that the rings are brittle and will snap if stretched too far. A safer method, and one which can be used to free gummed rings, is shown in the accompanying line drawing.
6 Carefully remove accumulated carbon from the grooves, then measure the groove width with feeler gauges. The ring thickness can be checked using a micrometer, and both readings compared with those given in the specifications.
7 The general condition of the rings is checked by measuring the free end gap using a vernier caliper. The installed end gap is measured by pushing the ring into the bottom (unworn) area of the bore, and checking the end gap with feeler gauges. This will indicate the degree of ring wear. If within tolerance in all other respects it is possible to fit new rings to compensate for normal wear.
8 Note that the wear ridge at the top of each bore must be removed, or the new rings may be broken by it. This job is done using a special tool, and is best done professionally along with glaze busting. This latter operation is essential if the new rings are to bed into the bores, and may be carried out using one of the proprietary tools designed for this work.

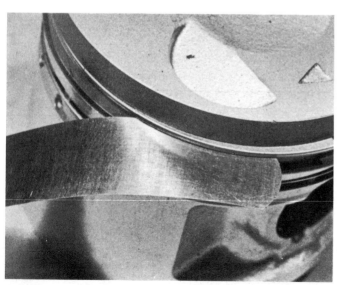

21.4 Measure the ring to groove clearance using feeler gauges

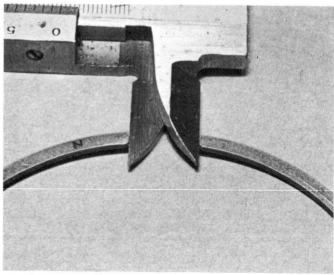

21.7 Ring free end gap can be measured as shown using a vernier caliper

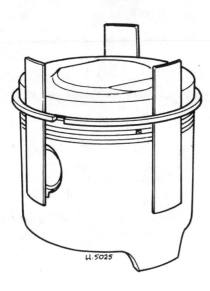

Fig. 1.17 Freeing gummed piston rings

22 Cylinder head and valves: examination and renovation

1   Before commencing any dismantling work on the head, have ready a suitable container for the valve components. This should take the form of a box divided into 16 compartments, each marked so that the relevant valve is clearly identified; 'IN/ 1/L' to denote cylinder 1, inlet, left-hand, for example. On no account allow the valve components to be mixed up.
2   Pivot the rocker arms clear of the valves, then remove each valve in turn using a valve spring compressor. With the valve spring compressed, displace and remove the collet halves (a pair of tweezers or a small magnet is invaluable for this) then lift away the spring retainer, springs and spring seat. The valve can now be displaced and removed.
3   To remove the rocker arms, unscrew the shaft locating bolt, then the shaft end cap. Screw a 6 mm bolt or screw into the shaft end, and use this to draw the shaft out of the head. Remove the rocker components, noting their relative positions, and place them in

sequence on the shaft to which they belong. Mark each shaft to ensure that it is refitted correctly.

Cylinder head
4   Degrease the head casting and remove accumulated carbon from the combustion chambers and ports. Check carefully for cracks, especially near the valve seats and spark plug holes. If cracking is detected, seek professional help.
5   If there has been any indication of warpage, such as a blown head gasket, check by using a straightedge and feeler gauges. If at any point the 0.2 mm (0.008 in) service limit is exceeded, the head will have to be skimmed flat or renewed.

Valves
6   Examine each valve, rejecting any that is obviously badly scored or burnt across the seating face. An indication of the degree of wear is given by the width of the 'face' (or more accurately the margin); the thin parallel face between the seating face of the valve and the valve head surface. If this is worn to 0.5 mm (0.02 in) or less, the valve must be renewed.
7   The valve stem runout can be checked using a dial gauge with the valve stem resting on V-blocks. The valve should be renewed if runout exceeds 0.05 mm (0.002 in), and the cause of the bending should be investigated. The radial runout of the valve head is checked in a similar fashion, the service limit being 0.03 mm (0.001 in).
8   Measure the valve stem diameter with a micrometer, renewing it if worn to or beyond the service limit. Note that stem wear will contribute to stem/guide clearance, and that guide wear cannot be assessed using a worn stem.

Valve guides
9   Guide wear is checked by measuring the 'wobble' between the valve guide and the stem, using a dial gauge. If this exceeds the service limit and the valve stem is unworn or within limits, the guide must be renewed.
10   To renew the guides it is necessary to have the various removal and fitting tools, a reamer to enlarge the bores in the cylinder head to take the oversized guides, another reamer to finish the valve guide bores, and the valve seat refacing equipment so that the seats can be cut to suit the new guides. In view of the sheer cost of this equipment, the work is best entrusted to a Suzuki Service Agent.

Valve springs
11   Measure the free length of the inner and outer valve springs, renewing them as pairs if worn to or beyond the service limit. It is unlikely that the springs will have weakened without becoming shorter, but this can be checked by measuring the spring pressures when compressed to specified lengths. This is not easy to do at home, but the resourceful owner should be able to contrive a suitable method using a spring balance and ruler.

22.2a Compress valve springs and displace collet halves ...   22.2b ... to free the spring retainer

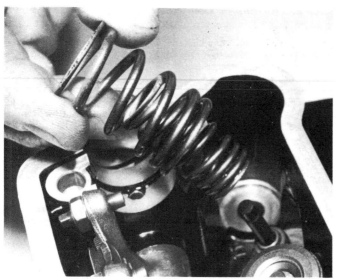

22.2c Lift away the valve springs noting that the tighter coils are fitted nearest the head

22.2d Valve can now be displaced and removed for examination

22.2e Valve stem oil seals are best renewed as a precaution against subsequent leakage

22.3a Rocker arm support shafts are located by a bolt and plain washer ...

22.3b ... and are retained by Allen-headed end caps

22.3c Use a bolt to draw shaft out of its bore in the head

22.3d Rockers and thrust spring can now be removed

3   Assemble each set of springs in turn. Fit the springs with the closer pitch end downwards, then fit the upper retainer. Compress the springs and fit the collet halves, ensuring that they engage properly in the groove in the valve stem. Release the compressor and check that the various components are seated correctly by tapping the end of the stem. Repeat the above sequence to fit the remaining valves.

4   Reassemble the rocker arms and shafts, ensuring that they are fitted in their original positions. Refit the shaft end plugs after securing the shaft locating bolts. If it proves necessary to turn the shaft to align the threaded hole for the locating bolt, this can be done using the 6 mm screw employed during removal.

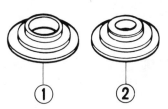

Fig. 1.18 When reassembling valves do not confuse the valve spring lower seat (1) with the spring retainer (2)

23 Valves and valve seats: refacing and grinding

1   If examination has shown the valve contact face to be badly pitted or eroded, it will be necessary to have them refaced by an engine reconditioner or to renew them. This work requires the use of a grinding wheel and the appropriate jigs, and is not worth attempting at home. Note that grinding or lapping the valves will not compensate for pitting, and if done to excess will pocket the valve in the valve seat.

2   It is likely that the valve seats will be in a similar state to the valve contact faces, and this work should be carried out at the same time as the valve refacing. Although a fairly simple operation, a good quality set of cutters is required, together with skill in their use. It should be noted that it is quite easy to take off too much material, rendering the seat and thus the head unserviceable. Unless experienced in this work, leave it to a professional.

3   Light wear or pitting can be removed by lapping the valve and seat, and this operation is undertaken during overhaul to restore the seal between the two. Apply a thin film of fine carborundum paste to the valve contact face, oil the valve stem and place the valve in its correct seat. Using a valve lapping tool, lap the valve using a semi-rotary motion. Lift the valve occasionally to redistribute the abrasive paste.

4   Remove the valve and wipe off the compound off the valve and seat. Examine the contact faces, each of which should show an unbroken light grey ring. Any deep pits will now be highlighted, as will an uneven contact area, and a decision can be made as to whether lapping should continue or if grinding is required. The standard contact width on the valve should be 0.9 – 1.1 mm (0.035 – 0.043 in), with a corresponding band evident on the valve seat.

5   If lapping seems adequate, repeat the operation on the remaining valves, making sure that all traces of the abrasive are removed; any compound finding its way into the engine will cause serious damage.

6   It is permissible to grind flat the end of the valve stem, provided that this does not reduce the length between the stem end and the upper edge of the collet groove to less than 2.9 mm (0.11 in). If the stem is ground it is essential that it is kept square, and when reassembled the stem end must still be proud of the collets.

24 Cylinder head components: reassembly

1   After examination and reconditioning has been completed, check that the head and valve components are quite clean. If the valve stem seals have hardened or were removed they must be renewed, pushing them over the guide ends using a stepped drift to avoid damage.

2   Place the valve spring seats in position, taking care not to confuse them with the upper retainers. Lubricate the valve stems with molybdenum disulphide grease, then slide them into their respective guides.

25 Camshafts and drive components: examination and renovation

Camshafts

1   Examine the cam lobes for wear or scoring. This will be most evident near the peaks of the lobes, and if present will require the renewal of the camshaft. Whilst the lobes will eventually wear down through normal use, scoring can usually be attributed to failure to change the oil at the specified interval.

2   If the lobes are undamaged, measure the overall cam lobe height to assess the degree of wear. The service limit for the inlet cam is 34.640 mm (1.3638 in) whilst that of the exhaust cam is 34.060 mm (1.3409 in).

3   The camshafts run directly in the cylinder head material, the bearing surfaces being formed by the head casting and the camshaft caps. The clearance between the bearing surfaces and the camshaft journals can be measured using Plastigage in the same way as has been described for the big-end and main bearings.

4   In the US, Plastigage is available from most large dealers, but availability is limited in the UK. Where the material is not available, it will be necessary to check the relevant dimensions directly, using internal and external micrometers, and comparing the readings obtained with those shown in the specifications.

5   Where Plastigage can be obtained, clean the bearing surfaces and place a strip of the material on each journal. Assemble the bearing caps, tightening the bolts to 0.8 – 1.2 kgf m (6.0 – 8.5 lbf ft), then remove them to allow the spread of the Plastigage to be read off against the scale provided. The measurement indicated at the widest point shows the clearance. If this exceeds the service limit, the camshafts, cylinder head or both may have to be renewed. In view of the expense that will be incurred it is suggested that the advice of an experienced Suzuki Service Agent is sought.

6   If the camshaft journal OD and the cylinder head/cap ID are to be measured directly using micrometers, the relevant dimensions are given below:

Camshaft journal OD .... 21.959 – 21.980 mm (0.8645 – 0.8654 in)

Cylinder head/cap ID:
    Except centre journal .... 22.012 – 22.025 mm (0.8666 – 0.8671 in)
    Centre journal only .... 22.030 – 22.043 mm (0.8673 – 0.8654 in)

7   Camshaft runout is measured with the shaft supported on V-blocks, using a dial gauge on the centre journal. If runout exceeds the 0.1 mm (0.004 in) service limit, the camshaft must be renewed.

Tensioner

8   The tensioner assembly is of the automatic type, an arrangement which ensures that cam chain tension is maintained as the chain wears and stretches during normal use. It is important that the mechanism operates smoothly and evenly in service, and this should be checked during overhauls.

64

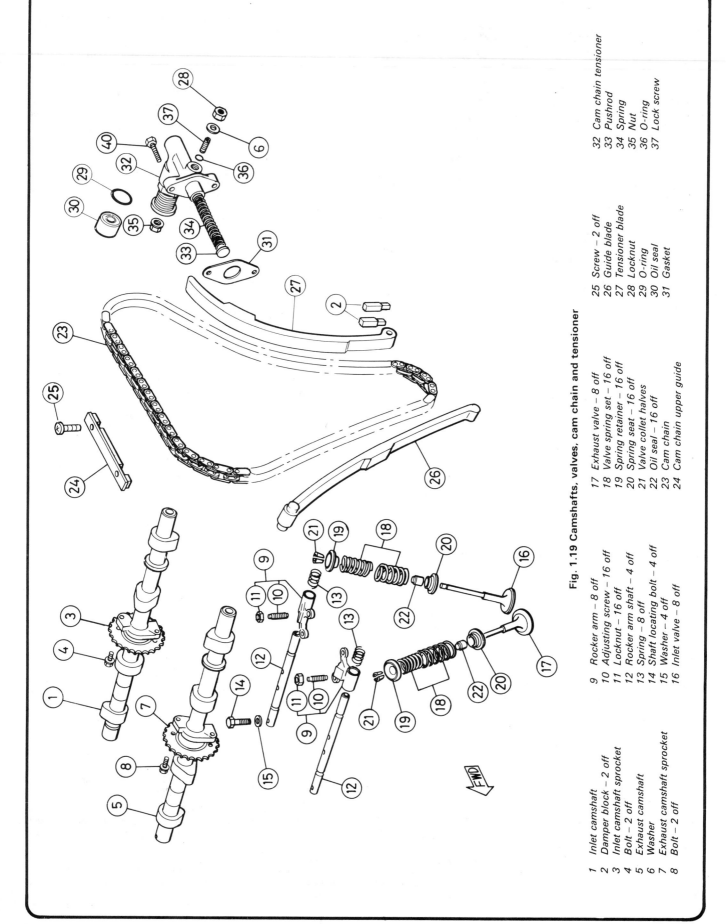

Fig. 1.19 Camshafts, valves, cam chain and tensioner

1 Inlet camshaft
2 Damper block – 2 off
3 Inlet camshaft sprocket
4 Bolt – 2 off
5 Exhaust camshaft
6 Washer
7 Exhaust camshaft sprocket
8 Bolt – 2 off

9 Rocker arm – 8 off
10 Adjusting screw – 16 off
11 Locknut – 16 off
12 Rocker arm shaft – 4 off
13 Spring – 8 off
14 Shaft locating bolt – 4 off
15 Washer – 4 off
16 Inlet valve – 8 off

17 Exhaust valve – 8 off
18 Valve spring set – 16 off
19 Spring retainer – 16 off
20 Spring seat – 16 off
21 Valve collet halves
22 Oil seal – 16 off
23 Cam chain
24 Cam chain upper guide

25 Screw – 2 off
26 Guide blade
27 Tensioner blade
28 Locknut
29 O-ring
30 Oil seal
31 Gasket

32 Cam chain tensioner
33 Pushrod
34 Spring
35 Nut
36 O-ring
37 Lock screw

9 Slacken by one or two turns the small locking screw which retains the tensioner plunger. Turn the knurled wheel anticlockwise against spring pressure, then check that the plunger can be moved smoothly and evenly. If resistance is noted, release the locking screw and examine and clean the plunger. If the plunger is bent or scored it should be renewed.

10 Turn the knurled wheel fully back against spring pressure, then release it, noting whether it returns fully to its rest position. If resistance or hesitation is noted, remove the lock shaft assembly from the tensioner body, remove the nut which retains the knurled wheel, then release the wheel and spring and displace the lockshaft.

11 Clean and lubricate the lockshaft components, then slide the lockshaft into its housing. Position the spiral ramps so that the stepped ends are 10 mm apart. Place the spring over the shaft end and hook the ends into the housing and the knurled wheel. Turn the knurled wheel one turn anticlockwise, fit the knurled wheel over the lockshaft end and fit the retaining nut, tightening it to 0.8 – 1.0 kgf m (6.0 – 7.0 lbf ft). Refit the assembled unit, tightening the body to 3.0 – 3.5 kgf m (21.5 – 25.5 lbf ft).

12 Refit the tensioner plunger, having first lubricated it with molybdenum disulphide grease, then turn the knurled wheel until the rod is fully home. Hold it in place, then secure the locking screw to secure it. Note that the locking screw must align with the slot on the side of the plunger.

Cam chain

13 Pull the cam chain taut, then measure the length of 20 links using a vernier caliper. If this exceeds the service limit of 128.90 mm (5.07 in), the chain must be renewed. The chain should be given a close visual inspection, renewing it if damage is evident.

Cam chain tensioner blade and guides

14 Examine the tensioner blade and guides for wear or damage, renewing them if necessary. No specific wear figures are available, but if the condition of any component is suspect it is best to compare it with a new part or to seek the advice of a Suzuki Service Agent. Note that the upper guide inside the cylinder head cover is retained by screws, and these should be coated with a thread locking compound during reassembly.

26 Gearbox components: examination and renovation

1 It will not be necessary to dismantle the gearbox input or output shafts unless damage to the pinions or the shafts themselves has occurred. Reference to the accompanying line drawing and photographs shows the precise sequence in which the shafts are assembled.

2 The shafts should be examined for indications of wear or damage. The gear teeth should be free from chipping. Each tooth should present a polished face with no indication of pitting. Ensure that the pinions turn smoothly with no tight spots or excessive play. If further examination proves necessary, proceed as follows.

Input shaft

3 Slide off the bearing and oil seal from the left-hand end of the shaft. Using a pair of circlip pliers with short angled tips, free the circlip which locates the 6th gear pinion, sliding it up towards the 3rd/4th gear pinion. The 6th and 2nd gear pinions can now be slid along the shaft to allow the 2nd gear pinion circlip to be removed. Slide off the 2nd, 6th and 3rd/4th gear pinions, laying them out in their correct relative positions. Remove the 5th gear pinion circlip, then slide the gear off the shaft.

Output shaft

4 Working from the right-hand end of the shaft, slide off the needle roller bearing and the plain thrust washer, followed by the large 1st gear pinion and the 5th gear pinion. Remove the circlip and splined washer which locate the 4th gear pinion and slide it off the shaft.

5 The 3rd gear pinion is secured by a splined washer which is in turn held by a special tanged washer. The tanged washer should be slid off the shaft and the splined washer turned until it clears the shaft splines. The 3rd gear pinion can now be removed, followed by another splined washer and a circlip.

6 Remove the 6th gear pinion, then release and remove the circlip which retains the 2nd gear pinion. The 2nd gear pinion runs on a headed bush which will slide off together with the pinion.

Reassembly

7 Examine the gearbox pinions for wear or damage, renewing as pairs those which show signs of chipping or burring of the teeth or the engagement dogs. Check that all components are clean, and lubricate the shafts with molybdenum disulphide grease prior to assembly.

8 The assembly sequence is shown in the accompanying photographs, and should be followed carefully. Pay particular attention to the disposition of the washers and circlips. In the case of the latter, note that the sharper edge must face towards the direction of thrust, the curved edge facing the pinion.

9 Note that a shim is fitted between the input shaft 2nd and 6th gear pinions. After assembly is complete, check the clearance between the shim and the 2nd gear pinion. If this is outside the range 0.1 – 0.3 mm (0.004 – 0.012 in), select and install the appropriate shim size to restore the correct clearance. Shims are available in 0.1 mm (0.004 in) increments from 0.5 – 0.8 mm (0.019 – 0.031 in).

10 In the case of the output shaft, fit the O-ring to its left-hand end, then position the spacer. Grease the oil seal lip before sliding it into place over the spacer.

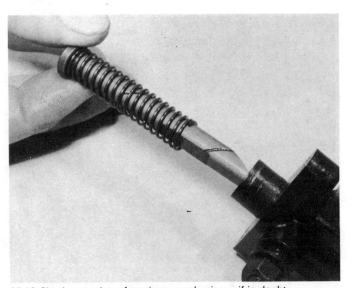

25.12 Check operation of tensioner mechanism – if in doubt dismantle it for cleaning and lubrication

26.8a Fit input shaft right-hand bearing with locating pin innermost as shown

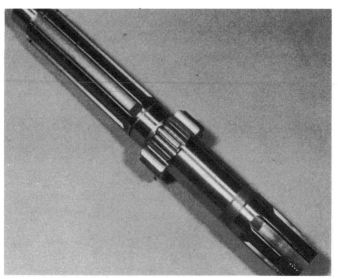

26.8b Input shaft 1st gear pinion is integral with shaft

26.8c Slide 5th gear pinion into position, followed by the headed bush on which it runs

26.8d Fit the locating circlip, ensuring that it seats correctly

26.8e The combined 3rd/4th gear is fitted next, the larger 4th gear pinion inwards

26.8f Fit the circlip near the pinion. DO NOT locate it in its groove at this stage. Fit the splined washer

26.8g Slide the 6th gear pinion with the grooved face outwards

26.8h Place the shim over the shaft ...

26.8i ... followed by the 2nd gear pinion

26.8j Locate the wire circlip in its groove and slide the 2nd and 6th gear pinions back against it

26.8k 6th gear pinion circlip can now be pushed into its groove

26.8l Fit the seal over the end of the input shaft ...

26.8m ... lubricate the sealed needle roller bearing ...

26.8n ... and place it in position

26.8o Note plain thrust washer on right-hand end of shaft

26.9a Renew O-ring on left-hand end of the output shaft where necessary

26.9b Fit the output shaft 2nd gear pinion and headed bush ...

26.9c ... and secure with a new circlip

26.9d Fit the 6th gear pinion, selector groove outwards

26.9e Fit a circlip in its groove, followed by the splined washer

26.9f Place the 3rd gear pinion against the washer ...

26.9g ... then fit the splined washer. Twist it to the position shown then lock it with the tanged washer

26.9h Slide the 4th gear pinion into place ...

26.9i ... followed by the splined washer ...

26.9j ... and secure it with a new circlip

26.9k The 5th gear pinion can now be displaced over the shaft ...

26.9l ... followed by the large 1st gear pinion

26.9m Finally, fit the plain washer ...

26.9n ... and the needle roller bearing

26.9o Do not omit the sleeve on the left-hand end of the shaft

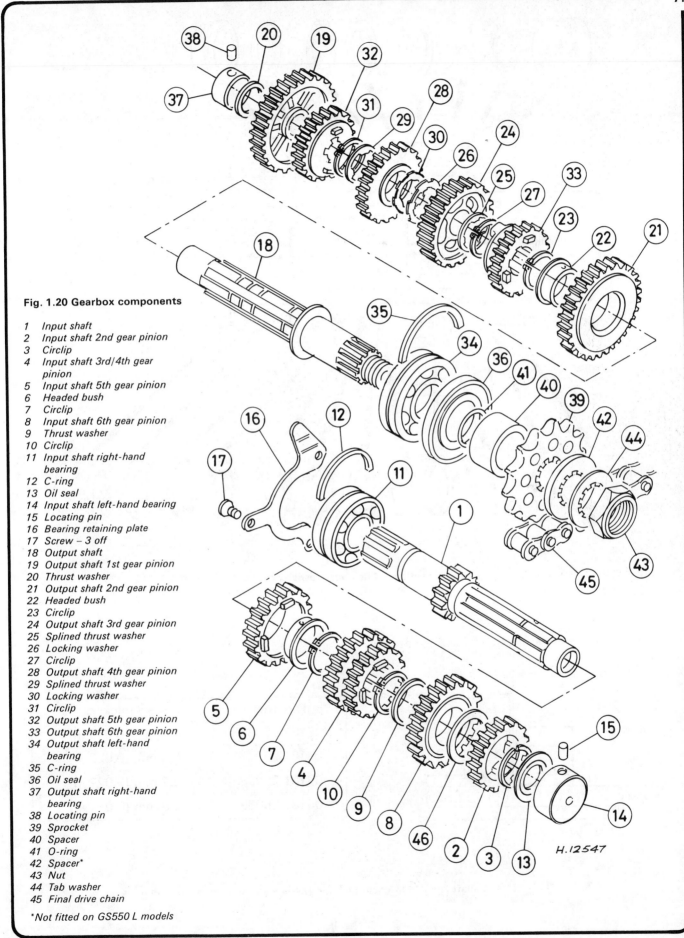

Fig. 1.20 Gearbox components

1 Input shaft
2 Input shaft 2nd gear pinion
3 Circlip
4 Input shaft 3rd/4th gear pinion
5 Input shaft 5th gear pinion
6 Headed bush
7 Circlip
8 Input shaft 6th gear pinion
9 Thrust washer
10 Circlip
11 Input shaft right-hand bearing
12 C-ring
13 Oil seal
14 Input shaft left-hand bearing
15 Locating pin
16 Bearing retaining plate
17 Screw – 3 off
18 Output shaft
19 Output shaft 1st gear pinion
20 Thrust washer
21 Output shaft 2nd gear pinion
22 Headed bush
23 Circlip
24 Output shaft 3rd gear pinion
25 Splined thrust washer
26 Locking washer
27 Circlip
28 Output shaft 4th gear pinion
29 Splined thrust washer
30 Locking washer
31 Circlip
32 Output shaft 5th gear pinion
33 Output shaft 6th gear pinion
34 Output shaft left-hand bearing
35 C-ring
36 Oil seal
37 Output shaft right-hand bearing
38 Locating pin
39 Sprocket
40 Spacer
41 O-ring
42 Spacer*
43 Nut
44 Tab washer
45 Final drive chain

*Not fitted on GS550 L models

H.12547

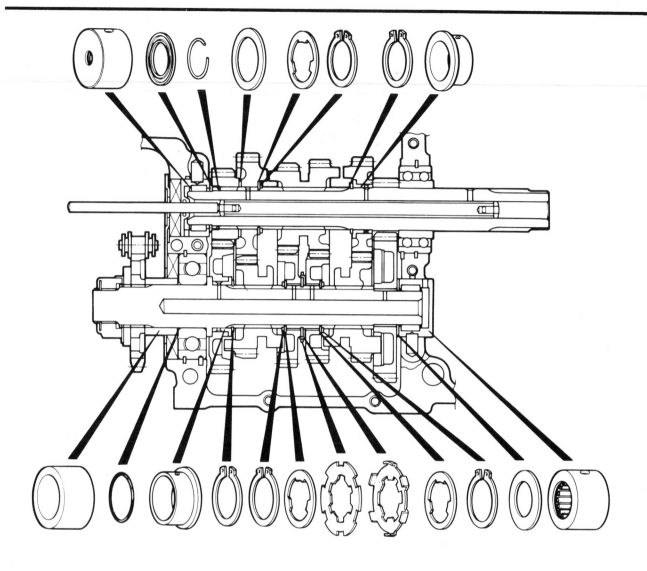

Fig. 1.21 Correct positions of gearbox washers, circlips and bushes

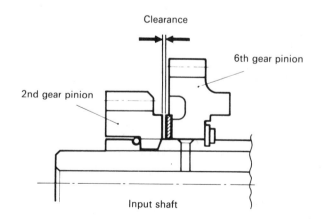

Part No.	Shim thickness
09181-25036	0.5 mm (0.019 in)
09181-25037	0.6 mm (0.023 in)
09181-25038	0.7 mm (0.027 in)
09181-25039	0.8 mm (0.031 in)

Shim selection table

Clearance

6th gear pinion

2nd gear pinion

Input shaft

Fig. 1.22 Input shaft 2nd and 6th gear pinion clearance and shim selection table

27 Gearchange mechanism: examination and renovation

1   Check the selector fork shafts for straightness by rolling them on a sheet of glass. Renew the forks if bent. Examine the selector forks for wear or damage, paying particular attention to the fork ends and the pegs which engage in the selector drum grooves.
2   Measure with feeler gauges the selector fork to groove clearance. The standard figure is 0.1 – 0.3 mm (0.004 – 0.012 in). The service limit is 0.5 mm (0.02 in), and if this is exceeded it will be necessary to check the selector fork thickness and the selector groove width to determine which component is in need of renewal. The standard dimensions are as follows:

   Selector fork thickness –   5.30 – 5.40 mm (0.209 – 0.213 in)
   Selector groove width –   5.50 – 5.60 mm (0.217 – 0.220 in)

3   The tracks in the selector drum should be free from signs of wear unless lubrication has been neglected. Examine the selector pawl assembly, renewing any component showing signs of burring. Wear on the pawl ends is the most probable cause of selection problems.

27.2 Selector groove width can be checked using a vernier caliper

28 Clutch assembly: examination and renovation

1   After extended use the clutch friction plates will wear, leading to clutch slip if wear is excessive. Measure the thickness of each plate, renewing them if worn to or beyond the service limit. If the locating tangs are worn below the service limit of 11.0 mm (0.43 in), the plates should be renewed as a set.
2   The plain steel plates are unlikely to wear, but may have warped due to overheating. This can be checked by placing each one on a surface plate or a flat glass sheet and measuring any distortion with feeler gauges. The innermost plain plate is retained on the clutch centre by a wire clip. The clip can be released to allow the removal of the plate, dished washer and seat.
3   The latter components provide a degree of shock absorption, making the clutch smoother in operation. It is unlikely that they will require attention, but if the assembly is dismantled, note that the piano wire retaining clip should be renewed.
4   The clutch springs will weaken in time, becoming shorter as they lose their elasticity. The free length should be measured and the springs renewed as a set if worn to or beyond the service limit.
5   Examine the clutch centre splines and also those of the clutch outer drum. In time, these will become indented by the clutch plates, causing the plates to catch on the resulting steps and making operation erratic.

Light damage may be corrected by dressing with a fine file or abrasive paper, but if wear is serious, the damaged component must be renewed.
6   The clutch drum incorporates the primary driven gear and a transmission shock absorber arrangement. If any of these items are worn, it will be necessary to renew the drum complete. In the case of the shock absorber assembly, the best way of assessing wear is to compare the amount of free play with that of a new component. In extreme cases the shock absorber springs will be loose and will rattle if the clutch drum is shaken.
7   The clutch centre bearing must be free from damage or indentations, however small. It is not practicable to measure wear in needle roller bearings, but any blemish on the rollers or race surfaces indicates the need for renewal.

29 Crankcases and covers: examination and renovation

1   The crankcase halves and the various outer covers are unlikely to become damaged unless the machine is dropped or accident damage is sustained. Small cracks can be repaired by a specialist welding process, providing that care is taken to avoid distortion, and expert advice should be sought regarding the viability of a proposed repair.
2   Damaged threads can be repaired relatively easily by tapping them oversize and fitting a Helicoil thread insert. This is a simple job which requires the relevant tap, insert and fitting tool. It is better, therefore to leave this work to a local dealer offering this service.
3   If the selector drum bearing requires renewal it can be driven out of the casing using a large socket as a drift. It is advisable to warm the casing with very hot water to expand the alloy, making removal easier.
4   The oil passages and galleries should be cleaned by flushing them through with a clean solvent. This should be done outside or in a well ventilated area, and care must be taken to avoid any risk of fire. Check and clean out the small oil jets which control the oil system pressure.

30 Engine reassembly: general

1   Before commencing reassembly, check that each component has been cleaned and that every gasket face is free from old gaskets or jointing compound. Removal of the latter is greatly facilitated by the use of solvent. This varies according to the composition of the compound, but methylated spirit, acetone or cellulose thinners are often effective. In some cases scraping may be the only answer, but take great care not to damage the gasket face itself.
2   Check that all gaskets, seals and O-rings are to hand and that they are of the correct type for the model in question; a dry run ro check this point may save time and frustration later. Clear the workbench of all unnecessary tools or parts, and make ready an oil can filled with clean engine oil for lubrication as assembly proceeds.
3   Make sure that a torque wrench is available and refer to the torque wrench settings at the front of this Chapter. Note that failure to observe torque settings may result in oil leakage, broken fasteners or distorted castings.

31 Engine reassembly: refitting the lower crankcase components

1   Assemble the selector pawl components and fit the unit to the end of the selector drum. It will be noted that the notch in each pawl is offset, and should be fitted towards the drum so that it aligns with the pawl spring. Lubricate the drum bearing surfaces, then slide the drum into the crankcase. When the drum is half way home, fit the detent cam, locating its notch over the projecting pin. Slide the spacer and thrust washer over the shaft end, then slide the drum fully home.
2   Install the selector fork shaft, fitting the forks in the correct order and position as shown in the accompanying photographs. Drop the neutral detent plunger into its bore, then fit the spring and detent bolt, tightening the latter to 1.8 – 2.8 kgf m (13.0 – 20.0 lbf ft). Hook the gear stopper arm spring over the edge of the lower crankcase half.
3   Fit the selector pawl guide plate and the selector drum bearing retainer, using thread locking compound on the retaining screws and tightening them securely. Turn the selector drum to the neutral position.

74

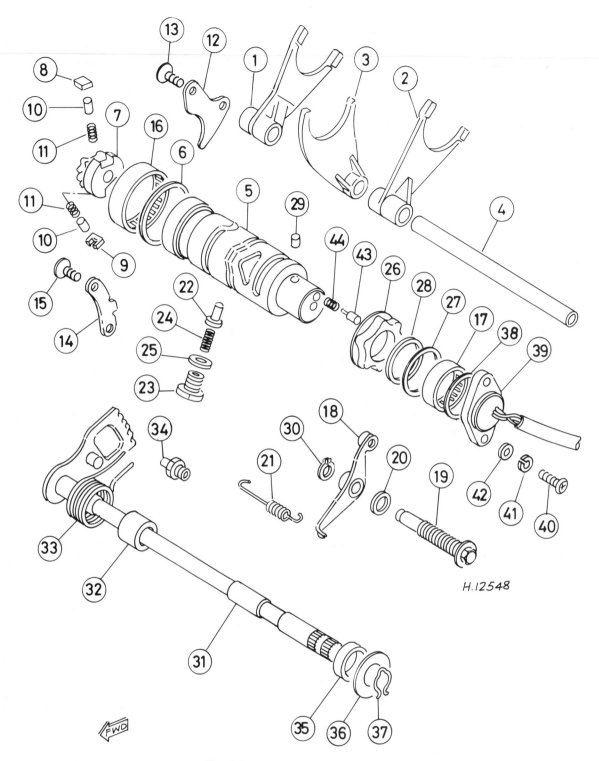

Fig. 1.23 Gearchange mechanism

1	Output shaft 6th gear fork	12	Bearing retainer	23	Detent plunger housing	34 Locating pin
2	Output shaft 5th gear fork	13	Screw – 2 off	24	Spring	35 Oil seal
3	Input shaft 3rd/4th gear fork	14	Guide plate	25	Sealing washer	36 Washer
4	Selector fork shaft	15	Screw – 2 off	26	Detent cam	37 Clip
5	Selector drum	16	Needle roller bearing	27	Thrust washer	38 O-ring
6	Washer	17	Bearing	28	Spacer	39 Gear indicator switch
7	Selector pawl	18	Stopper arm	29	Pin	40 Screw – 2 off
8	Pawl	19	Locating peg	30	Circlip	41 Spring washer – 2 off
9	Pawl	20	Washer	31	Gearchange shaft	42 Washer – 2 off (where fitted)
10	Pin – 2 off	21	Spring	32	Collar	43 Contact
11	Spring – 2 off	22	Detent plunger	33	Centralising spring	44 Spring

H.12548

31.1a Assemble the selector pawl assembly, noting that spring, pin and pawls are offset

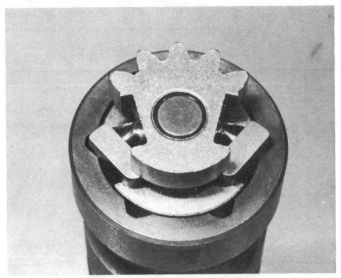

31.1b Pawl assembly can now be fitted into the end of the drum

31.1c Fit drum part way into the casing, then slide detent cam over the end

31.1d Fit spacer and thrust washer, then slide drum fully home

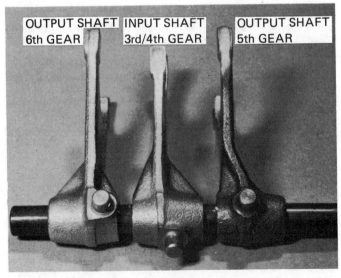

OUTPUT SHAFT 6th GEAR INPUT SHAFT 3rd/4th GEAR OUTPUT SHAFT 5th GEAR

31.2a Note relative positions of selector forks on shaft ...

31.2b ... then assemble in casing as shown

31.2c Drop the neutral detent plunger into its bore ...

31.2d ... followed by the spring, detent bolt and washer

31.2e Hook the stopper arm spring over the casing lip

31.3 Fit guide plate and bearing retainer, using Loctite on retaining screws

32 Engine reassembly: refitting the upper crankcase components

1   Fit the oil jets (one in each of the input shaft journals). Fit the bearing locating pins (one in the input shaft left-hand journal, one in the output shaft right-hand journal) and the C-rings (one in the input shaft right-hand journal and one in the output shaft left-hand journal).
2   Offer up the input and output shafts, ensuring that the C-rings and locating pins engage correctly. In the case of the bearings located by C-rings there is a small locating dowel fitted in the edge of the outer race. This should be positioned so that it engages in the small notch provided in the casing. Fit the end cap to the end of the left-hand end of the input shaft, sealing it with a smear of RTV sealant. Grasp the end of the output shaft and check that the input shaft can be turned freely. If necessary move the gears until neutral is located.
3   Where necessary, fit the main bearing shells in their respective recesses, ensuring that the locating pegs engage in their slots. Install the cam chain guide, ensuring that it locates correctly, and retain it with the two small rubber pegs (square ends towards the chain guide pin). Fit the plain washer followed by the O-ring to the oil gallery recess.
4   Apply a smear of molybdenum disulphide grease to each of the

crankshaft main bearing journals. Lubricate the lip of the crankshaft oil seal and slide it over the end of the crankshaft. Loop the cam chain around the crankshaft sprocket then lower the assembly into position in the lower crankcase half. Ensure that the oil seal locates correctly.
5   Fit the crankshaft thrust bearings to their recesses, noting that the oil grooves face outwards towards the crankshaft webs. Note that the crankshaft thrust clearance should be checked now if it has not already been measured. Refer to Section 18 for details.

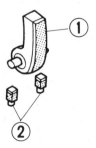

Fig. 1.24 Cam chain guide blade peg positions

1   Guide blade   2   Pegs

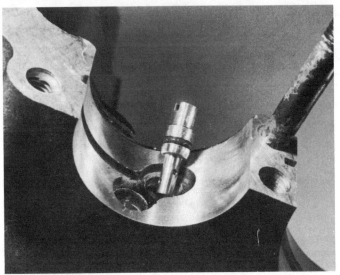

32.1a Fit the oil jets, using new O-rings as necessary

32.1b Fit the bearing locating dowels ...

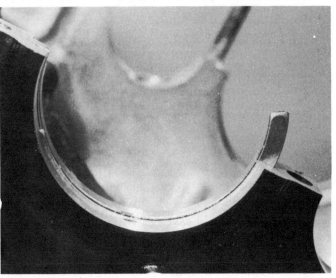

32.1c ... or C-rings, as appropriate

32.2a Install the gearbox output shaft ...

32.2b ... and input shaft, ensuring that the location pins (arrowed) are positioned in their recesses

32.3a Drop the tensioner blade into its recess ...

32.3b ... and fit rubber locating pegs as shown

32.3c Fit cam chain and lower crankshaft into position

32.5 Position thrust bearings with grooved face outwards

33 Engine reassembly: rejoining the crankcase halves

1   Check that the crankcase mating surfaces are clean and free from oil, then apply a thin, even film of sealant. Suzuki Bond No. 4 or any good quality silicone rubber RTV sealant can be used. Leave the sealant for about ten minutes to allow it to cure. Check that the locating dowels are in place (two at the front and one at the rear).

2   Offer up the lower casing half, placing it over the inverted upper half. Check that the forks engage correctly in the grooves in the gearbox pinions. These can be guided into place using a long screwdriver. Check that the casing halves seat fully and that the oil seals are located correctly. If necessary, the joint can be closed by tapping the casing with the palm of the hand, but if excessive force is needed, remove the lower half and rectify the cause of the problem.

3   Fit the 6 mm and 8 mm crankcase bolts, not forgetting the two Allen headed bolts inside the oil filter housing. Following the tightening sequence indicated by the numbers cast into the crankcase next to each bolt, tighten them evenly and progressively to the initial torque figure. Reset the torque wrench, then tighten to the final torque setting as shown below.

Crankcase torque settings	kgf m	lbf ft
6 mm bolts:		
Initial	0.6	4.5
Final	1.3	9.5
8 mm bolts:		
Initial	1.3	9.5
Final	2.4	17.0

4   When all the lower crankcase bolts have been secured, check that the gearbox shafts and crankshaft turn freely. If there are any problems in this respect, resolve them **now** before reassembly progresses further. If all is well, refit the oil strainer body, using a new O-ring. Fit the oil strainer, ensuring that the "FRONT" mark is positioned appropriately. Fit a new O-ring to the oil feed passage in the sump area. If it was disturbed during the overhaul, refit the oil pressure relief valve to the inside of the sump, using a new sealing washer. Tighten the valve to 2.5 – 3.0 kgf m (18.0 – 21.5 lbf ft). Place a new sump gasket in position and refit the sump. Secure the retaining bolts to a torque setting of 1.2 – 1.6 kgf m (8.5 – 11.5 lbf ft).

5   Invert the unit on the workbench and fit the upper crankcase securing bolts, noting the copper sealing washer fitted below the head of the bolt nearest the oil pressure switch, and the engine earth lead and cable clip fitted at the rear edge of the casing. Tighten them evenly and progressively in numerical sequence to the above torque figures.

6   Fit the input and output shaft bearing retainers, using thread locking compound on the retaining screws. If it was removed during the overhaul, fit the gear indicator spring and contact, then fit the switch body using a new O-ring.

33.3a Refit crankcase bolts, tightening them in the marked sequence

33.3b Do not omit the Allen headed bolts inside filter housing

33.3c Tighten the bolts to the appropriate torque setting

33.4a Fit the oil strainer body, using a new O-ring

33.4b Fit strainer (noting FRONT marking), gasket and O-ring (arrowed)

33.4c Clean and refit the oil pressure relief valve

33.6a Fit the input shaft bearing/selector shaft retainer ...

33.6b ... fit the output shaft bearing retainer and secure the locking tabs

33.6c Fit the spring and contact to the end of the selector drum ...

33.6d ... then offer up and secure the switch body

34.1 Refit the pump body, then slide the driving pin into the shaft end

34 Engine reassembly: refitting the oil pump and gear selector shaft

1   Fit the new O-ring to the pump body and install it in its recess. Apply a thread locking compound to the three retaining bolts, then tighten them evenly to 0.7 – 0.9 kgf m (5.0 – 6.5 lbf ft).

2   Place the driving pin through the pump spindle. Offer up the pump pinion, noting that the slot on its inner face must locate over the driving pin. Once in place, secure the pinion with its circlip.

3   Check that the gear selector pawl assembly is in position, then slide the selector shaft into the casing hole. Care should be taken to avoid damage to the shaft seal as it emerges from the left-hand side of the crankcase.

4   Arrange the claw assembly as shown in the accompanying photograph. Once the mechanism is aligned correctly, secure the end of the shaft with its plain washer and circlip. The ends of the centralising spring should be hooked over the locating pin as shown.

34.2 Offer up the pump pinion and retain it with the circlip

34.4a Slide the selector claw into place, noting how the ends of the centering spring fit over the locating pin

34.4b Secure the selector shaft with a plain washer and clip

35 Engine reassembly: refitting the clutch

1   Place the small diameter thrust washer over the projecting input shaft, sliding it up against the bearing inner race. Fit the larger thrust washer with its flat face outwards. Check that the oil pump drive pinion is in place on the back of the clutch drum, then manoeuvre the drum into position over the input shaft. Lubricate the clutch drum needle roller bearing assembly and slide it into position, followed by the centre sleeve. Fit the thrust washer with its flat face towards the clutch drum.
2   If the inner plain plate was removed from the clutch centre, this should now be refitted, using a new piano wire retaining clip. Fit the washer and its seat, then place the inner plate against them. Work the wire retaining clip into place, noting that the ends pass through a hole in the clutch centre (see photograph). The clutch centre can now be fitted over the end of the input shaft.

3   If new friction plates are to be fitted, they should be soaked in engine oil prior to installation. Meanwhile, fit the locking washer and the clutch centre nut on the shaft end. Hold the clutch centre securely and tighten the nut to 5.0 – 7.0 kgf m (36.0 – 50.5 lbf ft). Secure the nut by bending over the tab washer. Install the plain and friction plates alternately.
4   Fit the clutch pushrod into the end of the input shaft, followed by the headed end piece. Fit the needle roller release bearing and the plain thrust washer. The clutch pressure plate can now be placed in position. Fit the clutch springs, washers and bolts, tightening them evenly and in a diagonal sequence to the recommended torque setting of 1.1 – 1.3 kgf m (8.0 – 9.5 lbf ft).
5   Apply a thin film of Suzuki bond No. 4 or an RTV silicone sealant to the clutch gasket face in a strip of about 2 in across each crankcase joint, then fit a new clutch cover gasket. Check that the two locating dowels are in place, then offer up the cover. Tap the cover home and fit the cover securing screws.

35.1a Check that the smaller thrust washer is in position ...

35.1b ... then fit the larger thrust washer, flat face outwards

35.1c Fit the oil pump drive pinion over the clutch drum boss

35.1d Offer up the drum and fit the bearing and sleeve

35.1e Fit the thrust washer with its flat face towards the drum

35.2a Fit the spring seat to the clutch centre flange ...

35.2b ... followed by the large convex spring washer ...

35.2c ... and the inner plain plate

35.2d Secure the plate with the piano wire retaining clip

35.2e The clutch centre can now be fitted over the shaft end

35.3 Lock the clutch centre and tighten the retaining nut

35.4a Slide the clutch pushrod into the input shaft bore ...

35.4b ... followed by the headed push piece ...

35.4c ... the needle roller thrust bearing ...

35.4d ... and the plain washer

35.4e Install the clutch friction plates ...

35.4f ... and plain plates alternately

35.4g Refit the clutch cover and retain with the springs, washers and bolts

35.5 Apply RTV sealant to shaded areas, then fit a new gasket

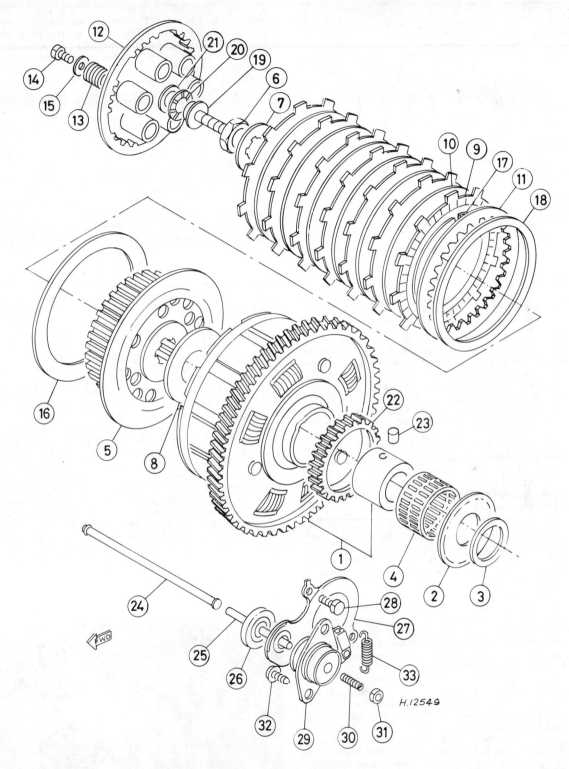

Fig. 1.25 Clutch

1	Clutch drum and sleeve	10	Plain plate – 6 off	18	Convex spring washer	26	Seal
2	Thrust washer	11	Plain plate	19	Headed push piece	27	Bearing retaining plate
3	Thrust washer	12	Pressure plate	20	Thrust bearing	28	Bolt – 3 off
4	Needle roller bearing	13	Spring – 6 off	21	Washer	29	Clutch release mechanism
5	Clutch centre	14	Bolt – 6 off	22	Oil pump drive gear	30	Adjusting screw
6	Nut	15	Washer – 6 off	23	Locating pin	31	Locknut
7	Tab washer	16	Spring seat	24	Pushrod	32	Screw – 2 off
8	Thrust washer	17	Wire clip	25	Pushrod	33	Return spring
9	Friction plate – 7 off						

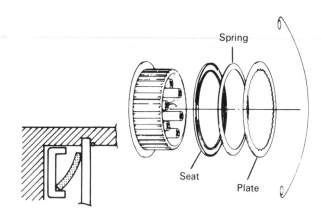

Fig. 1.26 Correct fitting of clutch inner plain plate, seat and spring

36 Engine reassembly: refitting the ignition pickup

1   Fit the pickup backplate into the casing recess, noting the slot for the wiring grommet at the bottom. It is a good idea to seal the grommet in its slot with a smear of RTV sealant to prevent the ingress of water. Fit the two backplate screws, tightening them firmly. Route the wiring down from the grommet, passing it through the cable clip. Note that the wiring now runs forward through the second cable clip before running down and back along the edge of the sump.
2   Offer up the pickup rotor, ensuring that it locates over the pin in the crankshaft end. Fit and tighten the securing bolt to 2.5 – 3.5 kgf m (18.0 – 25.5 lbf ft). Note that the inspection cover should **not** be fitted until the valve timing has been checked.

37 Engine reassembly: refitting the starter drive, starter motor and alternator assembly

1   Place the starter idler pinion in its recess, then slide the shaft through into the casing to retain it.
2   Check that the starter clutch rollers are located correctly in the clutch body, then fit the starter gear, easing the boss into engagement by turning it. Lubricate the clutch boss bearing with engine oil. Check that the crankshaft taper is clean and free from grease or oil contamination, then fit the rotor over the crankshaft end. Apply very sparingly thread locking compound to the rotor bolt threads, then fit the bolt. **Take extreme care to ensure that none of the locking compound finds its way between the rotor and crankshaft.** Lock the crankshaft by the same method used during removal, then tighten the bolt to 14.0 – 16.0 kgf m (101.5 – 115.5 lbf ft).
3   Check the condition of the starter motor O-ring and where necessary renew it. Fit the starter motor into the casing recess, ensuring that the motor shaft engages the idler pinion. Once in place, fit the two retaining bolts and tighten them securely. Thread locking compound should be used on the bolt threads.
4   Apply a 2 in strip of RTV silicone sealant across the crankcase joint areas of the alternator cover gasket face and check that the dowel pin is in place in either the cover or the crankcase. Fit a new gasket, then pass the wiring through the casing hole. Offer up the cover and fit and tighten the retaining screws.
5   Route the alternator wiring along the starter motor recess and out through the cutout in the casing. The wiring is held in place by the motor cover.

38 Engine reassembly: refitting the pistons and the cylinder block

1   Pack each crankcase mouth with clean rag to prevent debris or dropped circlips from entering the crankcase. Lay out the pistons in the

correct sequence to ensure that they are refitted in the correct relative positions. Note that new circlips should be used even where the old pistons are to be reused; the old clips will have been weakened during removal, and the expense incurred in the event of a failure does not justify making economies.
2   Where the rings have yet to be fitted, position the oil ring spacer, making sure that the ends of the spacer do not overlap. When fitting the 2nd and top rings, note that the 2nd ring is tapered in section and is fitted so that the wider diameter faces downwards. The top ring is of plain section, and like the second ring is marked 'N' on the top face. Note that on later engines the piston supplier was changed, and in this case the top face of the rings is marked 'R'. If new rings are to be fitted, make sure that they are of the same type as the originals; do not attempt to fit 'R' marked rings in place of 'N' marked rings or vice versa.
3   Lubricate the big-end bearings and the small-end eyes, then fit the pistons with the arrow mark on each crown facing forward. If the gudgeon pins are tight, warm the pistons using a rag soaked in near boiling water, taking suitable precautions to avoid scalding. Fit the circlips so that the ends are clear of the removal notch, and ensure that the circlips locate fully in their grooves.
4   Check that the locating dowels are in position in the underside of the cylinder block. Fit new O-rings to the grooves around each of the cylinder liners. When pushing them into their grooves, work each one in evenly, starting it at three or four points around the groove. This avoids the irritation of having a 'spare' loop of O-ring; if this happens, remove the O-ring and start again.
5   When fitting the cylinder block, note that a set of piston ring clamps will prove invaluable. Although each bore has a tapered lead in, it was found that this was quite abrupt in the case of the machine shown in the photographs. It is possible to introduce the rings manually, but this requires two people and is rather time consuming. Suzuki ring clamps, Part number 09916-74521, in conjunction with 55 – 65 mm bands (Part number 09916-74530) are ideal, or a proprietary set may be used.
6   Fit a new cylinder base gasket over the holding studs. Check that the piston ring ends are staggered, then fit a ring clamp to each piston, ensuring that all rings are enclosed. Lubricate the cylinder bores with engine oil, then position the cylinder block above the pistons and pass the cam chain loop through the tunnel.
7   Carefully lower the cylinder block over the pistons, keeping the pistons square to the bore as they enter. Once the pistons are well into the bores, the ring clamps may be removed. If fitting the rings manually, proceed as described above, but take great care to feed each ring into its bore. Avoid trapping the ring ends outside the grooves. Check that all the rings are fully engaged, then push the block down onto the gasket.

36.1 Fit the ignition pickup assembly, fitting the wiring grommet into the casing slot

37.1 Fit the starter idler pinion and shaft

37.2a Install the starter gear unit into the clutch body

37.2b Offer up the alternator rotor/starter clutch unit

37.2c Hold rotor with chain wrench and tighten retaining bolt

37.5 Refit the alternator cover, noting routing of wiring

38.2 Check the N or R mark on rings faces upwards

38.4 Fit a new O-ring to the bottom of each cylinder liner

38.6 Fit a new cylinder base gasket, noting bead of sealant on lower face

38.7 Lower cylinder block, feeding rings into bores by hand or with clamps

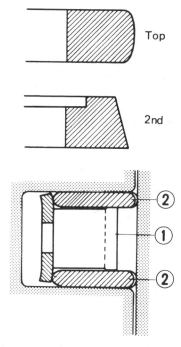

Fig. 1.27 Piston ring identification and position

Note different profiles of top and second ring. When fitting oil scraper ring fit spacer (1) first, followed by the side rails (2)

39 Engine reassembly: refitting the cylinder head, camshafts and tensioner

1   Place a new gasket on the cylinder head gasket face, ensuring that the face marked 'HEAD' is upwards. Lower the cylinder head into position, feeding the cam chain through the tunnel and securing it by passing a bar or screwdriver through the chain loop.

2   The cylinder head is retained by a total of twelve domed nuts and a single 6 mm bolt between the inner exhaust ports. Before fitting the main cylinder head nuts, place a new sealing washer over each stud. Be warned that these are non-ferrous and so cannot be retrieved with a magnet if dropped into a recess. To avoid such problems fit the washer over a screwdriver, holding it in place while the end of the screwdriver is placed against the end of a stud. The washer can now be freed and will run down over the stud.

3   Fit the twelve domed cylinder head nuts, then tighten them progressively in the sequence indicated by the numbers cast into the head material adjacent to each one. The final torque setting is 2.3 – 2.8 kgf m (16.5 – 20.0 lbf ft). Fit the single 6 mm bolt and tighten it to 0.7 – 1.1 kgf m (5.0 – 8.0 lbf ft). Slide the cam chain guide into the tunnel and position it in its locating pocket.

4   Using a 19 mm socket, turn the crankshaft clockwise to align the '1-4' cylinder 'T' mark with the fixed timing mark (the pole piece of the rear pickup coil – see Fig. 1.28 and photograph). When turning the crankshaft keep the chain taut to prevent it from bunching under the crankshaft sprocket.

5   The exhaust camshaft incorporates the tachometer drive pinion, and thus is easily distinguished from the inlet camshaft. Note also that the right-hand end of each camshaft has a notch in it.

6   Fit the exhaust camshaft through the chain loop, positioning the sprocket with the notch parallel to the gasket face and the '1' arrow mark pointing forward. The '2' arrow should face upwards. Fit the remaining camshaft, again with the notch lying parallel to the gasket face. The '3' arrow should face upwards and should be 23 pins from that indicated by the '2' arrow on the exhaust camshaft. The

arrangement is illustrated in Fig. 1.28, and should be checked carefully to ensure that the cam timing is correct. Note that it is all too easy to find that the cam chain has 'jumped' a tooth if it is not kept taut when turning the crankshaft – it was found helpful to temporarily refit the tensioner mechanism, fitting the holding bolts loosely.

7 Fit the camshaft bearing caps without disturbing the camshafts or the crankshaft. Each cap is marked with an arrow to indicate the front and is lettered to indicate its position; the three caps to the left of the cam chain on the exhaust cam are marked "A", those to the right being marked "B". In the case of the inlet camshaft, the corresponding caps are marked "C" and "D" respectively. A corresponding letter is cast into the cylinder head. Make sure that the locating dowels are in position when fitting the caps, and fit the retaining bolts finger tight only.

8 Tighten the cap bolts by a half turn at a time in a diagonal sequence. It is important that the camshafts are pulled down squarely to avoid damage to the caps or cylinder. Once the camshaft caps are all in contact with the cylinder head, tighten the bolts, again in a diagonal sequence, to the correct torque setting of 0.8 – 1.2 kgf m (6.0 – 8.5 lbf ft). Suzuki advise that the camshaft cap bolts are made from 'a special material' and are identified by the figure 9 stamped on the heads. On no account should other bolts be used.

9 Before proceeding further, turn the crankshaft through two full revolutions until the 1-4 T mark aligns, remembering to keep the cam chain taut. Check that the cam timing marks all align properly, and if necessary make any alterations at this stage. If all is well, refit the internal oil pipes using new sealing washers. Note that the left-hand pipe has a silver finish to distinguish it from the right-hand pipe, which has a yellowish cadmium finish. Note also that two different union bolts are used; the longer bolts must be fitted on the inlet side.

10 Check that the tensioner pushrod is fully retracted. Slacken the lock bolt and push the pushrod inwards whilst turning the knurled wheel anti-clockwise against spring pressure. Once the pushrod is fully home, tighten the lock bolt to retain it. Offer up the tensioner, using a new gasket, noting that the knurled wheel should face towards the right-hand side. If the tensioner will not seat fully, turn the crankshaft using the 19 mm hexagon on the crankshaft end to obtain chain slack on the tensioner side of the block. Fit and tighten the retaining bolts.

11 Slacken the lock screw to free the pushrod, which should move inwards to apply pressure to the chain, then tighten the locknut whilst holding the lock screw in position. Slowly turn the crankshaft anticlockwise whilst turning the knurled wheel anticlockwise to allow the chain to push the tensioner plunger inwards. Release the knurled wheel, then turn the crankshaft clockwise to check that the mechanism is operating normally. The wheel should revolve as the tensioner adjusts to take up chain slack. Having checked that all is well, do not disturb the knurled wheel further.

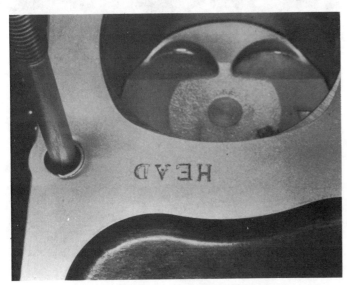

39.1a Note that HEAD marking on gasket faces upwards

39.1b Pass cam chain through tunnel then lower head into place

39.2 Use a screwdriver to guide washers over the cylinder head studs

39.3a Tighten the cylinder head nuts to the correct torque setting

39.3b Do not forget bolt between centre exhaust ports

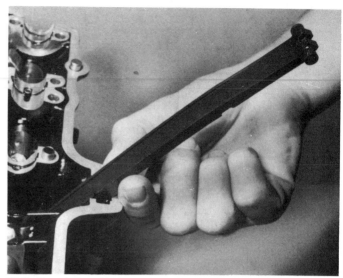
39.3c Cam chain guide can now be dropped into position

39.4 Align the '1.4 T' mark with pickup pole as shown

39.6a Fit the exhaust camshaft through chain loop ...

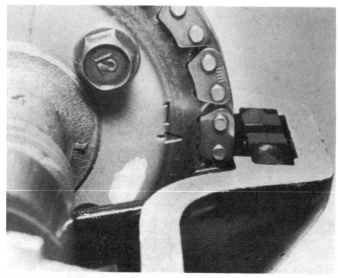
39.6b ... aligning the '1' mark as shown

39.6c Fit the inlet cam, with '3' and '2' marks positioned as shown

39.8 Tighten camshaft cap bolts evenly and progressively

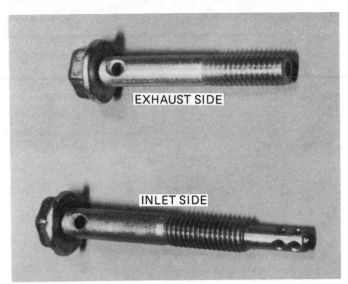
39.9a Note the type and position of the internal oil pipe union bolts

EXHAUST SIDE

INLET SIDE

39.9b Refit the pipes, using new sealing washers ...

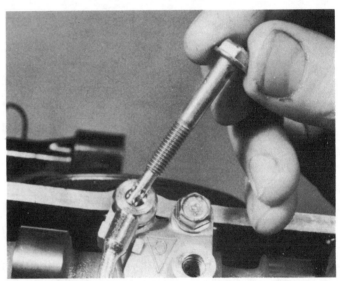
39.9c ... then fit the union bolts

39.10 Retract and lock tensioner plunger, then install mechanism

39.11 Release locknut and screw, checking that tensioner wheel indicates that mechanism has adjusted correctly

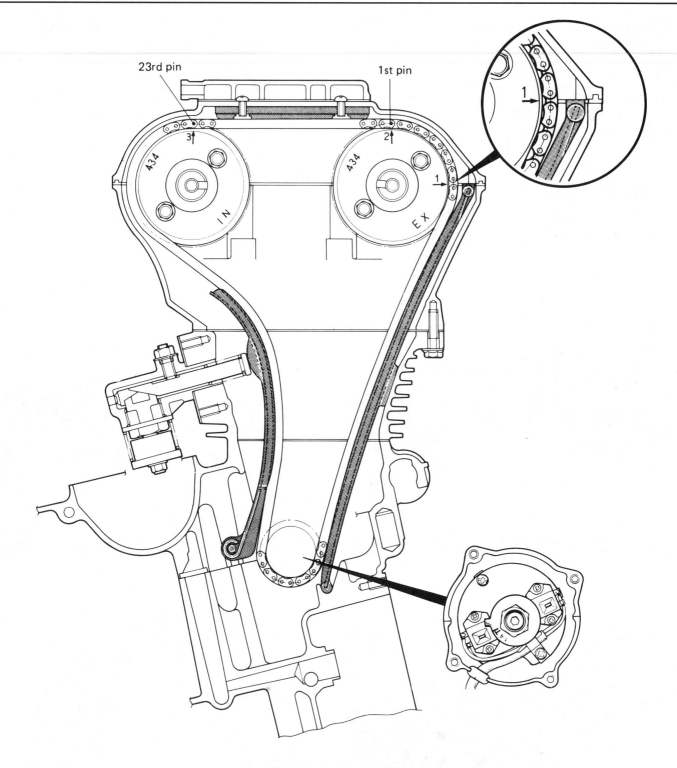

Fig. 1.28 Valve timing arrangement

40 Engine reassembly: setting the valve clearances

1   If the engine has been overhauled or if the valve train components have been disturbed for any reason, the valve clearances must be checked and reset. The correct clearance for both inlet and exhaust valves is 0.08 – 0.13 mm (0.003 – 0.005 in). Using the 19 mm hexagon on the ignition pickup end of the crankshaft, rotate it until the notches in the camshaft end face outwards and the '1-4 T' mark is aligned with

the centre pole of the rear pickup coil. Check and adjust the clearances for the following valves:

Cylinder No. 1 Inlet and exhaust
Cylinder No. 2 Exhaust only
Cylinder No. 3 Inlet only

2   Measure the clearance between each valve and its adjuster, using feeler gauges. Note that it is preferable to measure the clearances in pairs, rather than singly. This eliminates any possibility of a false reading due to movement in the forked rocker arm. If adjustment is

required, slacken the locknut with a ring spanner and set the clearance by turning the small square-headed adjuster. When set correctly, the feeler gauge should be a light sliding fit with no free play and no pressure on it from the valve springs. Hold the adjuster in this position and secure the locknut. Note that a Suzuki tool is available to fit the adjuster, Part number 09917-14910. It is useful but not essential.

3   Rotate the crankshaft through 360°, again aligning the '1-4 T' mark. The camshaft notches should now face inwards. Repeat the adjustment sequence on the remaining valves as listed below:

Cylinder No. 2 Inlet only
Cylinder No. 3 Exhaust only
Cylinder No. 4 Inlet and exhaust

41 Engine reassembly: refitting the oil filter, cylinder head cover and external oil hoses

Note: *If the engine unit has yet to be installed in the frame this*

operation is best left until it is in position to give extra clearance during fitting

1   Apply grease to the oil filter cover groove to hold the sealing ring in place. Fit a new filter element into its recess, then offer up the cover and spring. Apply thread locking compound to the domed nuts and tighten them evenly and securely.

2   Check that the sump drain plug is secure, then prime the oil pockets around the cam lobes with engine oil. Coat the gasket face of the head and cover with RTV sealant to ensure an oil-tight seal.

3   Fit a new cover gasket applying a thin film of RTV sealant to the end cap extensions of the gasket. Fit the two locating dowels, then place the cover in position. Place new O-rings in the bolt head recesses of the cylinder head cover, then fit the bolts. The bolts should be tightened evenly in a diagonal sequence to avoid warpage. The correct torque setting is 1.3 – 1.5 kgf m (9.5 – 11.0 lbf ft). On those machines fitted with a mechanically-driven tachometer, fit the tachometer drive gear assembly. If they have not yet been fitted, install the oil feed hoses between the rear of the cylinder block and the crankcase, using new sealing washers.

40.2 Set the valve clearances, using two feeler gauges to reduce chance of error

41.3a Connect upper ends of oil hoses as shown, noting guide clip

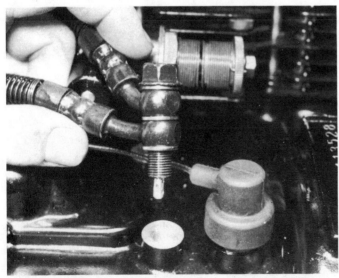
41.3b Lower union is fitted as shown. Use new sealing washers

41.3c Fit breather cover using a new gasket

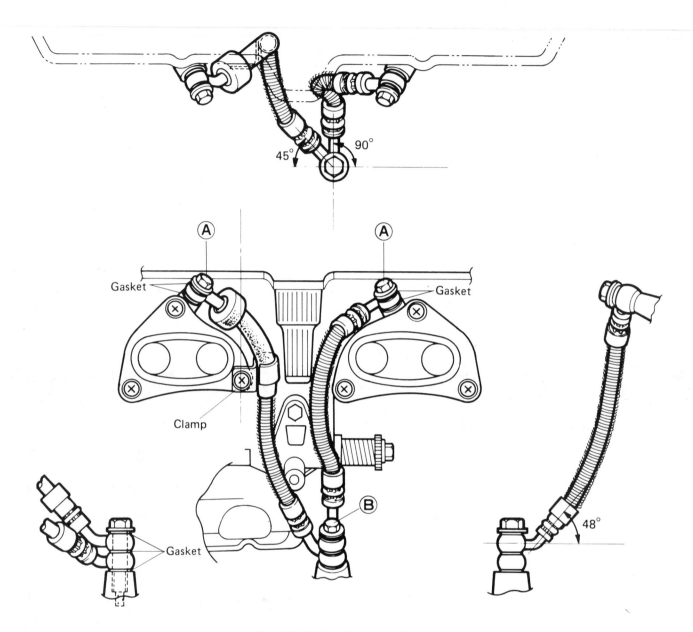

Fig. 1.29 Oil feed hose installation

Torque settings
A 0.8 – 1.2 kgf m (6.0 – 8.5 lbf ft)
B 2.0 – 2.4 kgf m (14.5 – 17.5 lbf ft)
Note: *no settings available for US GS550 ESE and ES3 models*

42 Engine reassembly: refitting the engine unit in the frame

1   As will be realised by those who have removed the engine unit, fitting it will be no easy task without some form of engine hoist, the use of which is recommended. In the absence of this, three persons will be required to lift it into position safely. Before starting work, tape some rag or card around the frame lower rails to protect them and the painted finish of the engine.

2   Lift the unit into position on the right-hand side of the frame and rest it against the frame lower rails. One person should now move to the left-hand side and guide the unit into position. Once it is resting in the frame cradle, the various engine bolts and plates can be fitted loosely. Lever the unit up in the frame using lengths of timber so that the bolt holes can be lined up.

3   When all fasteners are in position (see accompanying photographs), tighten them to the specified torque settings. The three long through bolts are fitted from the left-hand side, noting that the rear suspension hydraulic adjuster is fitted to the left-hand side of the rear upper bolt. Note also that the oil cooler hose guide brackets are secured by the upper front mounting bracket bolts. Fit new copper sealing washers to the hose unions, then fit the hose union bolts. Tighten the bolts to 2.5 – 3.0 kgf m (18.0 – 21.5 lbf ft).

4   Place the gearbox sprocket in the final drive chain loop and install

it. Fit the retaining nut with its recessed face inwards and tighten to 10.0 – 15.0 kgf m (72.5 – 108.5 lbf ft). Remember to reset the final drive chain free play.

5 Reassemble the exhaust system, using new sealing rings in the ports. These can be held in place with grease during installation. When in position, tighten the exhaust retainer nuts and the clamps below the crankcase, followed by the silencer mounting bolts.

6 Refit the footrests and the gearchange pedal. Reconnect the spark plug caps, noting that each lead is marked to indicate the cylinder to which it belongs (1 to 4 from left to right). Refit the cylinder head cover, if this was left off during installation. Fit the cylinder head breather cover, using a new gasket.

7 Refer to the accompanying line drawings and reconnect the alternator, ignition, side stand switch, gear position switch, neutral switch, oil pressure switch and starter motor wiring. When the battery has been refitted and connected (see below), check that the electrical system functions normally.

8 Check that the clutch cable is connected properly at the actuating lever end, then offer up the cover ensuring that the pushrod engages correctly. Slacken the clutch lever adjuster locknut and screw the adjuster fully inwards. Remove the clutch adjuster inspection cover on the sprocket cover and slacken the locknut. Back off the adjuster screw, then turn it clockwise until slight resistance can be felt. Back off

the screw by $1/4$ to $1/2$ of a turn, then tighten the locknut and refit the inspection cover. Using the adjuster at the lower end of the cable, set the handlebar lever free play to give 4 mm (0.16 in) clearance between the lever stock and blade.

9 Reconnect the throttle and choke cables and manoeuvre the carburettors into position. Check the routing of the fuel and breather hoses. Secure the carburettor retaining clips. Refit the air filter trunking and secure its retaining clip and bolts. Refit the battery tray and install the battery. Fit the igniter unit and plug in the two wiring connectors. Install the fuse box and reconnect the starter relay negative lead. Where appropriate, reconnect the tachometer drive cable. Top up the crankcase with 3.1 litres (6.6/5.5 US/Imp pint) of SAE 10W/40 motor oil, noting that the oil level must be checked after the engine has been run.

10 Before the fuel tank and bodywork are refitted, check that all wiring connections have been remade, and that the wiring, control cables and the various breather and drain hoses have been routed correctly. Lift the tank into position, propping it at the rear while the vacuum and fuel hoses are connected. Do not forget to reconnect the fuel gauge sender leads. Refit the fairing, remembering to feed the turn signal leads through the mounting slots. Reconnect the wiring, then fit the turn signal lamps.

42.3a Assemble rear right-hand mounting plate as shown

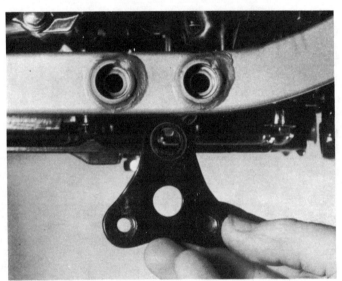

42.3b Right-hand lower plate is retained by two Allen bolts

42.3c Note that front mounting bolts also retain oil cooler hose brackets

42.3d Captive nuts fit into slots in crankcase

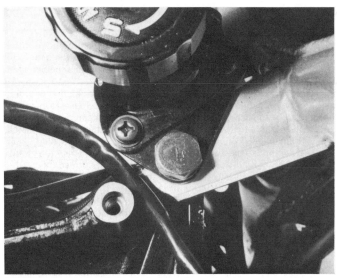
42.3e Rear mounting bolt also holds adjuster bracket

42.4 Use new tab washer when fitting sprocket

42.5a Grease can be used to hold exhaust port seals in place

42.5b Fit retainers and tighten bolts evenly

42.5c Fit and tighten silencer mounting bolts

42.9 Refit the carburettors and mounting rubbers

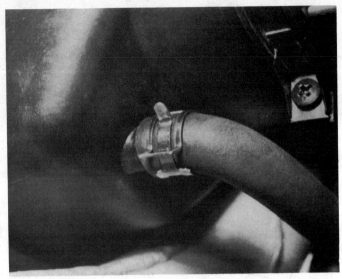

42.10 Do not forget to fit engine breather hose

Fig. 1.30 Engine mountings

1   Rear top mounting bolt – length 160 mm (6.29 in)
2   Rear bottom mounting bolt – length 165 mm (6.49 in)
3   Front top mounting bolt – length 195 mm (7.67 in)
A   Rear top mounting nut – torque setting 6.7 – 8.0 kgf m (48.5 – 58 lbf ft)
B   Rear bottom mounting nut – torque setting 6.0 – 7.2 kgf m (43.5 – 52 lbf ft)
C   Front top mounting nut – torque setting 6.7 – 8.0 kgf m (48.5 – 58 lbf ft)
D   Front bottom mounting bolts – length 35 mm – torque setting 6.0 – 7.2 kgf m (43.5 – 52 lbf ft)

Note: *no settings available for US GS550 ESE and ES3 models*

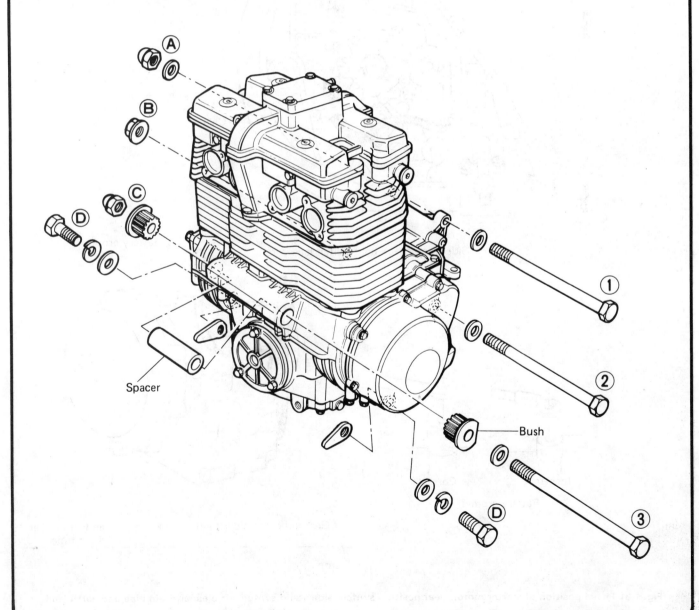

Spacer

Bush

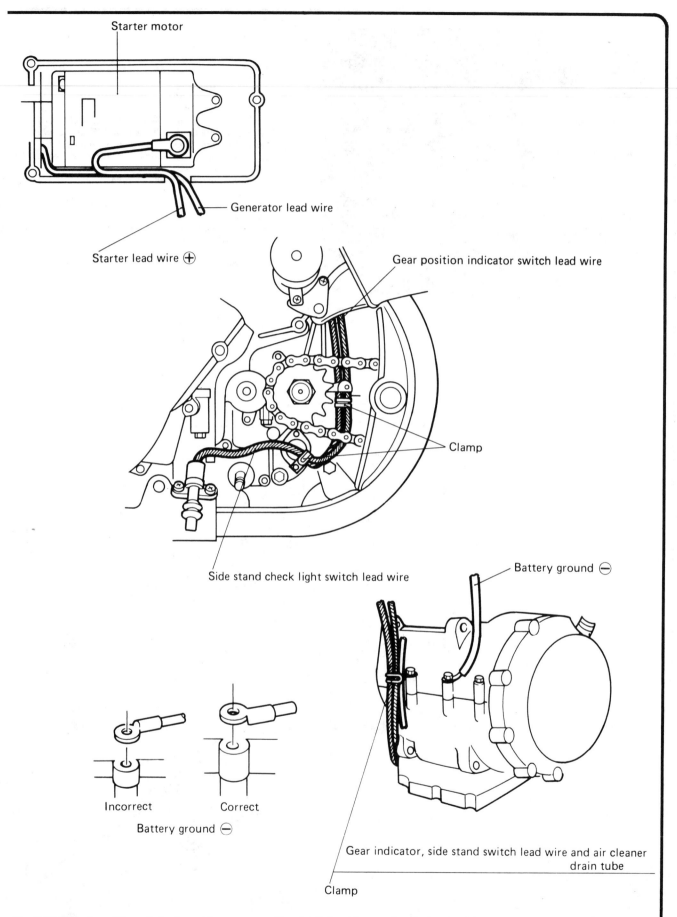

Starter motor

Generator lead wire

Starter lead wire ⊕

Gear position indicator switch lead wire

Clamp

Side stand check light switch lead wire

Battery ground ⊖

Incorrect

Correct

Battery ground ⊖

Gear indicator, side stand switch lead wire and air cleaner drain tube

Clamp

Fig. 1.31 Fitted position of starter motor, gear position switch, side stand switch, air cleaner drain pipe and earth lead

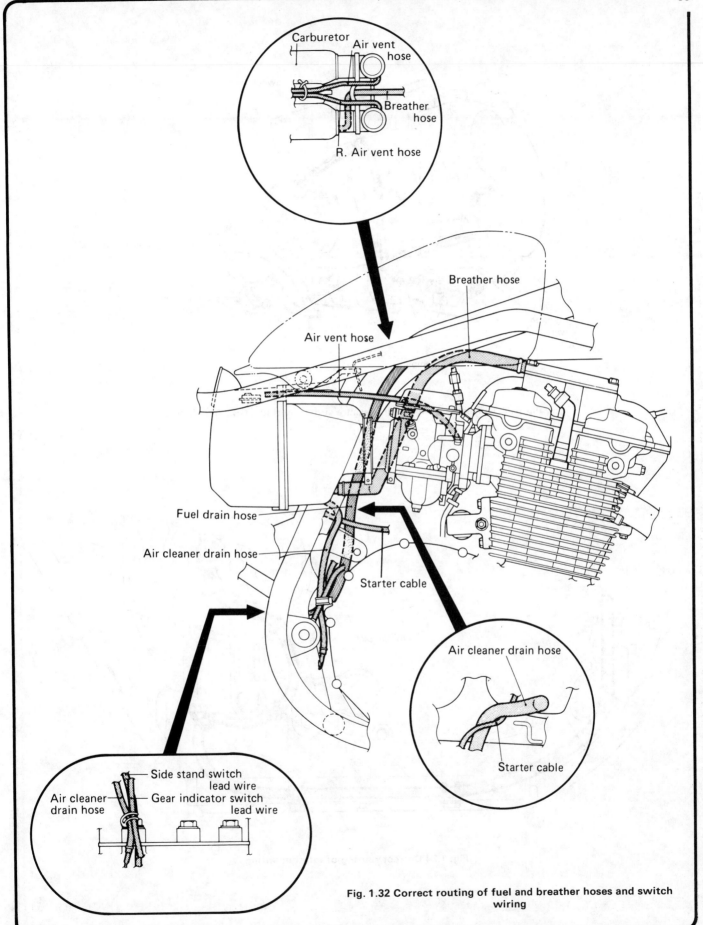

Carburetor   Air vent hose

Breather hose

R. Air vent hose

Breather hose

Air vent hose

Fuel drain hose

Air cleaner drain hose

Starter cable

Air cleaner drain hose

Starter cable

Side stand switch lead wire

Air cleaner drain hose   Gear indicator switch lead wire

Fig. 1.32 Correct routing of fuel and breather hoses and switch wiring

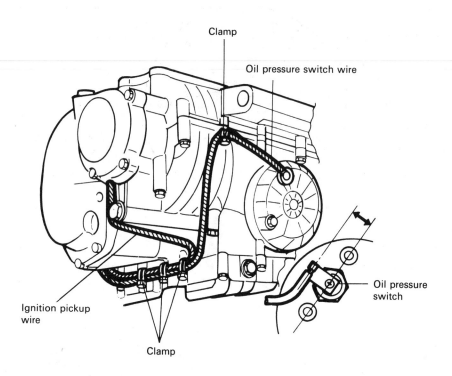

Fig. 1.33 Correct routing of oil pressure switch wiring – GS550 L models

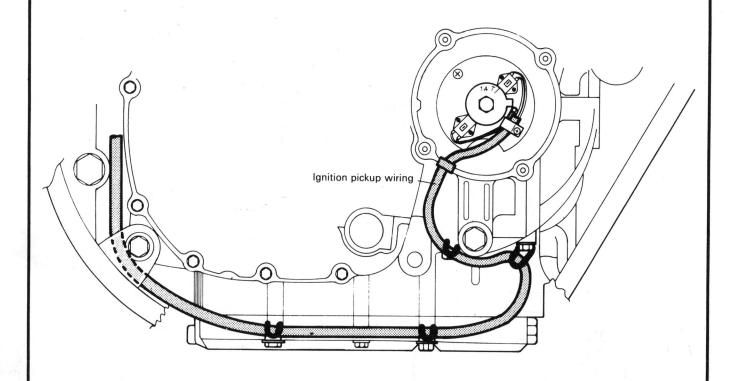

Fig. 1.34 Correct routing of ignition wiring

43 Starting and running the rebuilt engine

1 Attempt to start the engine using the usual procedure adopted for a cold engine. Do not be disillusioned if there is no sign of life initially. A certain amount of perseverance may prove necessary to coax the engine into activity even if new parts have not been fitted. Should the engine persist in not starting, check that the spark plug has not become fouled by the oil used during reassembly. Failing this go through the fault-finding charts and work out what the problem is methodically.

2 When the engine does start, keep it running as slowly as possible to allow the oil to circulate. The oil warning light should go out almost immediately the engine has started, although in certain instances a very short delay can occur whilst the oilways fill and the pressure builds up. If the light does not go out the engine should be stopped before damage can occur, and the cause determined. Open the choke as soon as the engine will run without it. During the initial running, a certain amount of smoke may be in evidence due to the oil used in the reassembly sequence being burnt away. The resulting smoke should gradually subside.

3 Check the engine for blowing gaskets and oil leaks. Before using the machine on the road, check that all the gears select properly, and that the controls function correctly.

4 Once the engine has settled down and is running normally, note that the following adjustments should be checked before the machine is used on the road:

   (a) Rear brake pedal height
   (b) Rear brake lamp switch
   (c) Clutch operation and adjustment
   (d) Final drive chain free play
   (e) Throttle operation and cable adjustment
   (f) Carburettor synchronisation (balance)
   (g) Idle speed adjustment

44 Taking the rebuilt machine on the road

1 Any rebuilt machine will need time to settle down, even if parts have been replaced in their original order. For this reason it is highly advisable to treat the machine gently for the first few miles to ensure oil has circulated throughout the lubrication system and that any new parts fitted have begun to bed down.

2 Even greater care is necessary if the engine has been rebored or if a new crankshaft has been fitted. In the case of a rebore, the engine will have to be run-in again, as if the machine were new. This means greater use of the gearbox and a restraining hand on the throttle until at least 500 miles have been covered. There is no point in keeping to any set speed limit; the main requirement is to keep a light loading on the engine and to gradually work up performance until the 500 mile mark is reached. These recommendations can be lessened to an extent when only a new crankshaft is fitted. Experience is the best guide since it is easy to tell when an engine is running freely.

3 If at any time a lubrication failure is suspected, stop the engine immediately, and investigate the cause. If any engine is run without oil even for a short period, irreparable engine damage is inevitable.

4 When the engine has cooled down completely after the initial run, recheck the various settings, especially the valve clearances. During the run most of the engine components will have settled into their normal working locations. Check the various oil levels, particularly that of the engine as it may have dropped slightly now that the various passages and recesses have filled.

Chapter 2 Fuel system and lubrication

Refer to Chapter 7 for information relating to the 1986 to 1988 GS/GSX550 ES and GS550 L models

Contents

Specifications

UK GSX550 ESD, EE, ESE and EFE models

Fuel tank

Overall capacity	18 lit (4.8/4.0 US/Imp gal)
Reserve capacity	3.5 lit (0.9/0.8 US/Imp gal)

Fuel grade .... Unleaded or low-lead, minimum octane rating 90 RON/RM

Carburettors

Make	Mikuni
Type	BSW30SS
Size	30 mm (1.18 in)
Identity number:	
ESD	43400
EE, ESE, EFE	43470
Idle speed	1100 $\pm$ 100 rpm
Fuel level	6.5 $\pm$ 0.5 mm (0.26 $\pm$ 0.02 in)
Float height	20.5 $\pm$ 1.0 mm (0.81 $\pm$ 0.04 in)
Main jet, ESD:	
Cylinders 1 and 4	95
Cylinders 2 and 3	102.5
Main jet, EE, ESE, EFE:	
Cylinders 1 and 4	90
Cylinders 2 and 3	97.5
Main air jet	1.0
Jet needle:	
ESD	5C7
EE, ESE, EFE	5C13
Clip position	3rd groove from top
Needle jet:	
ESD	P-2
EE, ESE, EFE	P-4
Throttle valve:	
ESD	120
EE, ESE, EFE	105
Pilot jet:	
ESD	40
EE, ESE, EFE	37.5
Bypass:	
ESD	0.8, 0.7, 0.8, 0.8
EE, ESE, EFE	0.9, 0.9, 0.8
Pilot outlet:	
ESD	0.7
EE, ESE, EFE	0.9
Float valve seat	2.5
Starter jet	55
Pilot screw:	
ESD	Preset (1⅝ turns out)
EE, ESE, EFE	Preset (2½ turns out)
Pilot air jet:	
ESD	145
EE, ESE, EFE	140

Throttle cable free play	0.5 – 1.0 mm (0.02 – 0.04 in)
Choke cable free play	0.5 – 1.0 mm (0.02 – 0.04 in)

Engine/transmission oil

Capacity:	
Dry	3.1 lit (7.0/5.5 US/Imp pint)
At oil change	2.4 lit (5.1/4.2 US/Imp pint)
Oil and filter change	2.9 lit (6.1/5.1 US/Imp pint)
Oil grade	SAE 10W/40 motor oil API class SE or SF

Oil pump

Type	Trochoid
Pump reduction ratio	1.703:1 (89/45 x 31/36 T)
Oil pressure:	
Minimum	2.5 kg cm² (35.6 psi) @ 60°C/140°F
Maximum @ 3000 rpm	5.5 kg cm² (78.3 psi) @ 60°C/140°F

US GS550 ED, ESD, LD, ESE, ES3, EF, ESF and LF models

Note: *Where a model suffix is shown thus: EF(ca) the specification relates to the Californian model fitted with an evaporative emission control system*

Fuel tank

Overall capacity:	
ED, ESD, ESE, ES3, EF, ESF	18 lit (4.8/4.0 US/Imp gal)
LD, LF	12 lit (3.2/2.6 US/Imp gal)
EF(ca), ESF(ca)	17.5 lit (4.6/3.9 US/Imp gal)
Reserve capacity:	
ED, ESD, ESE, ES3, EF, ESF	3.5 lit (0.9/0.8 US/Imp gal)
LD, LF	2.5 lit (0.7/0.6 US/Imp gal)
EF(ca) ESF(ca)	3.5 lit (0.9/0.8 US/Imp gal)

Fuel grade .... Unleaded or low-lead, minimum octane rating 90 RON/RM

Carburettors

Make	Mikuni
Type	BSW30SS
Size	30 mm (1.18 in)
Identity number:	
ED, ESD	43410
LD	43510
ESE	43440
EF, ESF	43560
EF(ca), ESF(ca)	43570
LF	43610
Idle speed	1100 ± 100 rpm
Fuel level	6.5 ± 0.5 mm (0.26 ± 0.02 in)
Float height	20.5 ± 1.0 mm (0.81 ± 0.04 in)
Main jet, ED, ESD, ESE, ES3:	
Cylinders 1 and 4	95
Cylinders 2 and 3	102.5
Main jet, LD:	
Cylinders 1 and 4	95
Cylinders 2 and 3	105
Main jet, EF, ESF, EF(ca), ESF(ca), LF:	
Cylinders 1 and 4	90
Cylinders 2 and 3	97.5
Main air jet	1.0
Jet needle:	
ED, ESD, LD, LF	5C64
ESE, ES3	5C10
EF, ESF, EF(ca), ESF(ca)	5C-15
Clip position:	
ED, ESD, LD	1st groove from top
ESE, ES3, EF, ESF, EF(ca), ESF(ca), LF	Not available
Needle jet:	
ED, ESD	P-2
LD, ESE, ES3, EF, ESF, EF(ca), ESF (ca),LF	P-3
Throttle valve:	
ED, ESD, LD	120
ESE, ES3	105
EF, ESF, EF(ca), ESF(ca), LF	110
Pilot jet:	
ED, ESD, LD	35
ESE, ES3, EF, ESF, EF(ca), ESF (ca), LF	37.5
Bypass:	
ED, ESD, LD	0.8, 0.7, 0.8, 0.8
ESE, EF, ESF, EF(ca), ESF(ca), LF	0.9, 0.9, 0.8

Pilot outlet:	
ED, ESD, LD	0.7
ESE, EF, ESF, EF(ca), ESF(ca), LF	0.9
Float valve seat	2.5
Starter jet	55
Pilot screw	Preset
Pilot air jet:	
ED, ESD	145
ESE, ES3	147.5
LD, LF, EF, EF (ca), ESF, ESF (ca)	150
Throttle cable free play	0.5 – 1.0 mm (0.02 – 0.04 in)
Choke cable free play	0.5 – 1.0 mm (0.02 – 0.04 in)

Note: *GS550 ES3 model – specifications are not available for the main air jet, float valve seat, starter jet, fuel level and float height.*

Engine/transmission oil

Capacity ED, ESD, ESE, ES3, EF, ESF, EF(ca), ESF(ca):	
Dry	3.1 lit (7.0/5.5 US/Imp pint)
At oil change	2.4 lit (5.1/4.2 US/Imp pint)
Oil and filter change	2.9 lit (6.1/5.1 US/Imp pint)
Capacity LD, LF:	
Dry	3.3 lit (6.9/5.8 US/Imp pint)
At oil change	2.6 lit (5.5/4.6 US/Imp pint)
Oil and filter change	3.1 lit (6.5/5.5 US/Imp pint)
Oil grade	SAE 10W/40 motor oil API class SE or SF

Oil pump

Type	Trochoid
Pump reduction ratio	1.703:1 (89/45 x 31/36 T)
Oil pressure:	
Minimum	2.5 kg cm² (35.6 psi) @ 60°C/140°F
Maximum @ 3000 rpm	5.5 kg cm² (78.3 psi) @ 60°C/140°F

1 General description

The fuel system comprises a tank from which fuel is fed by gravity to the float chambers of the two twin-choke carburettors. A single automatic vacuum-operated tap controls the flow of fuel to the carburettors. When the tap is set to the ON or RES positions, fuel can flow only if the engine is running. If the tank is run dry, the PRI position allows the vacuum diaphragm to be bypassed to permit the carburettors to be primed.

The carburettors are of twin-choke construction and are of the CV, or constant vacuum, type. Each instrument comprises a single float chamber, main body and diaphragm chamber, with twin pistons and fuel circuits. In this way, each cylinder is fed separately even though only two carburettors are fitted. The arrangement saves a certain amount of weight and complexity. For cold starting, a mixture-enriching circuit is brought into operation. This is controlled by a handlebar lever via cables.

Engine lubrication is by conventional wet sump design, the oil reservoir being contained in the bottom of the crankcase. A trochoid pump, driven from the back of the clutch assembly, draws oil from the sump via a strainer and full flow filter, supplying it under pressure to the engine and transmission components.

2 Fuel tank: removal and replacement

1 Unlock the seat and lift it away. The fixing bolts at the rear of the tank can now be removed. Lift the rear of the tank slightly and prop it in this position with a piece of wood or a screwdriver. Locate the fuel level sender leads and disconnect them.

2 Check that the fuel tap is set to the ON or RES positions. Squeeze together the ends of the fuel pipe retaining clip and slide it up the pipe, clear of the stub. The pipe can now be worked off the stub using a small screwdriver. The smaller diameter vacuum pipe is removed in a similar manner.

3 It is not normally necessary to drain the tank before it can be removed, though it should be noted that a full tank will be somewhat unwieldly. If draining is necessary, take care to avoid any risk of fire. The tank can be drained by turning the fuel tap to the PRI position.

4 The fuel tank is located at the front by two rubber buffers, and can be removed by pulling rearwards. It may help to rock the tank from side to side, but care should be taken to avoid damage to the paintwork as the tank comes free.

5 The tank is installed by reversing the removal sequence. Note that it will be much easier to locate the tank over the rubber buffers if these are lubricated with a little petrol, some WD40 or a similar lubricant.

3 Fuel tap: removal and replacement

1 In all but the PRI (prime) position, fuel flow is controlled by engine vacuum by means of a diaphragm assembly connected to the inlet tract. As soon as the engine is started, the diaphragm reacts to engine vacuum, opening a plunger valve against spring pressure. When the engine is stopped the valve closes, shutting off the fuel supply. The PRI setting allows fuel to flow even with the engine stopped, and is used to allow the carburettors to be primed after they have run dry or been drained.

2 It should be noted that replacement parts for the tap are not available, so in the event of failure of the diaphragm or internal seals, the whole unit must be renewed. Leakage around the tap mounting flange can be rectified by renewing the O-ring seal.

3 For obvious reasons, the tank should be drained prior to tap removal, and it is preferable to carry out the work with the tank removed and inverted on some soft cloth to protect the paintwork.

4 Remove the two securing bolts and lift the tap away. Examine the O-ring seal on the flange, renewing it if it appears indented or damaged. Examine the gauze strainer, noting any signs of water or dirt. Where necessary, flush out the tank with clean fuel and clean the gauze prior to reassembly.

5 If the tap has shown signs of leakage around the spindle, or if it has become obstructed by dirt or water, it is possible to dismantle it. The square diaphragm chamber can be lifted away after its four retaining screws have been removed, taking care not to tear the diaphragm which will be stuck to the cover. The tap spindle assembly should not be dismantled unless the only alternative is renewal, in which case there is little to lose by attempting a repair. Prise off the clip which secures the spindle assembly and lift it away, noting carefully the arrangement of the coil spring, tap rotor and the flat spring cam mechanism which opens the diaphragm in the "PRI" position; this latter must be refitted correctly and must not be bent or twisted. Where fuel has been leaking around the tap lever, fitting a new O-ring of the appropriate size will usually resolve the problem.

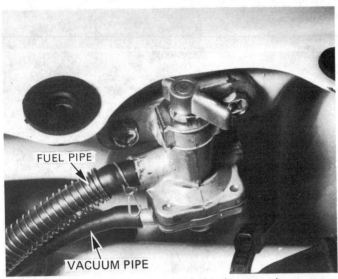

2.2 Lift rear of tank and disconnect the fuel and vacuum pipes

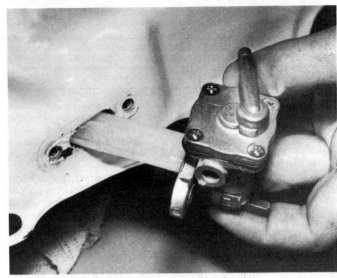

3.4 Tap is retained by two bolts to underside of tank

3.5a Peel diaphragm away from tap body, taking care not to damage it

3.5b Tap outlet incorporates one-way valve – check for obstructions

3.5c Tap rotor assembly is retained by clip. Note O-ring seal

4 Carburettors: removal

1   Remove the seat, fuel tank and side panels to gain access to the carburettor assembly. Note the position of the various drain and overflow pipes, making a sketch to simplify refitting. Disconnect the battery leads and remove the battery, noting the routing of its breather hose. Disconnect the igniter unit connectors and remove the igniter unit from the battery tray. Free the turn signal relay from its rubber mounting on the side of the tray, and free the fuse box from the right-hand side of the tray. Remove the two screws from the lower edge of the battery tray and lift it out from between the frame rails.

2   Remove the two bolts which locate the air filter casing; these are to be found just below the fuel tank mounting bracket. Slacken the hose clips which secure the carburettor assembly to the inlet and air filter stubs. Disengage the air filter stubs and pull the casing back and clear of the carburettors.

3   Pull the carburettor assembly back and twist it to disengage the carburettors from the inlet mounting rubbers. Once free of the rubbers, pull the assembly part way out to the right-hand side, taking care not to strain the throttle and choke cables.

4   Disconnect the throttle cable by disengaging the outer cable from its anchor point and unhooking the inner cable from the pulley.

Unscrew the cold start plungers on each instrument and withdraw them, together with the cables. The carburettors can now be lifted clear.

5 Carburettors: dismantling and reassembly

1   For most purposes it will not be necessary to separate the two instruments, access to the float bowl and vacuum chamber components being possible with the carburettors joined as an assembly. In the interests of clarity, however, a single instrument is shown in the accompanying photographs. If it is necessary to separate the carburettors for any reason, proceed as follows.

2   Using an impact driver, slacken and remove the four screws which retain the upper and lower support brackets. The brackets can now be removed and the carburettors pulled apart. As the two instruments separate, the throttle connecting linkage will pull apart, and the relative positions of the linkage components should be noted as a guide during assembly. The fuel connecting pipe, which is sealed at each end by an O-ring, will also pull free. Remove the vacuum, breather and fuel hoses, noting their positions.

3   As has already been mentioned, access to the various jets, the float assembly and the diaphragm assembly can be gained without separating the individual instruments. Whether working on the assembled instruments or having first separated them, always work on one carburettor at a time to ensure that components are not interchanged, or make certain that each part is placed in a marked container as it is removed.

4   Remove the four screws which retain the carburettor top. Lift the top away, taking care not to damage the diaphragm. Invert the assembly and tip out the diaphragm together with the valves and needles. The two valves are hooked onto a holder plate fixed to the underside of the diaphragm. Mark each valve, using a spirit-based felt marker to indicate the bore to which it belongs so that it can be refitted in its original position. The needle assembly can be released from each valve after the white plastic retainer has been removed. This can be pulled out using a pair of snipe-nosed pliers. Tip out the plastic seat, the needle and clip, the spring seat and the spring.

5   The diaphragm should only be removed from the valve holder assembly if it is in need of renewal. It is held by a flat plate which is secured by four screws. Before removing the screws, note the position of the diaphragm locating tab in relation to the slots on the valve holder plate; fit the new diaphragm in the same position.

6   The throttle butterfly plates should not normally be disturbed. If removal is necessary, slacken the two screws which retain each one to the throttle spindle. Turn the spindle through 90° and slide the plates out. The spindle can then be withdrawn. If the plates are to be refitted, mark each one to indicate the bore to which it belongs.

7   Slacken and remove the four float bowl screws and remove the float bowl. Displace the float pivot pin to free the float assembly. The float needle can now be tipped out of its seat. The seat can be removed by releasing the single retaining screw and washer which retains it.

8   The main jets are screwed into the pillars at the outer edge of the body and can be unscrewed for cleaning. As the main jet and the washer beneath its head is removed, the needle jet for that side of the instrument will be released and can be tipped out through the valve bore. The pilot jets are mounted together near the centre of the instrument and these too may be unscrewed for cleaning.

9   Reassembly is a straight-forward reversal of the above sequence, noting that care should be taken to avoid overtightening the jets. When fitting the needle jet, ensure that the notch aligns with the locating pin. Do not omit the washer which is fitted below the head of the main jet. When fitting the throttle valves and diaphragm, ensure that the valves locate correctly over the holder slots. Make sure that the diaphragm locating tab fits into its recess correctly, and that the diaphragm is not creased or twisted as the cover is refitted.

10 If the throttle butterfly plates were removed, they should be refitted with the identification number downwards and facing outwards. Use thread locking compound on the screws and tighten them firmly. Whenever the carburettors have been disturbed, they must be synchronised. Preliminary alignment is accomplished by setting the throttle valve plates so that they align with the bypass outlets in the carburettor throats, using the knurled throttle stop screw and the synchronising screw on the throttle shaft. Full synchronisation should be carried out after the carburettors have been refitted.

5.2 Fuel connecting pipe is sealed by O-rings

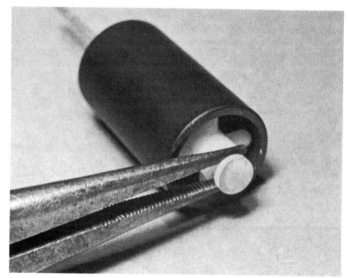
5.4a Grasp head of plastic retainer with pliers ...

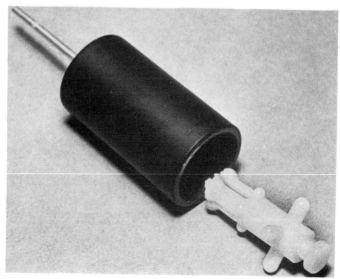
5.4b ... and pull it out of the piston

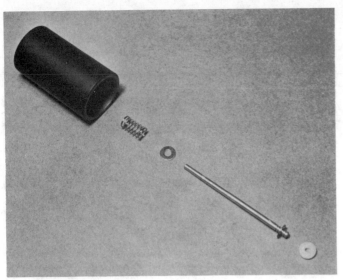

5.4c Plastic seat, needle, washer and spring can now be removed

5.7a Displace pivot pin to free the float assembly

5.7b Float needle can now be removed for examination

5.7c Float needle seat is retained by a single screw and washer (arrowed)

5.7d Seat incorporates fuel strainer. Note O-ring seal

5.8a Main jet can be unscrewed for cleaning. Note washer fitted under head

5.8b Note that main jet serves to retain the needle jet ...

5.8c ... which is located over a small pin (arrowed)

5.8d Needle jet can be displaced through main body and removed via piston bore

5.8e Pilot jets are located in adjacent bores

5.9a Ensure that the pistons locate over slots in the holder

5.9b Diaphragm has locating tab on outer edge

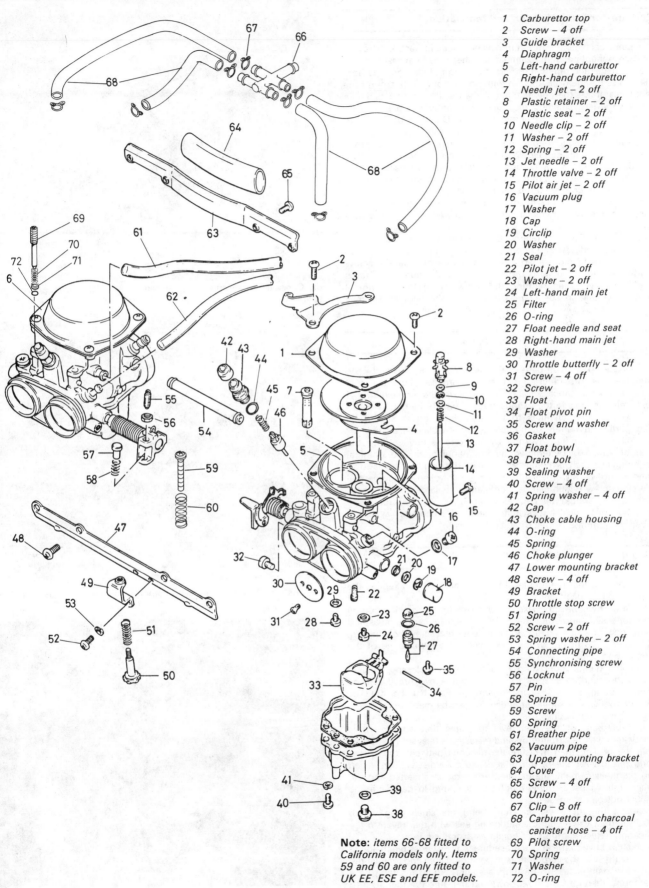

Fig. 2.1 Carburettors

1 Carburettor top
2 Screw – 4 off
3 Guide bracket
4 Diaphragm
5 Left-hand carburettor
6 Right-hand carburettor
7 Needle jet – 2 off
8 Plastic retainer – 2 off
9 Plastic seat – 2 off
10 Needle clip – 2 off
11 Washer – 2 off
12 Spring – 2 off
13 Jet needle – 2 off
14 Throttle valve – 2 off
15 Pilot air jet – 2 off
16 Vacuum plug
17 Washer
18 Cap
19 Circlip
20 Washer
21 Seal
22 Pilot jet – 2 off
23 Washer – 2 off
24 Left-hand main jet
25 Filter
26 O-ring
27 Float needle and seat
28 Right-hand main jet
29 Washer
30 Throttle butterfly – 2 off
31 Screw – 4 off
32 Screw
33 Float
34 Float pivot pin
35 Screw and washer
36 Gasket
37 Float bowl
38 Drain bolt
39 Sealing washer
40 Screw – 4 off
41 Spring washer – 4 off
42 Cap
43 Choke cable housing
44 O-ring
45 Spring
46 Choke plunger
47 Lower mounting bracket
48 Screw – 4 off
49 Bracket
50 Throttle stop screw
51 Spring
52 Screw – 2 off
53 Spring washer – 2 off
54 Connecting pipe
55 Synchronising screw
56 Locknut
57 Pin
58 Spring
59 Screw
60 Spring
61 Breather pipe
62 Vacuum pipe
63 Upper mounting bracket
64 Cover
65 Screw – 4 off
66 Union
67 Clip – 8 off
68 Carburettor to charcoal
    canister hose – 4 off
69 Pilot screw
70 Spring
71 Washer
72 O-ring

Note: *items 66-68 fitted to California models only. Items 59 and 60 are only fitted to UK EE, ESE and EFE models.*

6 Carburettors: examination and renovation

1   Dismantle each carburettor in turn as described in Section 5, laying out the component parts for examination. Check the float assembly for wear or damage, and renew it if there is any sign of leakage. The float needle and seat should be unworn with no sign of a ridge around the contact faces. If less than perfect, renew the needle and seat as a pair.
2   Inspect the jets, cleaning these and the carburettor passages by blowing them through with compressed air. On no account try to remove obstructions with wire; this will only score or enlarge the drilling, ruining the jet. Avoid the use of rag on the carburettors, because lint and fibres can easily block the jets.
3   The diaphragm must be in good condition with no cracks or splits in its surface. If renewal is required, note the comments made in the preceding Section concerning its removal and fitting.
4   The needle jet and the needle must be free of visible wear or scoring, and the two items should be renewed as a pair where necessary.
   Note: Do not disturb or remove the pilot screw. This is considered an emission-related part and is pre-set at the factory. No settings are available for the US models, so if removal is unavoidable, the screw should first be turned inwards until it seats and the number of turns counted carefully. When refitting the screw, set it to the original position. Note that in some areas, disturbing the pilot screw may violate local emission laws, and is therefore not advised.

7 Carburettors: settings and adjustment

1   The various component parts of the carburettors are chosen by the manufacturer as providing the best compromise between fuel economy and performance, and take into account the requirements of exhaust emission laws in the various areas in which the machines are sold. It follows that changes to the standard settings should be avoided, particularly where such changes might violate local laws.
2   The pilot mixture is governed by the pilot screw setting, the position of which is determined during manufacture. No nominal screw settings for the US models are given by the manufacturer, and so they should not be disturbed. Idle speed is controlled by the central throttle stop screw which can be identified by its large knurled knob. The idle speed should be kept between 1000 – 1200 rpm. The carburettors must be kept synchronised, a procedure which is described in Section 9 of this Chapter.

8 Carburettors: checking the fuel level

1   It is important that the fuel level in each carburettor is kept to the figure given in the specifications, otherwise the mixture for the relevant pair of cylinders will be either excessively weak or rich, making normal running impossible and adjustment futile. The level can be measured by connecting a fuel level gauge to each float drain screw hole in turn, and measuring the height of the fuel against the lower edge of the carburettor body.
2   A suitable gauge, consisting of a length of fuel pipe, a clear graduated tube and an adaptor to fit the drain screw thread, can be obtained through Suzuki Service Agents as Part Number 09913-14511. Alternatively, a similar arrangement can be made up at home without too much difficulty.
3   If measurement of the fuel level indicates that adjustment is necessary, remove the carburettors and release the relevant float bowl. Remove the gasket, then measure the distance between the gasket face and the lower edge of the float, using a vernier caliper. When making the measurement, the carburettor should be inverted and the float valve lightly closed, noting that the small spring-loaded pin in the latter must not be compressed.
4   To adjust the fuel level, carefully bend the small tang which operates the float valve until the setting agrees with that given in the Specifications. Recheck the float height as described above.
5   As an alternative to the above procedure, it is just possible to adjust the float height with the carburettors in position. Drain and remove the float bowl to gain access to the float assembly. Bend the tang by a small amount, then refit the float bowl and measure the fuel level to gauge the effect of the adjustment. Repeat until the prescribed setting is achieved.

6.1 Check condition of O-ring and remove any debris from gauze strainer

6.2 Jets should be cleaned using compressed air – do not use wire

6.4 If pilot screws are removed, first count number of turns before they seat as a guide during reassembly

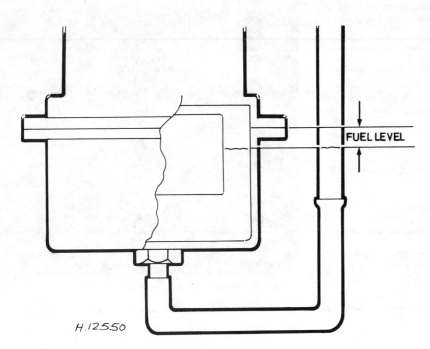

Fig. 2.2 Fuel level measurement

H.12550

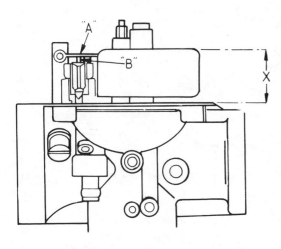

Fig. 2.3 Float height measurement

A Float tang   X Float height
B Float needle

9 Carburettors: synchronisation

1   It is of fundamental importance that air and fuel are delivered in identical quantities and proportions to each of the four cylinders. The fuel flow is governed by the jets of each carburettor, but it is essential that the flow of air through each is similar at all engine speeds and throttle openings. It will be appreciated that if this is not the case, one or more cylinders will have to be 'carried' by the remainder, resulting in reduced engine power and fuel efficiency. Poor synchronisation is usually characterised by hesitant throttle response, erratic running and increased engine noise, the latter due to the effects of otherwise normal backlash in the transmission components.

2   If the carburettors have been separated, the throttle plates must be roughly synchronised during assembly as described in Section 5 above. This is a necessary preliminary to full vacuum synchronisation (balancing) which is described below. This procedure should be carried out whenever the engine is running poorly and at the intervals specified in Routine Maintenance. It must be noted that synchronisation cannot be carried out successfully unless all other adjustments are normal, especially the remaining carburettor settings. Unless these are set correctly, any attempt at synchronisation will produce false readings.

3   Synchronisation requires the use of an accurate vacuum gauge set. This can be the Suzuki type, consisting of four calibrated tubes in which steel balls indicate the vacuum level and which can be ordered through Suzuki Service Agents under the following Part Numbers:

09913-13121 Carburettor balancer
09915-94511 Adaptor

4   As an alternative, any good quality clock or mercury column type vacuum gauge set may be used, provided that the appropriate adaptors are available. Note that no specific vacuum figures are available, but this does not prevent the two instruments being set to the same vacuum level. If a proprietary set is used, follow the maker's instructions regarding any initial calibration procedure which may be required. This is described below for the Suzuki gauge set.

5   Run the engine until it has reached its normal operating temperature. Remove the vacuum take-off screw from one cylinder and fit an adaptor in its place. Connect the hose from the first gauge, start the engine and set the idle speed to 1750 rpm, using the large knurled throttle stop control. Set the damper screw on the gauge so that the steel ball aligns with the centre line. Connect the next hose to the adaptor and repeat the procedure. It is not necessary to calibrate all four sections of the gauge; only two will be required.

6   During adjustment, access to the top of the instruments is required, and this will necessitate the removal of the tank. To maintain a supply of fuel, place the tank as near as possible to the machine and slightly higher than the carburettors. Use a length of fuel hose to arrange a temporary feed, and plug the fuel tap vacuum take-off point. Set the fuel tap to the PRI position.

7   With the engine stopped, remove the remaining vacuum take off screw and fit the second gauge adaptor. Connect the vacuum hoses to their respective adaptors, then start the engine and allow it to idle. The object of the test is to set the carburettor of the two pairs of cylinders so that the steel balls are bisected by the centre line of the gauge.

8   Start the engine, and set the idle speed to 1750 rpm using the large knurled throttle stop control. The steel balls should both align with the centre line on the gauge. If adjustment is required, locate the balance screw on the throttle spindle between the two carburettors. Slacken the locknut and turn the screw until balance is achieved. It is likely that this will affect the idle speed, and this should be reset to 1750 rpm. Open the throttle a few times, then allow the engine to resume idling

and recheck the synchronisation. When the carburettors are synchronised, tighten the balance screw locknut and reduce the idle speed to
1000 – 1200 rpm.

10 Air filter: removal and refitting

1   The air filter element is of the dry type, comprising a pleated,
resin-impregnated paper element, supported by a metal mesh inner
core. The element can be removed after releasing the seat and
removing the right-hand side panel. Pull off the filter casing end cover
and remove the single screw which retains the filter inside the casing.
The element can now be withdrawn for cleaning and examination.
2   The filter element must be cleaned at the intervals given in the
Routine Maintenance Section of this Manual. Using compressed air,
blow the element clean from the inside. Note that no attempt must be
made to clean the element using solvents.
3   If the element has become very dirty, or has already been cleaned 3
or more times, it should be renewed. It is also important to examine
very carefully the filter surface, looking for any indications of damage.
If torn or holes, renew the element without delay.
4   Note that if the machine is used with a damaged filter element, or if
the element is omitted, any airborne dust will be drawn into the engine
and will probably result in rapid wear. In addition, the resulting weak
mixture will upset the carburation.

10.1 Air filter element is retained by a single screw

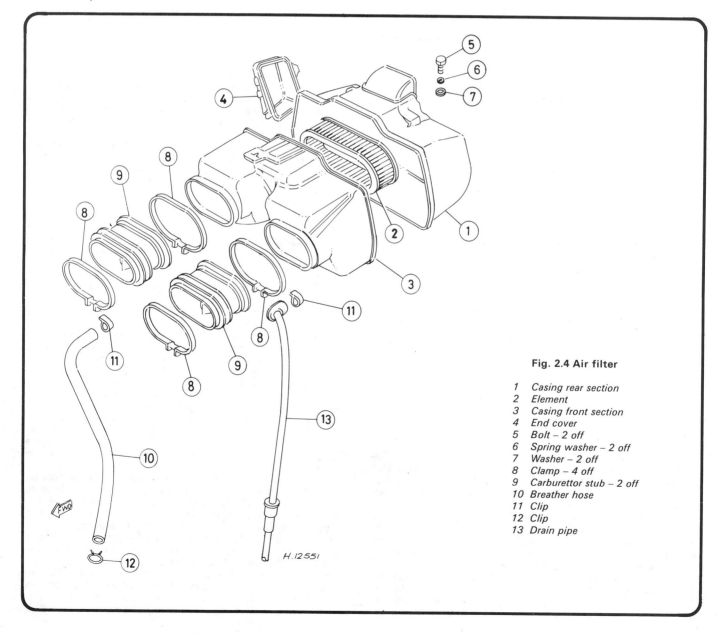

Fig. 2.4 Air filter

1   *Casing rear section*
2   *Element*
3   *Casing front section*
4   *End cover*
5   *Bolt – 2 off*
6   *Spring washer – 2 off*
7   *Washer – 2 off*
8   *Clamp – 4 off*
9   *Carburettor stub – 2 off*
10 *Breather hose*
11 *Clip*
12 *Clip*
13 *Drain pipe*

H.12551

11 Oil pump: examination and renovation

1 The engine and transmission components are dependent on the reliable supply of oil at the correct pressure. Provided that the oil is changed at the specified intervals and no catastrophic failure of internal components occurs, the oil pump will usually last the life of the engine.

2 In the event of a suspected oil pump fault, or if the oil pressure lamp comes on repeatedly or fails to go out, check the oil pressure immediately; running the engine with a faulty lubrication system will result in rapid and expensive engine failure. The test procedure is described in Section 12 below.

3 The oil pump should only require attention during major engine overhauls, or if indications of low oil pressure or unusual engine noises prompt further investigation. Access to the pump requires the removal of the clutch assembly, the relevant procedures for which are described in Sections 10 and 11 of Chapter 1.

4 With the pump removed from the crankcase, the end cover can be taken off. The cover is held in place by two recessed cross-head screws. Lift away the cover and displace the inner and outer rotors for further examination.

5 Inspect the pump rotors and the working faces of the body and cover for signs of excessive wear or damage. If scoring is found, the pump must be renewed and the source of the damage should be traced and rectified. Note that if debris remains in the oil passages, a new pump will soon be destroyed, and it will be necessary to dismantle the crankcases to ensure that all traces of swarf are removed.

6 It follows that if metal particles are found, an internal component has failed and will require renewal. No wear limit or clearance figures

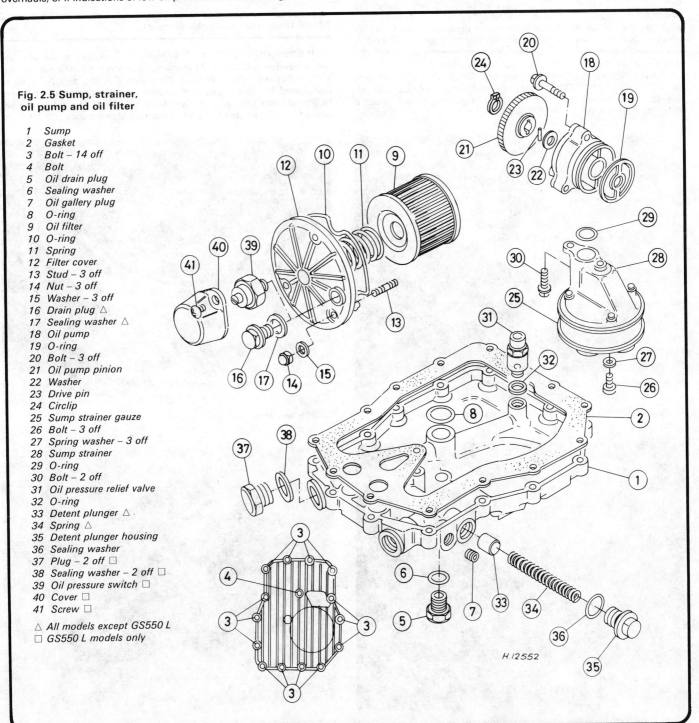

Fig. 2.5 Sump, strainer, oil pump and oil filter

1   Sump
2   Gasket
3   Bolt – 14 off
4   Bolt
5   Oil drain plug
6   Sealing washer
7   Oil gallery plug
8   O-ring
9   Oil filter
10 O-ring
11 Spring
12 Filter cover
13 Stud – 3 off
14 Nut – 3 off
15 Washer – 3 off
16 Drain plug △
17 Sealing washer △
18 Oil pump
19 O-ring
20 Bolt – 3 off
21 Oil pump pinion
22 Washer
23 Drive pin
24 Circlip
25 Sump strainer gauze
26 Bolt – 3 off
27 Spring washer – 3 off
28 Sump strainer
29 O-ring
30 Bolt – 2 off
31 Oil pressure relief valve
32 O-ring
33 Detent plunger △
34 Spring △
35 Detent plunger housing
36 Sealing washer
37 Plug – 2 off □
38 Sealing washer – 2 off □
39 Oil pressure switch □
40 Cover □
41 Screw □

△ All models except GS550 L
□ GS550 L models only

H.12552

are available for the pump components, so it is necessary to assess the amount of wear visually. If you are unsure about the condition of the pump, seek the advice of a Suzuki Service Agent.

7   When reassembling the pump, clean the body, cover and rotors with petrol or a cleaning solvent, then lubricate them with engine oil. Make sure that the inner rotor drive pin is correctly located in its slot in the rotor. Use a thread locking compound on the pump cover screws and tighten them firmly. Check the condition of the O-ring seal and renew it if necessary, prior to installation.

12 Checking the oil pressure

1   It is recommended that the oil pressure is checked if there is reason to suspect that there is a lubrication system fault. The test requires the use of a Suzuki pressure gauge, or an equivalent.

2   With the engine at normal running temperature, connect an oil pressure gauge to the take-off point on the oil filter cover. This is closed by a blanking plug on most models, though on some ''L'' models the oil pressure switch is fitted in this position.

3   Suzuki can supply an oil pressure gauge and adaptor, Part numbers 09915-74510 and 09915-77330. Failing this, any gauge with an adaptor of the correct size may be used. The pump should produce a reading of at least 2.5 kg cm² (35.6 psi) but not more than 5.5 kg cm²

(78.2 psi) at 3000 rpm with an oil temperature of 60°C (140°F). If the pressure is low, remove the pump and check for wear. Abnormally high pressure indicates a blockage or fault in the pressure relief valve which is screwed into the sump and which can be removed after the oil has been drained and the sump removed.

13 Checking the oil pressure switch

1   If the oil pressure lamp comes on and a subsequent check on the oil pressure shows this to be acceptable, it can be assumed that the oil pressure switch is at fault. If necessary, check the switch by substitution. The switch is screwed into the oil filter cover (US L models) or to the top of the crankcase on other models.

14 Oil filter: renewing the element

1   It is important that the oil filter element is renewed at the intervals recommended in Routine Maintenance. If renewal is postponed for too long, a bypass valve will open to ensure that the supply of oil is maintained, but this means that the oil now circulating in the engine is unfiltered, and engine wear will be accelerated. The filter renewal procedure is described in detail in Routine Maintenance.

11.5a Displace and remove driving pin from shaft end

11.5b Remove the two cover retaining screws ...

11.5c ... then lift away the cover and pump rotors

11.5d Check rotors and pump body for wear or damage

15 Oil cooler: general description

1   The oil cooler comprises a small frame-mounted radiator, connected to the lubrication system by hoses, and a pressure sensitive plunger valve in the sump. When the engine is first started the oil is cold and its viscosity high. The resulting high pressure closes the plunger valve, bypassing the oil cooler and allowing the engine to warm up quickly.

2   As the oil temperature rises its viscosity lowers. This allows the pressure on the plunger valve to drop, and when it falls to about 1 kg cm² it allows the oil to be routed through the oil cooler radiator. This arrangement ensures that engine warm-up is fast, but provides greater protection for the engine components at high engine temperatures. In this sense the oil cooler supplements the normal air-cooling of the engine.

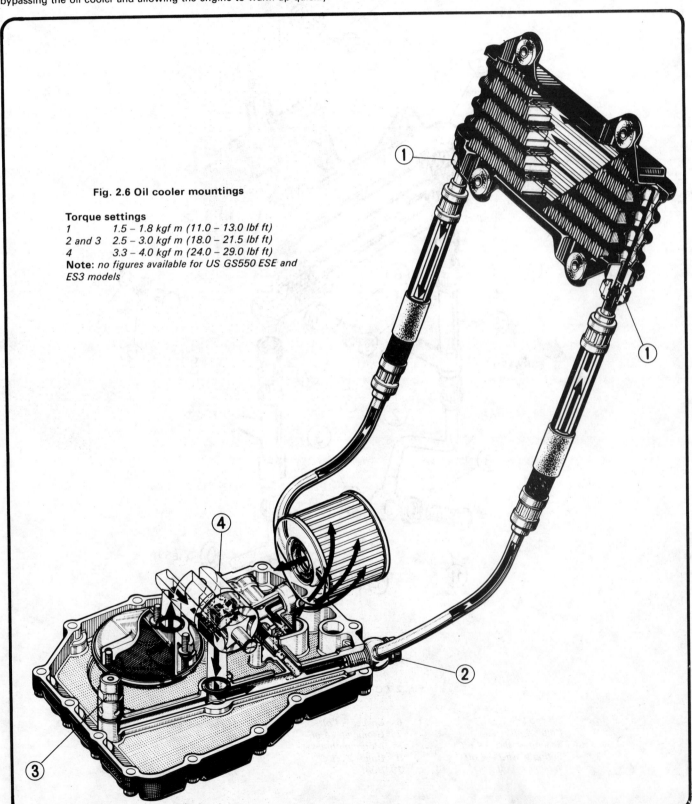

Fig. 2.6 Oil cooler mountings

Torque settings
1   1.5 – 1.8 kgf m (11.0 – 13.0 lbf ft)
2 and 3   2.5 – 3.0 kgf m (18.0 – 21.5 lbf ft)
4   3.3 – 4.0 kgf m (24.0 – 29.0 lbf ft)
Note: no figures available for US GS550 ESE and ES3 models

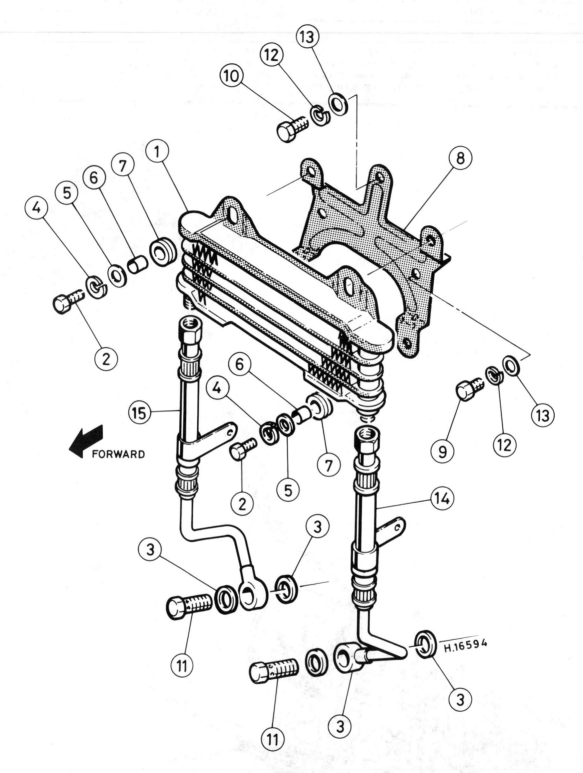

Fig. 2.7 Oil cooler assembly

1 Oil cooler	6 Spacer – 4 off	11 Union bolt – 2 off
2 Bolt – 4 off	7 Grommet – 4 off	12 Spring washer – 3 off
3 Sealing washer – 4 off	8 Mounting bracket	13 Washer – 3 off
4 Spring washer – 4 off	9 Bolt – 2 off	14 Left-hand hose
5 Washer – 4 off	10 Bolt	15 Right-hand hose

15.1a Oil cooler radiator is retained by rubber-bushed bolts

15.1b Oil cooler hoses are held by brackets on front engine mounting bolts

16 Evaporative emission control system: California models

1   The later California models of the GS550 are equipped with an evaporative emission control system designed to prevent the escape of unburnt hydrocarbons in the form of fuel vapour. Instead of a conventional vented filler cap, a separator unit inside the fuel tank is connected to a charcoal canister at the rear of the machine by a hose. A second hose leads from the canister to the carburettors.
2   When the machine is at rest, any expansion in the tank causes fuel vapour to be forced through the vapour hose and into the canister, where any hydrocarbon molecules are held by the charcoal. When the engine is next started, air and the residual fuel vapour are drawn through the purge hose and into the engine, where the fuel is burnt.
3   The system is automatic in operation and requires no maintenance other than occasional checking and renewal of the hoses. The charcoal canister is a sealed unit and should require no attention during the life of the machine, unless it becomes badly contaminated with large quantities of fuel. If this occurs it will be necessary to renew the canister.

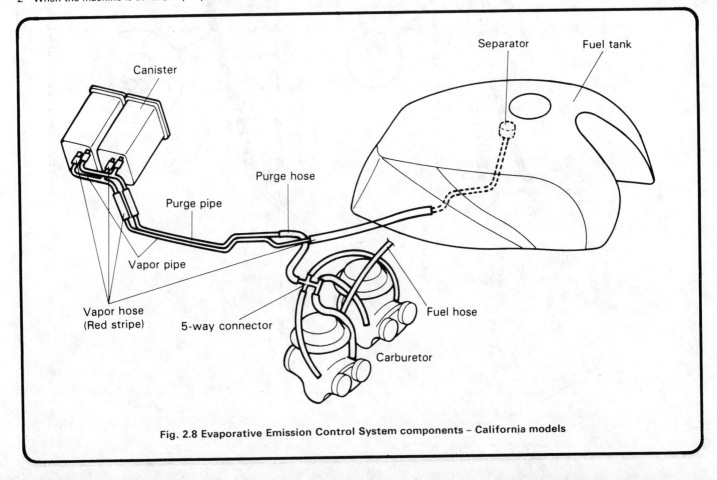

Fig. 2.8 Evaporative Emission Control System components – California models

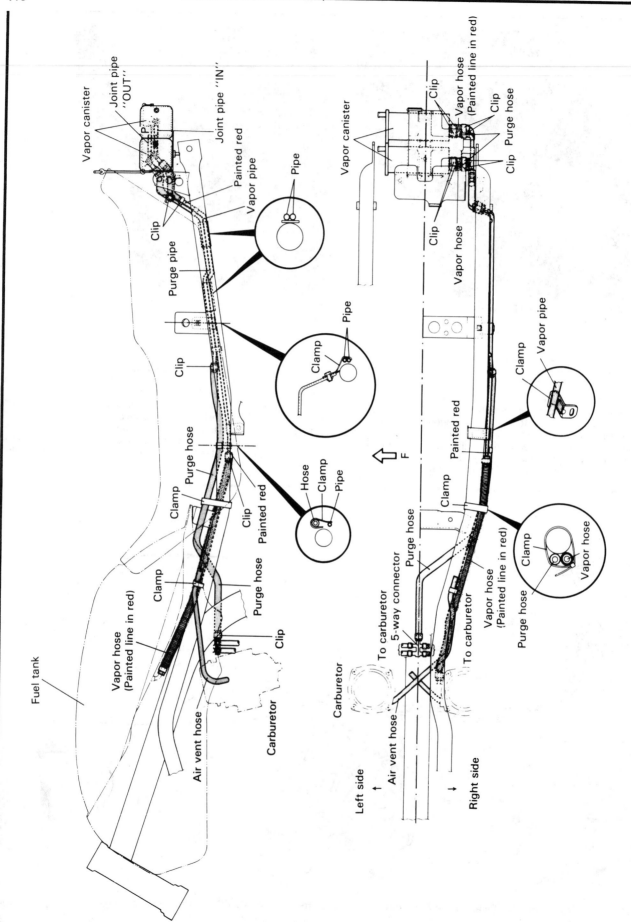

Fig. 2.9 Correct routing of Evaporative Emission Control System hoses – California models

Chapter 3 Ignition system

Contents

Specifications

Ignition system
Type .... Electronic
Minimum spark performance .... 8 mm (0.3 in) @ 1 atmosphere
Firing order 1,2,4,3

Ignition timing
Below 1650 ± 100 rpm:
   UK models .... 15° BTDC
   US models .... 11° BTDC
Above 3000 ± 100 rpm:
   UK models .... 35° BTDC
   US models .... 31° BTDC

Spark plug

	NGK	ND
Make		
Type:		
UK models	DR8ES	X27ESR-U
US models	D9EA	X27ES-U
Electrode gap	0.6 – 0.7 mm (0.024 – 0.028 in)	

Ignition coil resistances
Primary windings .... 3 – 5 ohms approx
Secondary windings .... 30 – 60 k ohms approx

Pickup coils
Resistance .... Approx 250 – 500 ohms

1 General description

The machines featured in this manual are equipped with a transistorised ignition system of the type which has become well established in motorcycle applications. An ignition pickup assembly is mounted on the right-hand end of the crankshaft. This comprises a rotor, mounted on the right-hand end of the crankshaft, and a stator unit with two small pickup coils. The pickup induces a trigger pulse as it sweeps past the two pickup coils. The trigger pulses are fed to a sealed ignition amplifier, the resulting pulse being routed to the appropriate ignition coil.

Two ignition coils are fitted, each coil firing two plugs in a 'spare spark' arrangement. In this system, plugs 1 and 4 spark simultaneously, combustion occurring only in the cylinder in which the fuel/air mixture is under compression, the remaining spark occurring in a cylinder on the exhaust stroke. The same arrangement applies to cylinders 2 and 3. As the engine speed rises it is necessary to advance the point at which the ignition spark occurs. This is accomplished automatically by the igniter unit.

The ignition system is depicted in the accompanying circuit diagram. It will be seen that the system is very simple in design, and given the inherent reliability of transistor circuits, the arrangement will be found to require little attention in normal use.

2 Testing the ignition system: general

1 In the event of a fault developing in the ignition system, the spark plugs should always be checked first as described below. Where the fault cannot be attributed to the plugs, plug caps or the high tension leads, further testing of the system will require the use of a simple multimeter. In the absence of the Suzuki 'Pocket Tester', Part Number 09900-25002, any similar device will be adequate for most purposes.

Note that a multimeter should be considered an essential piece of equipment for ignition and electrical tests. In view of the low cost, it can be considered a good investment.

2 As has been mentioned above, most ignition faults can be traced to the plugs or the high tension side of the system, and will have resulted from normal wear or from corrosion. The second most likely culprit will be damaged, broken or shorted wiring, or a fault in a connector. Failure of the pickup assembly or the igniter unit is rare, but it is worth noting that the nature of the fault will often give a good indication of the source of the problem.

3 If the fault is evident on cylinders 1 and 4, or on cylinders 2 and 3 only, check the relevant pickup coil and ignition coil. In the event of complete ignition failure, the above components are unlikely to be responsible, and attention should be directed towards the supply, switches and the ignitor unit.

3 Checking the alternator output and battery

It will be appreciated that the ignition system will not operate normally if the supply to the ignition unit is unstable or non-existent. If other electrical problems are evident, always investigate the alternator output and the condition of the battery before the ignition system is checked. For details, refer to Chapter 6.

4 Checking the wiring and connections

Using the wiring diagrams at the end of Chapter 6, trace and examine the ignition wiring, repairing and re-routing any wires which have been damaged or trapped. The associated connectors should be separated and checked for corrosion. This should be removed by scraping it off, and further corrosion prevented by coating the metal parts with silicone grease.

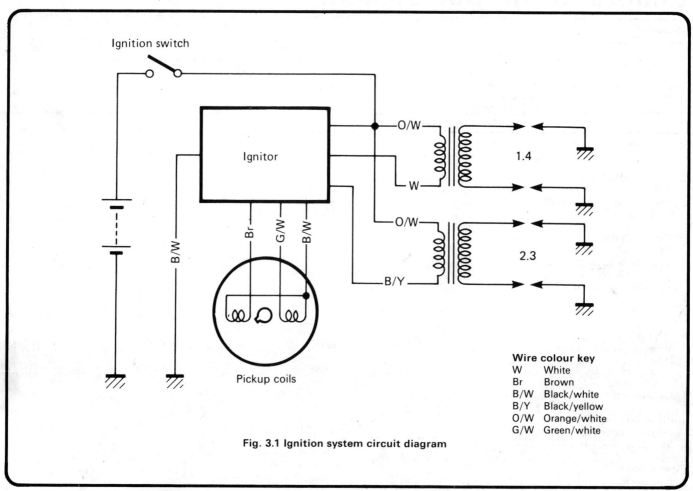

Fig. 3.1 Ignition system circuit diagram

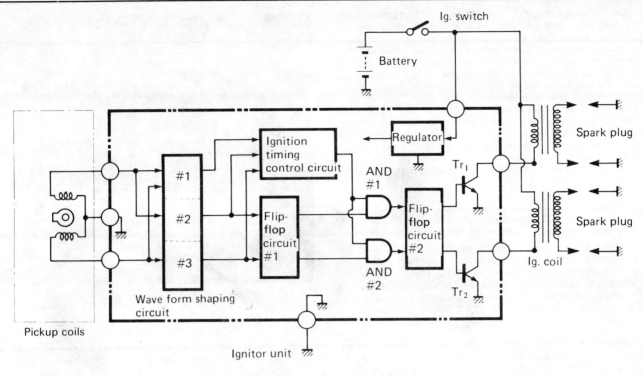

Fig. 3.2 CDI unit/schematic diagram

5 Spark plugs: checking and resetting the gaps

1 As has been mentioned, the single most common cause of ignition faults is defects in the spark plugs. The plug condition should be checked regularly at the intervals given in Routine Maintenance, and whenever misfiring or poor starting is evident.

2 The UK models are fitted with NGK DR8ES or ND X27ESR-U plugs. The US versions are equipped with NGK D9EA or ND X27ES-U plugs. In all cases the electrode gap is 0.6 – 0.7 mm (0.024 – 0.028 in).

3 Remove the plugs and examine the electrodes and insulator nose, comparing the appearance with the examples shown in the accompanying colour photographs, as a guide to the general condition of the engine. With experience, a great deal of information may be obtained in this way.

4 Light carbon deposits can be scraped off, taking care not to crack the rather brittle ceramic insulator. If the carbon build-up is heavy, it is preferable to renew the plugs as a set, given the relatively low cost involved.

5 With both new and used plugs, check the electrode gaps prior to installation, using feeler gauges. If adjustment is required, carefully bend the outer earth (ground) electrode only. On no account attempt to bend the inner electrode or the insulator nose will be damaged.

6 Check that the threads are clean and apply a thin film of molybdenum disulphide or copper grease to ease subsequent removal. Fit each plug finger tight only, then use a plug socket or box spanner to tighten them by about a quarter turn; just enough to seat the sealing washer firmly, and no more.

7 If previous overtightening of the plugs has stripped the plug threads in the head casting, they can be reclaimed by fitting Helicoil inserts. This is an inexpensive and convenient service offered by many dealers.

8 It is good practice to carry one or two new spark plugs of the correct type, correctly gapped, with the toolkit. This can save a lot of time in the event of a roadside breakdown.

6 Plug caps and leads: examination and renovation

1 The plug caps incorporate suppressors to limit radio frequency (RF) interference and form a sealed connection between the plugs and the high tension leads. The most likely problems are failure of the suppressor or tracking and shorting. If a suppressor fails, the increased resistance will usually prevent or reduce sparking at the associated plug.

2 Check first that the plug is operating normally, then check the cap by substitution, swapping it with a sound cap and noting whether this resolves the problem. The seal around the bottom edge of the cap is important because it excludes dirt and moisture at the otherwise vulnerable plug connection. If it is damaged, renew the cap.

3 Another form of shorting, known as tracking, can develop along the HT lead. This is initially due to dirt and moisture on the lead providing an alternative path for the high tension current, and may be visible at night. In time, the repeated discharge will cause a carbon build up, worsening the problem. If tracking is suspected, clean the leads carefully using a rag moistened with WD40 or a similar silicone-based water dispersal spray.

4 Care should be taken to avoid damage to the leads, being especially careful to prevent chafing against the cylinder head cover. Note that the leads are moulded into the coils, and will have to be renewed as an assembly if seriously damaged.

7 Ignition coils: checking

1 A fault in an ignition coil will almost invariably be indicated by weak or erratic sparking on one pair of plugs only; the chances of both coils failing simultaneously being most unlikely. Always check first that the plugs, plug caps and leads are not at fault (see above) before testing the coils.

2 The spark performance is tested with the coils removed from the machine, using an Electro Tester, a piece of equipment used by most Suzuki Service Agents, but not worth buying for infrequent home use. An approximate indication of performance can be obtained with the coils in place on the machine.

3 Remove the relevant plugs and lodge them securely against the cylinder head with the plug caps attached. Crank the engine and note the spark at the electrodes. If all is well, a fat blue spark should be produced, whilst a weak coil will show a weak or erratic spark at both

plugs, possibly orange in colour. It should be noted that partial failure of the igniter unit could produce similar effects, so check the coil resistances as described below.

4   Remove the fuel tank and separate the low tension connector to the suspect coil, and disconnect the plug caps. Using a multimeter set on the resistance scale, connect the probes to the thin low tension leads and note the primary winding resistance reading. An approximate value of 3 – 5 ohms should be shown.

5   Connect the meter probes to the two HT leads at the plug caps and note the secondary winding resistance reading. A figure of approximately 30 – 60 kilo ohms should be indicated. Note that the above resistance figures are not intended to be exact, but if the readings obtained differ radically, the coil can be assumed to be defective. A Suzuki Service Agent will be able to confirm this by performing a spark test.

8   Ignition pickup coils: checking

Trace the wiring from the ignition pickup assembly back to the connector on the underside of the igniter unit. Separate the connector and measure the resistance between the green/white lead and the black/white lead. Repeat the check, this time between the brown lead and the black/white lead. In each case the standard figure is 250–500 ohms, a very high or zero reading indicating that the pickup coils are faulty.

7.4 Coil assembly is mounted on bracket below fuel tank

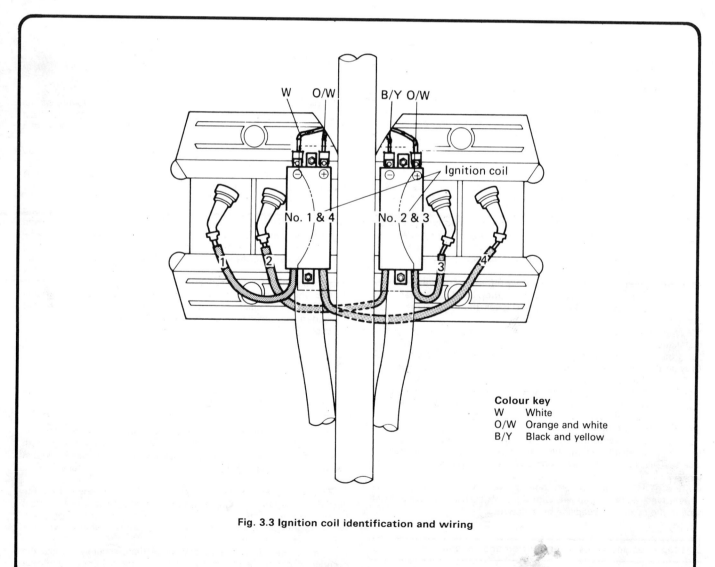

Colour key
W   White
O/W Orange and white
B/Y   Black and yellow

Fig. 3.3 Ignition coil identification and wiring

Spark plug maintenance: Checking plug gap with feeler gauges

Altering the plug gap. Note use of correct tool

Spark plug conditions: A brown, tan or grey firing end is indicative of correct engine running conditions and the selection of the appropriate heat rating plug

White deposits have accumulated from excessive amounts of oil in the combustion chamber or through the use of low quality oil. Remove deposits or a hot spot may form

Black sooty deposits indicate an over-rich fuel/air mixture, or a malfunctioning ignition system. If no improvement is obtained, try one grade hotter plug

Wet, oily carbon deposits form an electrical leakage path along the insulator nose, resulting in a misfire. The cause may be a badly worn engine or a malfunctioning ignition system

A blistered white insulator or melted electrode indicates over-advanced ignition timing or a malfunctioning cooling system. If correction does not prove effective, try a colder grade plug

A worn spark plug not only wastes fuel but also overloads the whole ignition system because the increased gap requires higher voltage to initiate the spark. This condition can also affect air pollution

Unit: kΩ

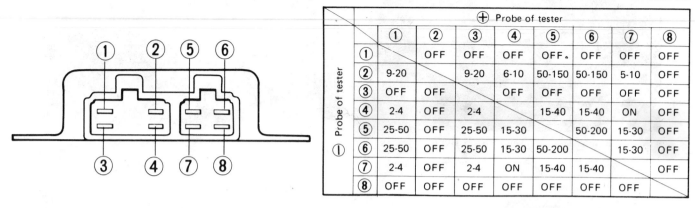

		⊕ Probe of tester							
		①	②	③	④	⑤	⑥	⑦	⑧
Probe of tester ⊖	①		OFF	OFF	OFF	OFF.	OFF	OFF	OFF
	②	9-20		9-20	6-10	50-150	50-150	5-10	OFF
	③	OFF	OFF		OFF	OFF	OFF	OFF	OFF
	④	2-4	OFF	2-4		15-40	15-40	ON	OFF
	⑤	25-50	OFF	25-50	15-30		50-200	15-30	OFF
	⑥	25-50	OFF	25-50	15-30	50-200		15-30	OFF
	⑦	2-4	OFF	2-4	ON	15-40	15-40		OFF
	⑧	OFF	OFF	OFF	OFF	OFF	OFF	OFF	

Fig. 3.4 Ignitor unit test table

9 Ignitor (ignition amplifier) unit: checking

Note: *The following check of the ignitor unit assumes that the coils, leads, plug caps and plugs are not at fault.*

1 Remove the seat and the left-hand side panel. Pull off the two wiring connectors from the underside of the ignitor unit. Remove the two screws which retain the unit to the battery tray and lift it away.
2 Using a multimeter set on the kilo ohms (ohms x 1000) scale, measure the resistances between the various terminals, according to the accompanying line drawing and table. Note that in the table 'ON' denotes full conductivity, or zero resistance, whilst 'OFF' indicates no conductivity, or infinite resistance. If the unit shows markedly different readings across any pair of terminals it is likely that it has failed internally and must be renewed. It is worth checking this by substitution. Note that the unit is sealed and thus cannot be repaired.

10 Ignition timing: checking and adjustment

The ignition timing is controlled electronically by the ignitor unit and cannot be adjusted; the position of the pickup coils being fixed. In the event of a suspected timing fault, check the igniter resistances as described above. No further checks or maintenance is possible or should be required.

10.1 "F" mark should align as shown if checked with strobe, but note that no adjustment is possible

Chapter 4 Frame and forks

Refer to Chapter 7 for information relating to the 1986 to 1988 GS/GSX550 ES and GS550 L models

Contents

Specifications

UK GSX550 ESD, EE, ESE and EFE models

Frame
Type .... Tubular, double cradle

Front forks
Stroke .... 150 mm (5.9 in)
Oil grade .... 15W fork oil
Oil quantity (per leg):
    ESD, EE .... 297 cc (10.5/10.0 Imp/US fl oz)
    ESE, EFE .... 307 cc (10.8/10.4 Imp/US fl oz)
Oil level:
    ESD, EE .... 160 mm (6.3 in)
    ESE. EFE .... 151 mm (5.9 in)
Fork spring free length (service limit) .... 490 mm (19.3 in)

Rear suspension
Type .... Cantilever (Suzuki Full Floater)
Rear wheel travel .... 117 mm (4.61 in)
Suspension unit .... Single oil-damped coil spring unit with remote hydraulic spring preload adjustment
Swinging arm pivot shaft runout (service limit) .... 0.3 mm (0.012 in)

Torque wrench settings

Component	kgf m	lbf ft
Steering stem top bolt	2.0 – 3.0	14.5 – 21.7
Steering stem clamp bolt	1.5 – 2.5	10.8 – 18.1
Front fork upper clamp bolt	2.0 – 3.0	14.5 – 21.7
Front fork lower clamp bolt	1.5 – 2.5	10.8 – 18.1
Front fork cap bolt	1.5 – 3.0	10.8 – 21.7
Front fork damper rod Allen bolt	2.0 – 2.6	14.5 – 18.8
Front wheel spindle nut	3.6 – 5.2	26.0 – 37.6
Front wheel spindle clamp nut	1.5 – 2.5	10.8 – 18.1
Handlebar clamp bolt	1.5 – 2.5	10.8 – 18.1
Handlebar mounting bolt	5.0 – 6.0	36.2 – 43.4
Handlebar mounting bolt locknut	2.0 – 3.0	14.5 – 21.7
Front brake caliper mounting bolt	2.5 – 4.0	18.1 – 28.9
Front brake anti-dive components:		
Modulator to plunger housing bolt	0.6 – 0.8	4.3 – 5.8
Plunger housing to fork bolt	0.4 – 0.5	2.9 – 3.6
Rear suspension components (see Fig. 4.19):		
Swinging arm pivot nut	5.5 – 8.8	39.8 – 63.7
Rear suspension unit mountings	4.8 – 7.2	34.7 – 52.1
Rear cushion lever nut	8.4 – 10.0	60.8 – 72.3
Rear cushion rod upper nut	4.8 – 7.2	34.7 – 52.1
Rear cushion rod lower nut	8.4 – 10.0	60.8 – 72.3
Rear brake caliper mounting bolt	1.5 – 2.5	10.8 – 18.1
Rear brake pedal pinch bolt	1.5 – 2.5	10.8 – 18.1
Rear torque arm nut	2.0 – 3.0	14.5 – 21.7
Rear master cylinder mounting bolt	1.5 – 2.5	10.8 – 18.1
Rear wheel spindle nut	5.0 – 8.0	36.2 – 57.9

US GS550 ED, ESD, LD, ESE, ES3, EF, ESF, LF models

Frame
Type .... Tubular, double cradle

Front forks
Stroke:
    ED, ESD, ESE, ES3, EF, ESF .... 150 mm (5.9 in)
    LD, LF .... 160 mm (6.3 in)
Oil level:
    ED, ESD .... 125 mm (4.9 in)
    LD .... 190 mm (7.5 in)
    ESE .... 119 mm (4.7 in)
    EF, ESF .... 114 mm (4.5 in)
    LF .... 179 mm (7.0 in)
Oil grade .... 15W fork oil
Oil quantity (per leg):
    ED, ESD .... 321 cc (10.9/11.3 US/Imp fl oz)
    LD .... 288 cc (9.7/10.1 US/Imp fl oz)
    ESE .... 330 cc (11.2/11.6 US/Imp fl oz)
    EF, ESF .... 345 cc (11.6/12.1 US/Imp fl oz)
    LF .... 276 cc (9.3/9.7 US/Imp fl oz)
Fork spring free length (service limit):
    ED, ESD, ESE, ES3, EF, ESF .... 490 mm (19.3 in)
    LD .... 513 mm (20.2 in)
    LF .... 564 mm (22.2 in)
Air pressure:
    ED, ESD .... Not applicable
    ESE, ES3, LD, EF, ESF, LF .... 0.3 kg cm² (4.2 psi)

Rear suspension
Type .... Cantilever (Suzuki Full Floater)
Rear wheel travel:
    ED, ESD, ESE, ES3, EF, ESF .... 117 mm (4.61 in)
    LD, LF .... 100 mm (3.94 in)
Suspension unit .... Single oil-damped coil spring unit with remote hydraulic spring preload adjustment
Swinging arm pivot shaft runout (service limit) .... 0.3 mm (0.012 in)

Torque wrench settings

Component	kgf m	lbf ft
Steering stem top bolt	2.0 – 3.0	14.5 – 21.7
Steering stem clamp bolt:		
ED, ESD, EF, ESF	1.5 – 2.5	10.8 – 18.1
LD, LF	1.2 – 2.0	8.5 – 14.5
Front fork upper clamp bolt	2.0 – 3.0	14.5 – 21.7
Front fork lower clamp bolt:		
ED, ESD, EF, ESF	1.5 – 2.5	10.8 – 18.1
LD, LF	1.2 – 2.0	8.5 – 14.5
Front fork cap bolt:		
ED, ESD	1.5 – 3.0	10.8 – 21.7
LD, LF	Not applicable	
EF, ESF	2.0 – 3.0	14.5 – 21.5
Front fork damper rod Allen bolt:		
ED, ESD, ESF	2.0 – 2.6	14.5 – 18.8
LD, LF	1.5 – 2.5	11.0 – 21.5
Front wheel spindle nut	3.6 – 5.2	26.0 – 37.6
Front wheel spindle clamp nut	1.5 – 2.5	10.8 – 18.1
Handlebar clamp bolt:		
ED, ESD, EF, ESF	1.5 – 2.5	10.8 – 18.1
LD	Not applicable	
LF	1.2 – 2.0	8.5 – 14.5
Handlebar mounting bolt:		
ED, ESD, EF, ESF	5.0 – 6.0	36.2 – 43.4
LD	1.5 – 2.5	11.0 – 18.0
LF	Not applicable	
Handlebar mounting bolt locknut:		
ED, ESD, EF, ESF	2.0 – 3.0	14.5 – 21.7
LD	1.0 – 1.5	7.0 – 11.0
LF	Not applicable	
Front brake caliper mounting bolt	2.5 – 4.0	18.1 – 28.9
Front brake anti-dive components (ED, ESD):		
Modulator to plunger housing bolt	0.6 – 0.8	4.3 – 5.8
Plunger housing to fork bolt	0.4 – 0.5	2.9 – 3.6
Front fork 'Posi-damp' bolt (EF, ESF)	0.6 – 0.8	4.5 – 6.0
Rear suspension components (see Fig. 4.19):		
Swinging arm pivot nut:		
ED, ESD, EF, ESF	5.5 – 8.8	39.8 – 63.7
LD, LF	5.0 – 8.0	36.0 – 58.0
Rear suspension unit mountings	4.8 – 7.2	34.7 – 52.1
Rear cushion lever nut	8.4 – 10.0	60.8 – 72.3
Rear cushion rod upper nut	4.8 – 7.2	34.7 – 52.1
Rear cushion rod lower nut	8.4 – 10.0	60.8 – 72.3
Rear brake caliper mounting bolt	1.5 – 2.5	10.8 – 18.1
Rear brake pedal pinch bolt	1.5 – 2.5	10.8 – 18.1
Rear torque arm nut	2.0 – 3.0	14.5 – 21.7
Rear master cylinder mounting bolt:		
ED, ESD, EF, ESF	1.5 – 2.5	10.8 – 18.1
LD, LF	Not applicable	
Rear wheel spindle nut	5.0 – 8.0	36.2 – 57.9

Note: *At the time of writing no torque settings were available for the GS550 ESE and ES3 models*

1 General description

The Suzuki GS/GSX models employ a full duplex cradle frame of welded tubular steel construction, much of which uses the currently fashionable square section tubing. Front suspension is by oil damped, coil sprung telescopic forks. These vary in sophistication and complexity according to the model, and are generally similar on both US and UK versions.

In the case of the UK models, conventional oil-damped coil spring telescopic forks are fitted, all of which are equipped with hydraulically operated anti-dive units. The system uses hydraulic pressure from the braking system to vary the fork compression damping rate, reducing the tendency for the machine to pitch forward under heavy braking. This in turn permits a more compliant initial rate for the forks, giving an improved ride.

The forks fitted to the US ED, ESD, ESE and ES3 models are similar to those of the UK models and employ the same anti-dive system. The UK models are not fitted with air valves in the top bolts. The LD and LF models do not use the anti-dive system, but are equipped with air-assisted forks. The EF and ESF models employ a similar fork to that fitted to the previous non-custom variants, but a new type of anti-dive system (Suzuki Posi-Damp) is fitted. This is not interconnected with the braking system, but instead relies on an adjustable valve which increases the damping rate in response to unusually high pressure in the damping system. In other words, under heavy braking the damping rate is increased, but not under direct control of the braking system.

Rear suspension is a rising rate design comprising an arrangement of bellcranks and links acting on a single, central suspension unit. The suspension unit is so arranged that the initial few inches of wheel travel compress the unit only slightly. As wheel deflection increases, the corresponding movement of the rear suspension unit becomes greater, and thus the springing and damping effect increases with deflection. This allows a soft and compliant ride initially, becoming much stiffer and more heavily damped under more demanding conditions.

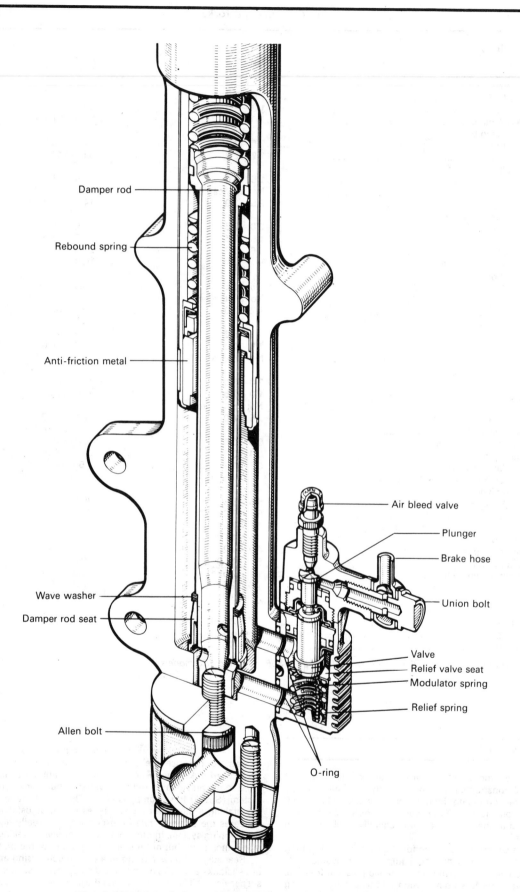

**Fig. 4.1 Sectioned view of front fork internals and linked anti-dive unit –
UK models and US ED, ESD, ESE and ES3 models**

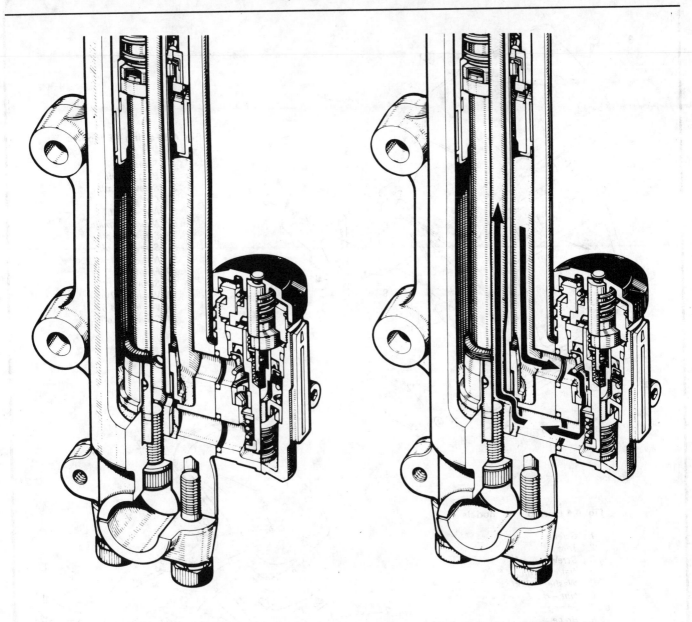

Fig. 4.2 Front fork anti-dive system (Suzuki Posi-damp) operation – US EF and ESF models

2 Fairing: removal and replacement

1   All models except the L (custom) versions are fitted with a fairing. In the case of the 'E' models, this is a small handlebar fairing. The ES variants have a slightly larger half fairing with short lower sections, whilst the EF version has a full length fairing with the lower sections extending under the bottom of the crankcase. In all cases it is best to remove the fairing component parts completely before attempting any front suspension work. This will provide much better access and will avoid any risk of damage to the fairing.

Handlebar fairing – E models
2   Remove the single screw on each side of the fairing, followed by the two screws which pass up through the fairing just below the headlamp unit. The fairing can now be lifted away.

Half fairing – ES models
3   Remove the short lower sections on each side of the upper half of the fairing. These are secured by short pegs which push through rubber bushed eyes. Pull each peg out of its rubber bush taking care not to strain it or the surrounding material. Trace the turn signal wiring under the front lip of the fairing and disconnect it. Remove the turn signal lamp mounting screws; these are reached through holes in the underside of the fairing. Lift the lamps clear of the fairing and place them to one side. Remove the two screws which secure the fairing sides to the frame, followed by the two screws below the front edge of the fairing. The fairing upper half can now be lifted forward and clear of the mounting frame.

Full fairing – EF models
4   Release the lower cover after slackening the two screws below the upper frame section. Remove the two cross-headed screws which secure each lower section to the fairing upper half, then remove either one of the two screws which secure the lower sections to the bottom joining bracket below the front of the crankcase. Turn the slotted-head Dzus-type fasteners (3 on each side) through 90° to free the lower sections and lift them away from the frame.
5   The upper part of the fairing can now be removed in the same way as has been described above for the half fairing type. When refitting the lower sections, note that all screws should be fitted loosely and the Dzus-type fasteners secured. The screws can then be tightened.

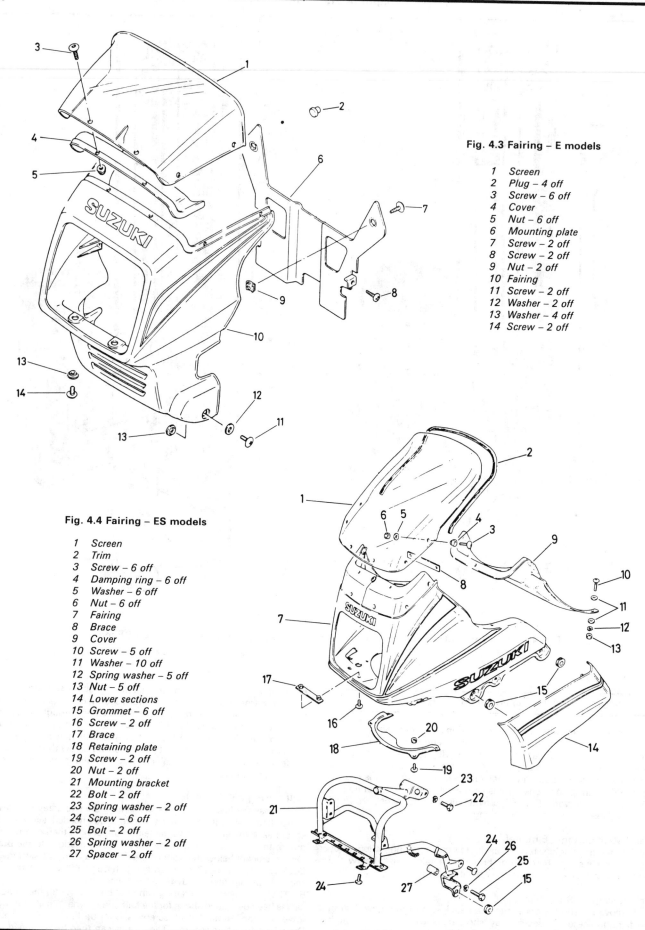

Fig. 4.3 Fairing – E models

1 Screen
2 Plug – 4 off
3 Screw – 6 off
4 Cover
5 Nut – 6 off
6 Mounting plate
7 Screw – 2 off
8 Screw – 2 off
9 Nut – 2 off
10 Fairing
11 Screw – 2 off
12 Washer – 2 off
13 Washer – 4 off
14 Screw – 2 off

Fig. 4.4 Fairing – ES models

1 Screen
2 Trim
3 Screw – 6 off
4 Damping ring – 6 off
5 Washer – 6 off
6 Nut – 6 off
7 Fairing
8 Brace
9 Cover
10 Screw – 5 off
11 Washer – 10 off
12 Spring washer – 5 off
13 Nut – 5 off
14 Lower sections
15 Grommet – 6 off
16 Screw – 2 off
17 Brace
18 Retaining plate
19 Screw – 2 off
20 Nut – 2 off
21 Mounting bracket
22 Bolt – 2 off
23 Spring washer – 2 off
24 Screw – 6 off
25 Bolt – 2 off
26 Spring washer – 2 off
27 Spacer – 2 off

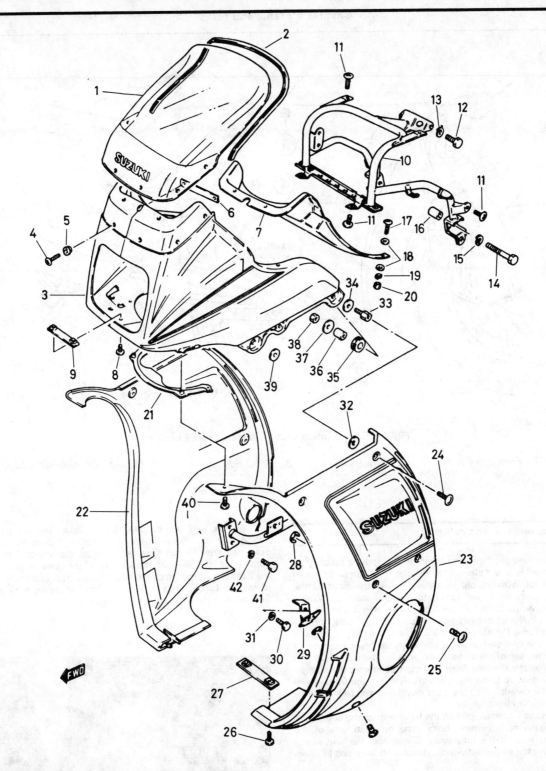

Fig. 4.5 Fairing – EF model

1	Screen	12	Bolt – 2 off
2	Trim	13	Spring washer – 2 off
3	Fairing	14	Bolt – 2 off
4	Screw – 6 off	15	Spring washer – 2 off
5	Damping ring – 6 off	16	Spacer – 2 off
6	Brace	17	Screw – 5 off
7	Cover	18	Washer – 5 off
8	Screw – 2 off	19	Spring washer – 5 off
9	Brace	20	Nut – 5 off
10	Mounting bracket	21	Retaining plate
11	Screw – 6 off	22	Right-hand lower section

23	Left-hand lower section	33	Mounting bolt – 4 off
24	Screw – 4 off	34	Washer – 4 off
25	Dzus-type fastener – 6 off	35	Grommet – 6 off
26	Bolt – 2 off	36	Spacer – 4 off
27	Brace	37	Washer – 4 off
28	E-clip – 3 off	38	Nut – 4 off
29	Bracket	39	Washer – 2 off
30	Bolt – 2 off	40	Screw – 2 off
31	Spring washer – 2 off	41	Bolt – 4 off
32	Washer – 4 off	42	Spring washer – 4 off

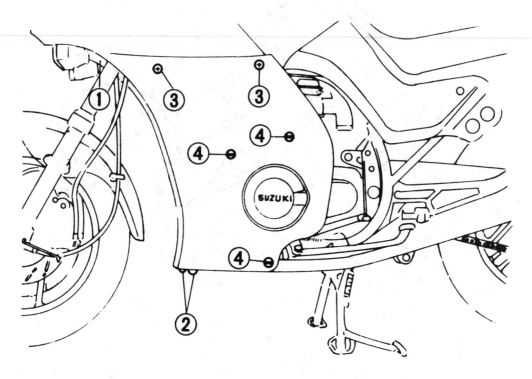

Fig. 4.6 Fairing lower section fasteners – EF model

1   *Front upper screws*   2   *Lower screws*   3   *Upper side screws*   4   *Dzus-type fastener – 3 off*

3   Front forks: removal and refitting

1   Place the machine on the centre stand and support it securely so that the front wheel is raised clear of the ground. This can be achieved by using a jack or wooden blocks placed below the front of the crankcase but care must be taken to ensure stability. Where appropriate, remove the fairing as described in Section 2 above.
2   Release both brake calipers (single caliper, on L models) and tie them clear of the forks. Do not allow the weight of the calipers to hang from the hoses, and take care to avoid operating the brake lever whilst they are off. In the case of machines fitted with hydraulically operated anti-dive units, remove the two Allen screws which retain the plunger units to the anti-dive units on the fork legs. Remove the front wheel (See Chapter 5 for details). Free the front mudguard and fork brace by removing the retaining bolts.
3   In the case of the E models, pull off the headlamp wiring connector, free the two headlamp mounting bolts (one on each side of the mounting frame) and lift the unit away. Disconnect the turn signal leads, then remove the single nut which retains each lamp and lift them away.
4   On L models, remove the two screws which retain the headlamp unit in the shell, disconnect the wiring connector and place the unit to one side. Push the wiring out through the holes in the back of the shell, remove the shell mounting bolts and lift it clear. Disconnect the turn signal wiring and remove the lamps from the headlamp brackets.
5   Slacken the upper and lower yoke clamp bolts and withdraw the fork legs by pulling them downwards. To facilitate removal, twist the stanchions to and fro. In the case of L models, the lower clamp bolts may be obstructed by the side marker reflectors; unscrew them if necessary.
6   In the case of all but the L models, if the fork legs are to be dismantled, leave them partly in position through the lower yoke and temporarily retighten the pinch bolts. Held in this way, it is relatively easy to slacken the fork cap bolts by one or two turns, making subsequent removal much easier.

7   The fork legs are installed by reversing the removal sequence noting that the oil level should be checked prior to installation as described later in this Chapter. Position the stanchions so that the upper edge is in line with the top face of the upper yoke. In the case of the L models, once the clamp bolts are secured, and before any weight is applied to the forks, check the fork air pressure as described in Section 9.

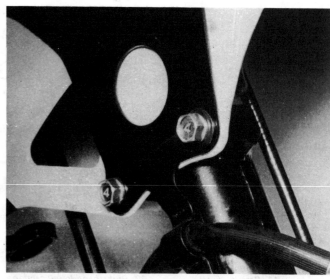

3.2a Mudguard and fork brace are retained by four bolts. Note hydraulic hose guide (anti-dive models)

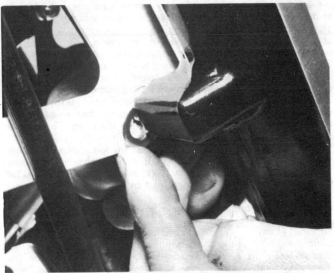

3.2b Take care not to lose headed spacers – they prevent damage to the plastic mudguard

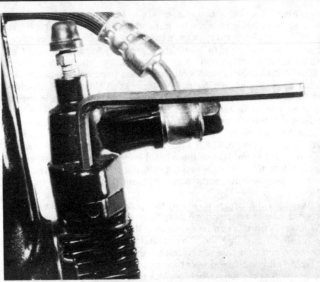

3.2c On machines with linked anti-dive, remove the two Allen bolts which retain each modulator to the fork leg

3.5a Slacken the single upper pinch bolt ...

3.5b ... and the two lower pinch bolts to free the fork leg

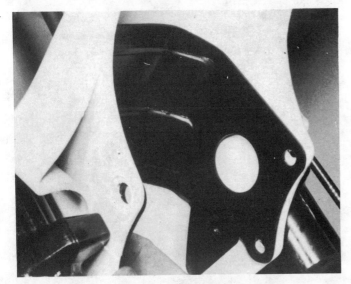

3.7 Remember to fit fork brace when refitting mudguard

4 Front forks: dismantling and reassembly – UK models and US ED, ESD, ESE and ES3 models

1 Dealing with one fork leg at a time to avoid interchanging the internal components, unscrew and remove the fork top bolt. Note that where air valves are fitted, fork air pressure should first be released by depressing the valve core. Remove the fork spring, then invert the leg and 'pump' it to expel the damping oil. Leave the leg inverted for a while to allow residual oil to escape.

2 To separate the stanchion and lower leg it is necessary to release the damper bolt from the underside of the lower leg. This screws into the damper rod which is free to rotate in the stanchion, and it will be necessary to hold the rod to prevent it from turning.

3 Suzuki produce a T-handle (Part number 09940-34520) and an adaptor (Part number 09940-34561) which locates in the head of the damper rod. In most cases an improvised holding tool can be made by grinding a coarse taper at the end of a length of wooden dowel. This can then be held with a self-locking wrench and pushed hard against the damper rod whilst the bolt is unscrewed. Alternatives to this method are to grind a pointed end on a length of square section bar or to make up the nut and bolt arrangement shown in the accompanying

photograph. The latter consists of a nut (22 mm across the flats) clamped firmly between a smaller nut and bolt. The bolt head can then be held in a socket fitted with the necessary extension bars. Note that a 22 mm socket will not fit inside the stanchion, hence the use of the smaller nut and bolt shown.

4 Once the damper rod bolt has been removed, separate the stanchion and lower leg by pulling them apart. Invert the stanchion and tip out the damper rod and the rebound spring, then invert the lower leg and tip out the damper rod seat.

5 Suzuki recommend that the fork oil seal and both fork bushes are renewed each time the fork leg is dismantled. The split lower bush can be slid off the stanchion after it has been spread, using a screwdriver to open the split seam. To free the oil seal and the top bush first remove the dust seal, the wire retaining clip and the plain washer. The oil seal can now be prised out, and the second plain washer and the top bush removed.

6 Assemble the leg by reversing the dismantling sequence, having first ensured that all components are clean and dust free. When fitting a new lower bush this can be eased over the end of the stanchion and then pushed home by hand. Do not stretch the bush any more than is necessary, and take care not to scratch the Teflon-coated surface.

7 Fit the rebound spring over the damper rod and slide the assembly into position in the fork stanchion. Use the holding tool to ensure that the damper rod does not get pushed back up into the stanchion. Fit a

wave washer, the plain washer and a second wave washer to the end of the damper rod, then fit the damper rod seat (oil lock piece) with the taper facing towards the stanchion. This arrangement is shown in the accompanying photograph. Invert the stanchion and damper rod assembly and slide the lower leg down over it.

8 The theads of the damper bolt must be clean and dry and should be coated with a thread locking compound. Tighten the bolt to the specified torque figure. Slide the top bush down over the stanchion, again taking care not to damage the Teflon-coated surface. Fit the plain washer, oil seal and the second plain washer, then use a length of tubing to tap them home in the top of the lower leg. Fit the wire retaining clip and press the dust seal into position.

9 Before fitting the fork spring, compress the fork fully and add the prescribed quantity of fork oil, Check that the oil level is the correct distance below the top of the stanchion (refer to the Specifications for details). This check should be made with the fork held vertical, using a dip stick marked to the correct level, or a steel ruler as shown in the accompanying photograph. Add or remove oil to bring it to the correct level.

10 When fitting the fork spring, note that the closer pitched coils must be uppermost. Fit the top bolt, leaving final tightening until the fork has been refitted in the lower yoke and temporarily clamped in place. On those models fitted with air pressure valves in the top bolts, check and set the air pressure as described later in this Chapter.

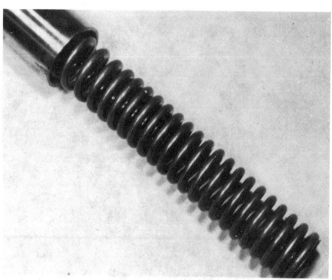
4.1 Note fork spring has tighter coils towards top (except L models – see text)

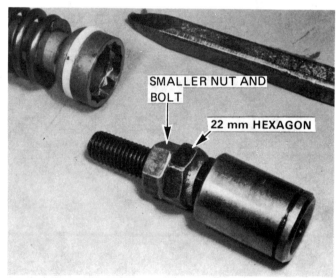
4.3a Two methods of holding the damper rod whilst bolt is removed

4.3b Lock damper rod, then remove Allen bolt in base of leg

4.7a Fit rebound spring over damper rod and install in stanchion

PLAIN WASHER

WAVE WASHER

4.7b Note arrangement of washers at base of damper rod

4.8a Fit top bush, plain washer and oil seal ...

4.8b ... followed by second plain washer and retaining clip

4.8c Finally, fit a new dust seal as shown

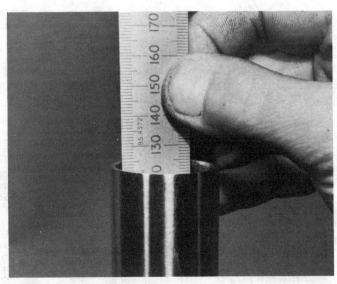

4.9 Check the fork oil level using steel rule

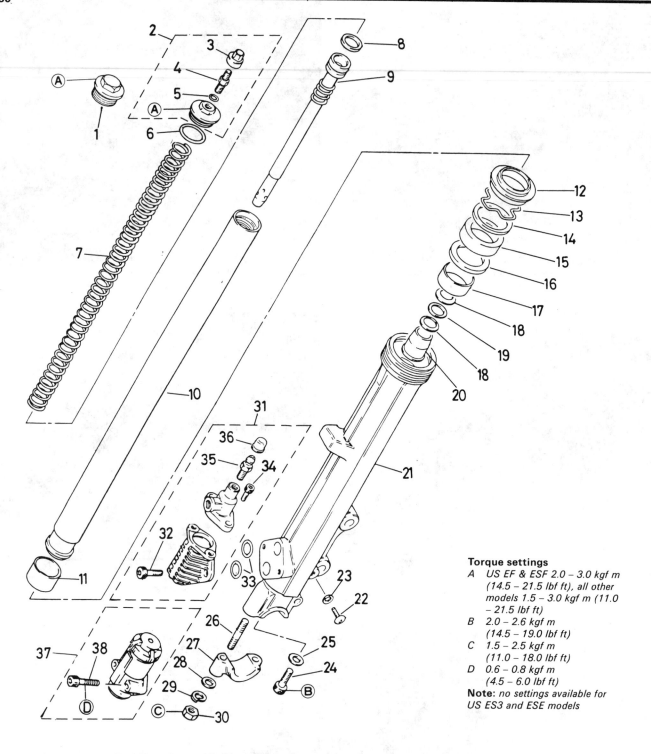

Torque settings

A   US EF & ESF 2.0 – 3.0 kgf m
(14.5 – 21.5 lbf ft), all other
models 1.5 – 3.0 kgf m (11.0
– 21.5 lbf ft)

B   2.0 – 2.6 kgf m
(14.5 – 19.0 lbf ft)

C   1.5 – 2.5 kgf m
(11.0 – 18.0 lbf ft)

D   0.6 – 0.8 kgf m
(4.5 – 6.0 lbf ft)

Note: no settings available for
US ES3 and ESE models

Fig. 4.7 Front forks – GS/GSX550 ED, EE, EF, ESD, ESE, ES3, ESF and EFE models

1   Top bolt – UK
2   Top bolt – US
3   Cap
4   Air valve
5   O-ring
6   O-ring
7   Fork spring
8   Damper rod piston ring
9   Damper rod and rebound
spring
10 Stanchion

11 Bottom bush
12 Dust seal
13 Retaining clip
14 Washer
15 Oil seal
16 Washer
17 Top bush
18 Wave washer – 2 off
19 Washer
20 Damper rod seat

21 Lower leg
22 Drain screw
23 Sealing washer
24 Allen bolt
25 Sealing washer
26 Stud – 2 off
27 Clamp
28 Washer – 2 off
29 Spring washer – 2 off
30 Nut – 2 off

31 Anti-dive modulator – All UK
models and US ED, ESD,
ESE, ES3
32 Allen bolt – 2 off
33 O-ring – 2 off
34 Allen bolt – 2 off
35 Bleed valve
36 Cap
37 Anti-dive modulator – US EF,
ESF models
38 Allen bolt – 2 off

5 Front forks: dismantling and reassembly – US L models

1 The dismantling and reassembly procedure is generally similar to that described in the previous Section. The forks used on the L models differ in certain respects, however, and the following points should be noted. Start by removing the air valve dust cap and releasing air pressure by depressing the valve core. The fork spring is held by a plug which is retained by a wire circlip. To free the plug, push it downwards against spring pressure and prise out the clip. This can be done using a length of tubing fitted over the air valve. Once removed, the clip should be discarded and a new one fitted during reassembly.

2 Invert the fork and allow the damping oil to drain, 'pumping' the fork to help force out the oil. Prise out the dust seal, then remove the circlip which retains the fork oil seal. Remove the damper rod bolt as described in the previous section, using the same method to prevent the rod from turning as the bolt is unscrewed. Note that the damper rod seat is similar in design but is not fitted with the two wave washers and the single plain washer.

3 When reassembling the fork, note that new top and bottom bushes and a new oil seal and dust seal should be fitted. These can be dealt with in the same way as has been described in the previous Section, noting that the oil seal has no upper washer, and that a lipped seat fits between the seal and top bush. Take care not to damage the Teflon surface of the two bushes when fitting them.

4 When refitting the top plug, fit the spring with the tapered end downwards, and on LD models only fit the spring seat and spacer. Fit and compress the plug to allow a new wire circlip to be installed. Make sure that this fits into its groove correctly. When fitting the leg into the yokes, align the top edge of the stanchion with the top surface of the handlebar holder. Set the air pressure as described later in this Chapter before the dust caps are refitted.

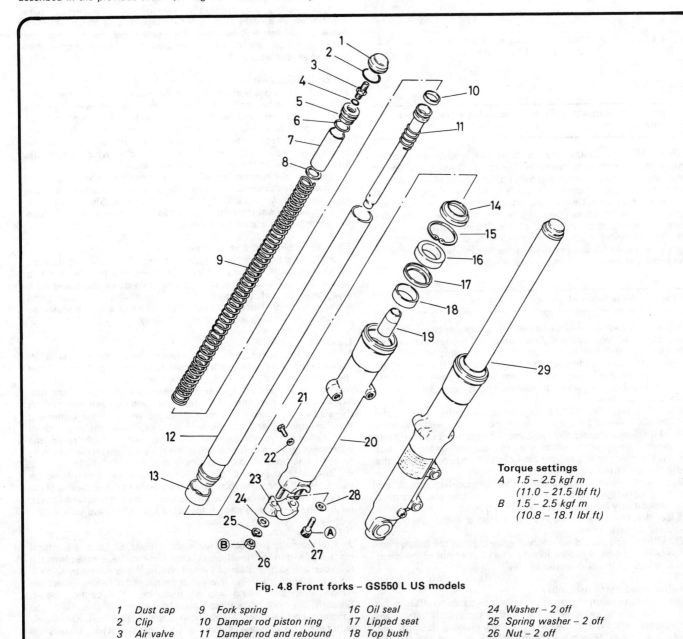

Fig. 4.8 Front forks – GS550 L US models

1 Dust cap	9 Fork spring	16 Oil seal	24 Washer – 2 off
2 Clip	10 Damper rod piston ring	17 Lipped seat	25 Spring washer – 2 off
3 Air valve	11 Damper rod and rebound spring	18 Top bush	26 Nut – 2 off
4 O-ring	12 Stanchion	19 Damper rod seat	27 Allen bolt
5 Top plug	13 Bottom bush	20 Lower leg – right-hand	28 Sealing washer
6 O-ring	14 Dust seal	21 Drain bolt	29 Left-hand fork leg
7 Spacer*	15 Circlip	22 Sealing washer	
8 Spring seat*		23 Clamp	* LD model only

Torque settings
A 1.5 – 2.5 kgf m (11.0 – 21.5 lbf ft)
B 1.5 – 2.5 kgf m (10.8 – 18.1 lbf ft)

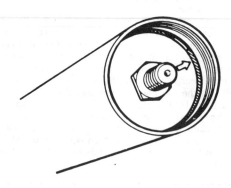

Fig. 4.9 Correct installation of wire circlip retaining fork top plug – GS550 L models

6 Front forks: dismantling and reassembly – US EF and ESF models

1 The forks used on the 1985 EF and ESF models are virtually identical to those fitted to the earlier ED and ESD machines, and in general the procedure described in Section 4 can be applied. The main change on the later machines is the use of 'Posi-Damp', a front suspension anti-dive system which, unlike the earlier version, is not connected to the front brake hydraulic system. Both types of anti-dive system are described in Section 7 of this Chapter. One other point worth noting is that a different adaptor needs to be used with the T-handle to prevent the damper rod from turning when the bolt is unscrewed. The new part number is 09940-34581.

7 Front forks: examination and renovation

1 Inspect the sliding surfaces of the fork components for signs of wear or damage. Wear of the sliding surfaces of the top and bottom bushes is easily dealt with by renewing the affected parts, and it should be noted that Suzuki recommend the renewal of both bushes and the fork oil seals whenever the legs are dismantled. In cases where the stanchion has become worn or damaged, this must be renewed together with the bushes.
2 Check the stanchion surface for scoring, particularly around the area normally covered by the dust seal. Scoring here will invariably cause oil leakage and rapid seal wear, and if found the stanchion must be renewed. Damage of this nature is usually found when the fork dust seals have worn or split, allowing road dirt to be trapped against the moving surface of the stanchion.
3 If the forks have been stripped after an accident, check the stanchions for straightness by rolling them on a flat surface. If damage is very slight it may be possible to have them trued by a specialist with press facilities, but it is preferable to renew them to avoid any risk of a subsequent stress fracture.
4 The damper rod should be cleaned, ensuring that the oilways are clear. Any residual oil or sediment should be cleaned out of the lower leg and the stanchion prior to reassembly.

Anti-dive modulator assembly
5 The modulator assembly serves to control the damping effect in the forks in response to pressure in the front brake system, effectively modifying the behaviour of the forks to reduce pitching (diving). The modulator unit can be removed from the fork leg and the O-rings renewed in the event of oil leaks, but if defective it must be renewed as a unit, replacement parts not being available separately.

Posi-damp unit (1985 EF and ESF models)
6 This arrangement performs a similar function to the anti-dive system described above, but is not connected to the front brake

hydraulic system. Under most normal road conditions the device allows the forks to operate with little damping effect, giving smooth and compliant fork action. Under abrupt or heavy loadings, however, the sudden increase of pressure closes a valve in the unit, giving significantly increased damping effect. This allows the forks to cope with sudden or unusual loading (including heavy braking loads) which might otherwise cause the forks to 'bottom'. Like the earlier anti-dive unit, little can be done in the event of leakage or failure of the unit unless the fault is attributable to the O-rings between the unit and the fork leg. If this fails to cure the problem, the unit must be renewed.
7 Refer to Section 9 for details of adjustment.

8 Steering head assembly: overhauling and adjustment

1 It is not normally necessary to dismantle the steering head assembly unless the taper roller steering head bearings require attention or as a result of accident damage. On all models, start by removing the seat and fuel tank, the front wheel, the fork legs and where applicable, the fairing, as described earlier in this Chapter, then proceed as follows.

ED and EF models
2 If it is still in position, disconnect the headlamp wiring connector, then remove the two bolts which secure the headlamp assembly to the headlamp brackets and lift it away. Separate the instrument panel wiring connectors, manoeuvre the wiring clear of the fork yokes. Unscrew the tachometer drive cable from the underside of the instrument head, then release the two bolts which retain the instrument panel to the top yoke and lift it away.
3 Separate the ignition switch wiring connector, then remove the two 5 mm Allen screws which retain the switch to the underside of the top yoke. Remove the switch and place it to one side. Prise off the rectangular cover at the centre of the top yoke cover, remove the two mounting screws and lift the cover away.

ESD, ESE, ES3 and ESF models
4 Pull off the headlamp wiring connector and free the wiring from the cable clips on the fairing subframe. Remove the four bolts which secure the subframe to the steering head and down tubes and lift it away together with the headlamp. Disconnect the instrument panel wiring connector, then remove the two bolts which secure the panel to the underside of the top yoke and lift it away.

L models
5 Remove the two screws which retain the headlamp to its shell, lift the unit clear and disconnect the headlamp wiring. Push the wiring out through the holes in the back of the shell, then remove the shell mounting bolts and lift it clear of the brackets. Disconnect the turn signal wiring, remove the single nut which retains each one, and lift them away. Trace back and disconnect the wiring to the instrument panel assembly. Free the tachometer drive cable from the underside of the instrument head. Remove the two bolts which retain the instrument heads to the underside of the top yoke and lift them away as an assembly. Unscrew the reflectors from the sides of the lower yoke.
6 Disconnect the ignition switch wiring connector, then remove the two 5 mm Allen screws which retain the switch to the underside of the top yoke and lift it away. Prise off the two caps on the top yoke cover, remove the two screws and lift the cover clear of the top yoke.

All models
7 It is normally possible to leave the various cables and electrical leads attached to the handlebars. These can then be released from the top yoke and lodged clear of the fork yokes. If it is necessary to clear the area around the yokes it will first be necessary to disconnect the handlebar switch wiring and to disconnect the control cables. Similarly, the front brake master cylinder can be left attached to the handlebar end, provided that the hose guide clips are freed. On models with twin front disc brakes, remove the single bolt which secures the hose union block to the underside of the top yoke.
8 Remove the handlebar holders from the top yoke by unscrewing the Allen bolts which retain them. Lift each handlebar assembly clear of the yoke and lodge or tie it clear. Where cables or wiring run between the two yokes, make a note of their positions as a guide during reassembly. Check that no remaining wiring or cables are held by clips to either yoke.

9 Slacken the top yoke clamp bolt and remove the steering stem top bolt. Using a hide mallet, tap the top yoke upwards and lift it away from the steering stem.

10 Using a special tool, Part number 09940-14911, or a C-spanner, slacken the steering stem adjuster nut. Support the lower yoke, then remove the adjuster nut and lift the yoke clear of the frame. Lift out the upper race and wipe off any grease from the bearings and races.

11 The tapered roller steering head bearings will not normally wear quickly, but should be checked closely for indications of wear or damage. If there is any sign of ridging or indentation of the rollers or races, the bearings must be renewed as a pair. Unless the bearings are to be renewed they should not be disturbed.

12 The bearing outer races can be driven out using a long drift passed through the steering head, working around the race to keep it square to the recess. Fit the new race using a stepped drift or a drawbolt arrangement, again ensuring that the race is kept square to the sides of the recess.

13 The lower bearing inner race can be drawn off the steering stem with a bearing extractor. In the absence of the relevant Suzuki tool, Part

numbers 09941-54911 and 09941-74910, many tool hire shops will be able to provide a suitable item.

14 Fit the new outer races using a drawbolt arrangement as shown in the accompanying line drawing. Tap the lower bearing inner race into position using a tubular drift, and grease both bearings prior to installation.

15 Assemble the steering head by reversing the dismantling sequence. Where the special peg socket is available, tighten the steering stem adjuster to 4.0 – 5.0 kgf m (29.0 – 36.0 lbf ft). Note that if a C-spanner is being used, this setting will have to be approximated. Turn the steering stem from lock to lock several times to seat the bearings, then back off the adjuster by a half turn. When working without a torque wrench, note that the purpose of the adjustment is to leave just a light loading on the bearings to eliminate any free play. It is easy to overload the bearings, and this will result in rapid wear and poor steering reponse.

16 Continue reassembly, remembering to route the various cables and wiring between the two yokes. Tighten the various fasteners to the correct torque figures, and check the action of the steering and front suspension before taking the machine on the road.

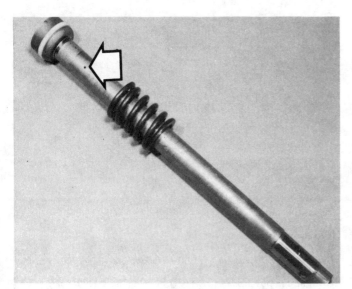

7.4 Check that small hole in damper rod is clear

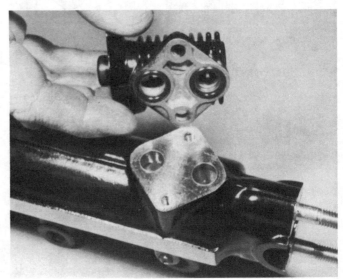

7.5a Anti-dive unit is held by two Allen bolts to fork leg

7.5b Renew O-rings if damaged, but do not attempt to dismantle the unit

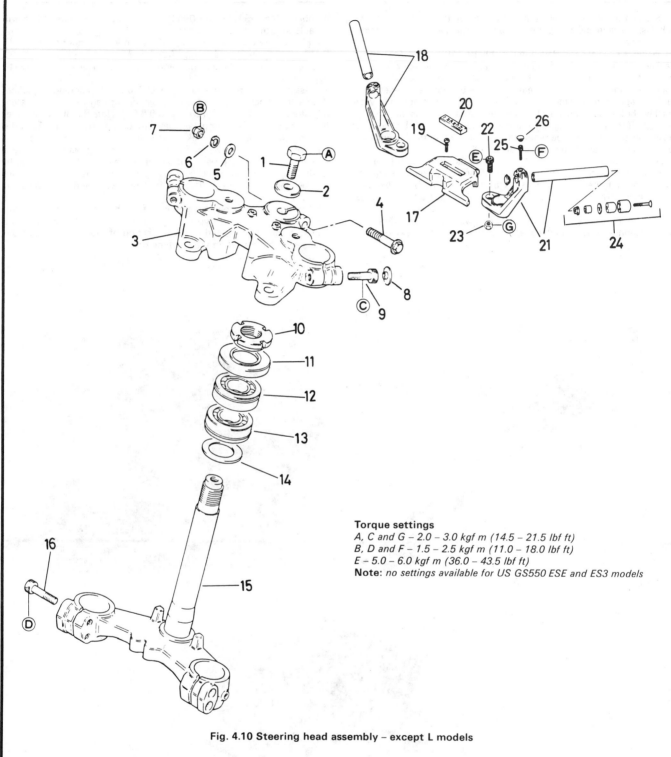

Torque settings
A, C and G – 2.0 – 3.0 kgf m (14.5 – 21.5 lbf ft)
B, D and F – 1.5 – 2.5 kgf m (11.0 – 18.0 lbf ft)
E – 5.0 – 6.0 kgf m (36.0 – 43.5 lbf ft)
Note: *no settings available for US GS550 ESE and ES3 models*

Fig. 4.10 Steering head assembly – except L models

1 Top bolt
2 Washer
3 Top yoke
4 Clamp bolt
5 Washer
6 Spring washer
7 Nut
8 Cap – 2 off
9 Allen bolt – 2 off
10 Adjuster nut
11 Dust cover
12 Upper bearing
13 Lower bearing
14 Washer – where fitted
15 Lower yoke/steering stem
16 Allen bolt – 4 off
17 Cover
18 Right-hand handlebar
19 Screw – 2 off
20 Cover/emblem
21 Left-hand handlebar
22 Allen bolt – 2 off
23 Nut – 2 off
24 Handlebar end assembly
25 Bolt – 2 off
26 Cap – 2 off

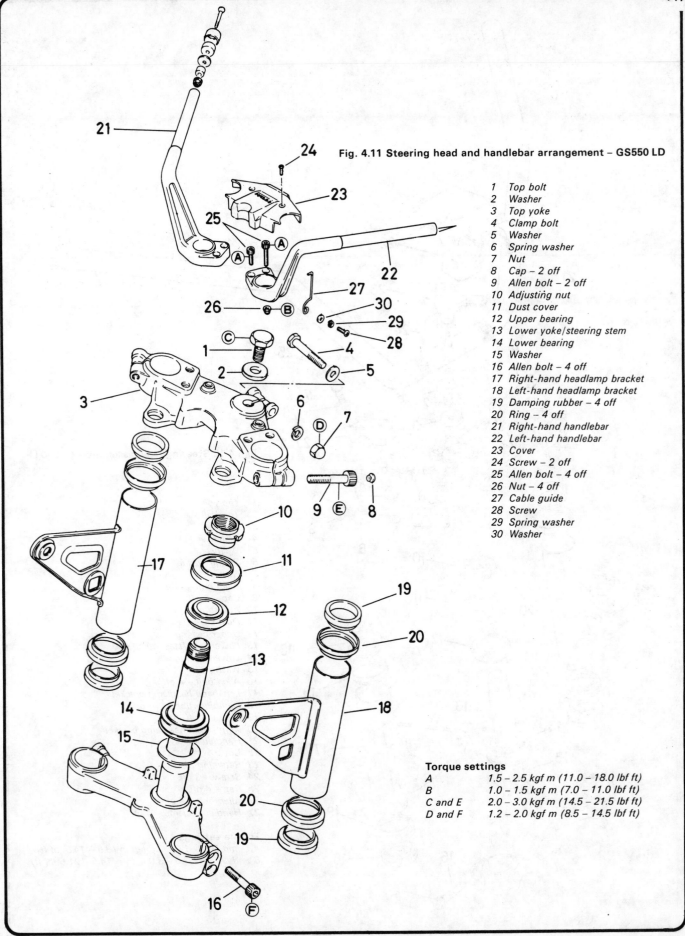

Fig. 4.11 Steering head and handlebar arrangement – GS550 LD

1 Top bolt
2 Washer
3 Top yoke
4 Clamp bolt
5 Washer
6 Spring washer
7 Nut
8 Cap – 2 off
9 Allen bolt – 2 off
10 Adjusting nut
11 Dust cover
12 Upper bearing
13 Lower yoke/steering stem
14 Lower bearing
15 Washer
16 Allen bolt – 4 off
17 Right-hand headlamp bracket
18 Left-hand headlamp bracket
19 Damping rubber – 4 off
20 Ring – 4 off
21 Right-hand handlebar
22 Left-hand handlebar
23 Cover
24 Screw – 2 off
25 Allen bolt – 4 off
26 Nut – 4 off
27 Cable guide
28 Screw
29 Spring washer
30 Washer

Torque settings

A	1.5 – 2.5 kgf m (11.0 – 18.0 lbf ft)
B	1.0 – 1.5 kgf m (7.0 – 11.0 lbf ft)
C and E	2.0 – 3.0 kgf m (14.5 – 21.5 lbf ft)
D and F	1.2 – 2.0 kgf m (8.5 – 14.5 lbf ft)

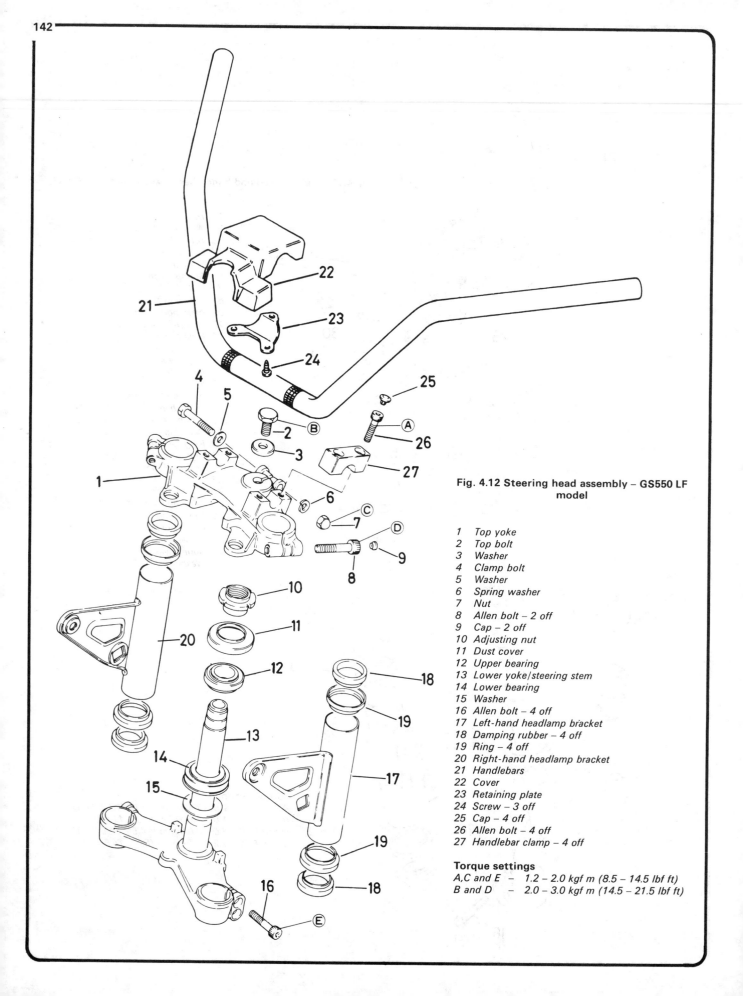

Fig. 4.12 Steering head assembly – GS550 LF model

1 Top yoke
2 Top bolt
3 Washer
4 Clamp bolt
5 Washer
6 Spring washer
7 Nut
8 Allen bolt – 2 off
9 Cap – 2 off
10 Adjusting nut
11 Dust cover
12 Upper bearing
13 Lower yoke/steering stem
14 Lower bearing
15 Washer
16 Allen bolt – 4 off
17 Left-hand headlamp bracket
18 Damping rubber – 4 off
19 Ring – 4 off
20 Right-hand headlamp bracket
21 Handlebars
22 Cover
23 Retaining plate
24 Screw – 3 off
25 Cap – 4 off
26 Allen bolt – 4 off
27 Handlebar clamp – 4 off

Torque settings
A,C and E – 1.2 – 2.0 kgf m (8.5 – 14.5 lbf ft)
B and D – 2.0 – 3.0 kgf m (14.5 – 21.5 lbf ft)

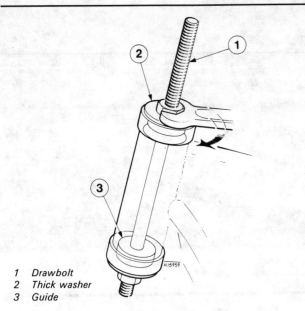

1 Drawbolt
2 Thick washer
3 Guide

Fig. 4.13 Drawbolt arrangement for removing and refitting steering head bearings

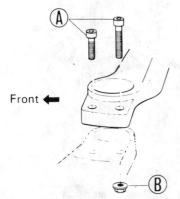

Fig. 4.14 Location of handlebar retaining bolts

A Bolt – note different lengths – torque to 1.5 – 2.5 kgf m (11 – 18 lbf ft)
B Locknut – torque to 1.0 – 1.5 kgf m (7 – 11 lbf ft)

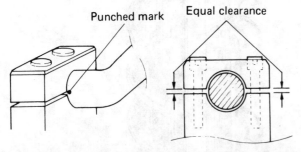

Fig. 4.15 Correct fitting of handlebar clamps – GS550 LF

9 Front fork adjustment: US models

Air pressure

1   Before attempting to adjust the front fork air pressure it is important that the general condition of the fork is sound and that the oil level is set correctly. If the oil level is incorrect or unequal in the two legs, any air pressure setting will be correspondingly unbalanced. If the oil has not been changed for some time this should be carried out before any further adjustment is attempted. To ensure accuracy, remove the fork legs, drain the oil and add oil to the level indicated in the specifications

section. For details refer to the preceding Sections.
2   The total volume of each fork leg is small, and in consequence accurate setting of the fork air pressure will require the use of a hand pump and gauge designed for this purpose. It is particularly important to note that it is not possible to use an air line without risk of applying excessive pressure, with the possibility of seal damage, and that a tyre pressure gauge is likely to waste so much pressure in taking a reading that the resulting fork pressure will not be accurately predictable.
3   Suzuki Service Agents should be able to order an official Suzuki fork pressure gauge and pump assembly. An alternative available through most large dealers, is the S&W equivalent. Both are designed to give an accurate indication of air pressure without losing a significant proportion of the air when the gauge is released.
4   Before attempting adjustment, place the machine on its centre stand and then raise the front wheel clear of the ground using wooden blocks or a jack placed below the crankcase. Make sure that the machine is secure and in no danger of toppling over. Remove the air valve dust cap and assemble the gauge and pump as indicated in the manufacturer's instructions. Pressurise the forks, taking care not to exceed the maximum safe pressure of 35.0 psi (2.5 kg/cm²) at any time. The standard air pressure for all US models is 0.3 kg/cm² (4.2 psi). Gradually release the air until the correct pressure is indicated. Remove the gauge assembly, losing as little pressure as is possible. Repeat the sequence on the remaining fork leg, noting that it is essential that each leg is set at the same pressure. Remember to refit the dust cap(s) after adjustment.

Posi-damp unit

5   The Posi-damp unit has four settings, designed to vary the duration of the damping effect. The standard setting is position 3, but this may be altered to suit the rider's needs; position 4 will bring the unit into operation earlier whereas positions 2 or 1 will have the opposite effect. To alter the setting, depress the top of the unit and turn the adjuster until the number required is positioned at the front of the unit; ensure that it locates in the detent provided. Always set the adjuster to the same position on each leg otherwise uneven damping and poor roadholding will result.

10 Frame: examination and renovation

1   The frame is unlikely to require attention unless accident damage has occurred. In some cases, renewal of the frame is the only satisfactory remedy if the frame is badly out of alignment. Only a few frame specialists have the jigs and mandrels necessary for resetting the frame to the required standard of accuracy, and even then there is no easy means of assessing to what extent the frame may have been overstressed.
2   After the machine has covered a considerable mileage, it is advisable to examine the frame closely for signs of cracking or splitting at the welded joints. Rust corrosion can also cause weakness at these joints. Minor damage can be repaired by welding or brazing, depending on the extent and nature of the damage.
3   Remember that a frame which is out of alignment will cause handling problems and may even promote 'speed wobbles'. If misalignment is suspected, as a result of an accident, it will be necessary to strip the machine completely so that the frame can be checked, and if necessary, renewed.

11 Rear suspension overhaul: general information

1   Rear suspension on all models is by Suzuki's fully floating arrangement; a cantilever rising rate design controlled by a single central suspension unit. Under most circumstances it will be necessary to remove either the swinging arm unit alone, or the complete rear suspension linkage. In the latter case the swinging arm is usually removed first, though it is possible to remove the complete assembly. In the interests of clarity, the two operations are described separately, but owners may wish to adapt the procedures to suit particular jobs, and the best approach to a particular task can best be gauged after examining the assembled linkage.

11.1a Rear suspension assembly can be removed complete if necessary

11.1b The complete suspension linkage showing the various pivot points and central suspension unit

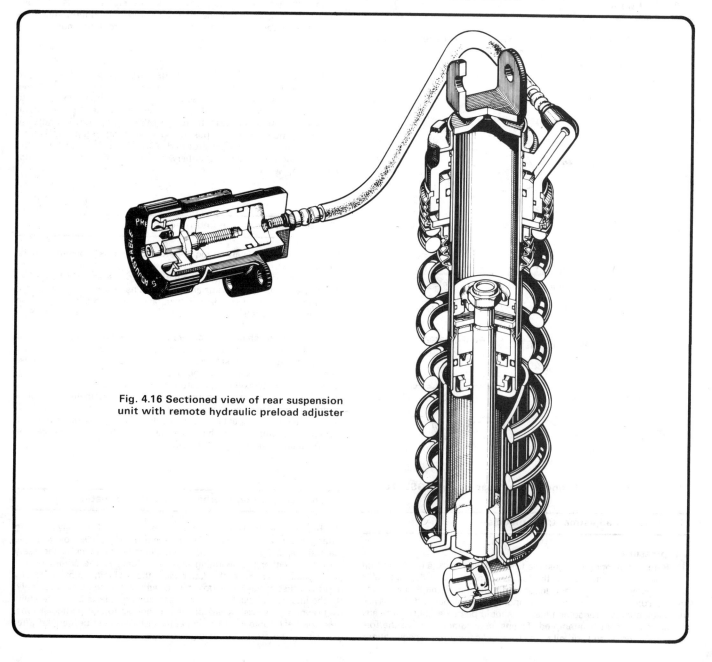

Fig. 4.16 Sectioned view of rear suspension unit with remote hydraulic preload adjuster

12 Swinging arm unit: removal and refitting

1   Place the machine securely on its centre stand. Unlock and remove the seat, then pull off the side panels. Referring to Chapter 5 where necessary, remove the rear wheel and place it to one side. Remove the two bolts which retain the chainguard and lift it away. Unscrew the three bolts which retain the front section of the rear mudguard and manoeuvre it clear of the frame.

2   Unscrew the rear brake hose union bolt and separate the hose from the caliper. Pump the brake pedal repeatedly to expel the hydraulic fluid into a suitable container. **Note:** Hydraulic fluid must not be allowed to come into contact with painted or plastic parts; these are quickly attacked by the fluid, and any accidental splashes should be washed off promptly with a water and detergent solution. Free the hose from the two guide clips on the top edge of the swinging arm, then feed it back through the torque arm bracket, lodging it clear of the swinging arm. Straighten and remove the split pin which secures the brake torque arm rear nut. Remove the nut and lift the caliper clear.

3   Free the suspension unit lower mounting by unscrewing the single bolt and nut. Free the 'cushion rod' (the short link between the suspension linkage bellcrank and the swinging arm) at its lower end. This too is retained by a single bolt and nut. Prise the swinging arm pivot end caps, then remove the pivot bolt nut. Pull out the pivot bolt, if necessary after tapping it through to start it. Take care not to damage the threads. As the bolt comes free, support the swinging arm, then lower it clear of the frame.

4   Before the swinging arm is refitted, check and renew or regrease the pivot bearings as described below. Grease and refit the bearing spacers and the dust seals. Offer up the swinging arm and refit the pivot bolt, tightening the nut to 5.5 – 8.8 kgf m (40.0 – 63.5 lbf ft). When refitting the brake hose, route it back through the torque arm bracket and guide clips. Fill the reservoir with new hydraulic fluid, then place the open end in a container and pump the pedal to fill the system. Reconnect the hose, using new sealing washers on the union bolt. Install the rear wheel and adjust the final drive chain. Bleed the hydraulic system (see Chapter 5) to remove any residual air.

12.1 Remove front section of mudguard to gain access to suspension components

12.2a Drain brake system and free hose from clips ...

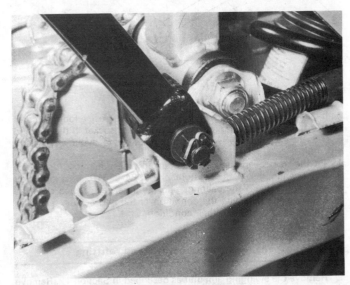

12.2b ... then pass hose through torque arm bracket

12.3 Remove pivot shaft to free the swinging arm

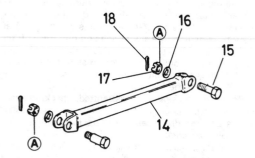

Fig. 4.17 Swinging arm

1	End cap	10	Nut
2	Pivot bolt	11	End cap
3	Dust seal – 2 off	12	Swinging arm
4	Bearing spacer – 2 off	13	Chain protector
5	Inner race – 2 off	14	Torque arm
6	Needle roller bearing – 2 off	15	Bolt – 2 off
7	Bearing spacer – 2 off	16	Spring washer – 2 off
8	Dust seal – 2 off	17	Nut – 2 off
9	Washer	18	Split pin – 2 off

Note: *On GS550 L models the bolts (item 15) pass through torque arm from the opposite side*

Torque settings
A – 2.0 – 3.0 kgf m (14.5 – 21.5 lbf ft)
B – 5.5 – 8.8 kgf m (40.0 – 63.5 lbf ft)
Note: *no settings available for US GS550 ESE and ES3 models*

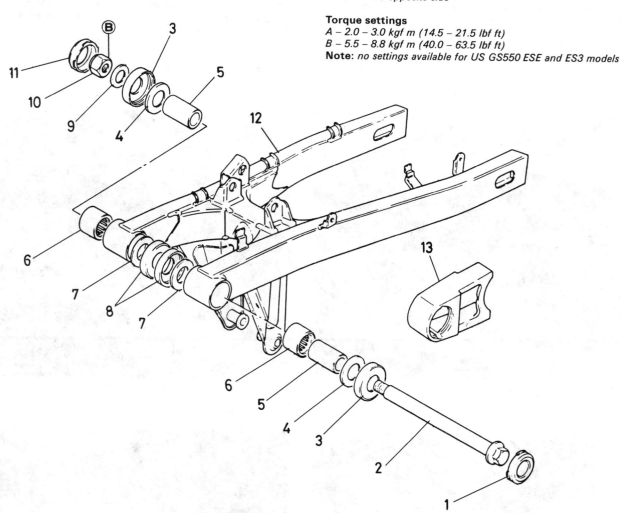

13 Swinging bearings: examination and renewal

1   Lift off the dust covers and then pull out the pivot bearing inner races. Wipe off any grease to allow inspection of the needle roller bearings and races. The outer surface of the inner races should be unmarked, with no sign of corrosion, scoring or indenting. If damage is noted, the bearings must be renewed.

2   Any excessive play noted during removal can be checked by temporarily refitting the inner races and rotating them by hand in the bearings. It is not practicable to assess wear by direct measurement, but if play or unevenness can be felt the bearings must be renewed.

3   It should be noted that the bearings will probably be destroyed during removal, so do not attempt this unless new ones are to hand. A bearing extractor will be required to draw out the old bearings, though

with care and patience it might just be possible to use a long thin drift passed through the swinging arm eye ends, or a socket. If this method is chosen, support the swinging arm securely to avoid any risk of distortion.

4   Fit the new bearings with the marked face outermost, using the Suzuki bearing installer, Part number 09924-84510, or a drawbolt arrangement. Grease the bearings and the inner races, then slide the latter into place. Examine the condition of the end covers, renewing them if in any doubt as to their condition.

14 Rear suspension linkage: removal and refitting

1   Remove the swinging arm unit as described in Section 12. Remove the two screws which retain the remote preload adjuster unit to the rear

left-hand engine mounting plate. Check that the adjuster unit can be passed between the frame members during removal; on the example shown in accompanying photographs it was necessary to remove the adjacent engine mounting bolt to provide clearance. **On no account** attempt to separate the adjuster from the suspension unit. If the hose connections are unscrewed, pressure will be lost and the assembly will have to be renewed.

2 Remove the suspension bellcrank ('cushion lever') pivot bolt and nut, leaving the suspension unit attached. The suspension linkage together with the suspension unit and adjuster can now be lifted away. The suspension mounting bracket will be left held in place by two bolts, and should not be removed unless it requires attention or removal.

3 Reassembly is a reversal of the removal sequence, noting the following points. If the bracket was removed for any reason, offer it up and locate it by temporarily refitting the swinging arm pivot shaft. Fit the two mounting bolts and tighten them securely. Check and renew the various linkage bushes and bearings as described below. Where spherical bearings are used apply molybdenum paste or grease to the bearings and seals, whilst on all other pivots use general purpose grease. Tighten the various fasteners according to the accompanying line drawing and table (Fig. 4.19).

13.1a End caps prevent dirt or water from entering bearings – renew if damaged

13.1b Central sleeve can be displaced ...

13.1c ... to allow bearing to be checked and lubricated

14.1 Rear engine mounting bolt must be removed to allow adjuster to pass through frame – DO NOT DISCONNECT HOSE

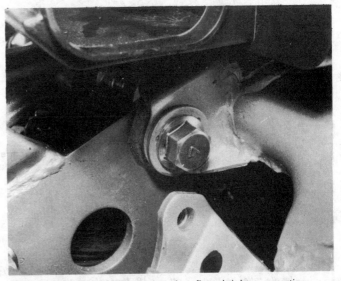

14.3 Fit pivot shaft to align bracket, then fit and tighten mounting bolts

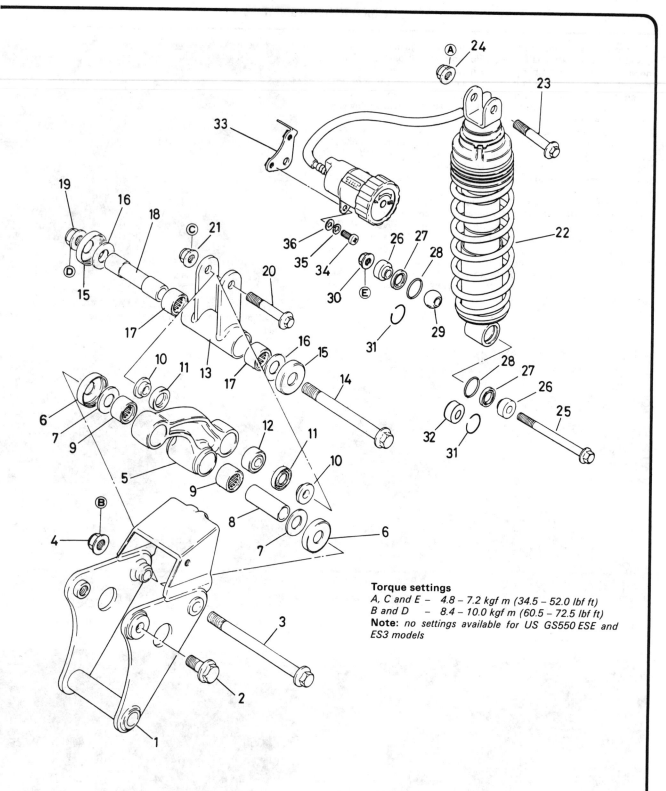

Fig. 4.18 Rear suspension unit and linkage

Torque settings
A, C and E – 4.8 – 7.2 kgf m (34.5 – 52.0 lbf ft)
B and D – 8.4 – 10.0 kgf m (60.5 – 72.5 lbf ft)
Note: no settings available for US GS550 ESE and ES3 models

1	Mounting bracket	10	Headed spacer – 4 off	19	Nut
2	Bolt – 2 off	11	Seal – 4 off	20	Bolt
3	Bolt	12	Bearing – 2 off	21	Nut
4	Nut	13	Cushion rod	22	Suspension unit and adjuster
5	Bellcrank	14	Bolt	23	Bolt
6	Dust cap – 2 off	15	Dust cap – 2 off	24	Nut
7	Washer – 2 off	16	Washer – 2 off	25	Bolt
8	Inner sleeve	17	Needle roller bearing – 2 off	26	Collar – 2 off
9	Needle roller bearing – 2 off	18	Inner sleeve	27	Seal – 2 off

28 O-ring – 2 off – E models
29 Bush – E models
30 Nut
31 Circlip – 2 off – L models
32 Bush – L models
33 Mounting bracket
34 Screw – 2 off
35 Spring washer – 2 off
36 Washer – 2 off

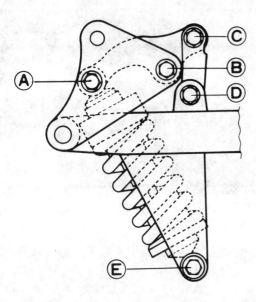

Fig. 4.19 Rear suspension linkage torque settings

A, C and E –   4.8 – 7.2 kgf m (34.5 – 52.0 lbf ft)
B and D   –   8.4 – 10.0 kgf m (60.5 – 72.5 lbf ft)
Note: *no settings available for US GS550 ESE and ES3 models*

15 Rear suspension unit: examination and adjustment

1   The rear suspension unit is of the oil-damped, coil spring type, located centrally in the rear suspension linkage. The unit features a remote hydraulically-operated spring preload adjuster located on the left-hand side of the machine. The two components are connected by a pressure hose and must not be separated. It is not possible to repair the assembly in any way; if it develops a fault it must be renewed. The unit offers five preload settings which are selected by turning the large adjuster knob. Turn the knob until the desired setting is shown on the scale on the unit's body, noting that position 1 provides the softest setting and position 5 the stiffest. The standard setting for UK models is position 3, and position 2 for US models.

2   The only serviceable part is the spherical bearing at the lower mounting point of the main unit. This can be renewed after the unit has been detached from the frame. It is just possible to gain access to the bearing if the lower mounting is freed and the unit allowed to hang from the top mounting, though access is limited.

3   Remove the headed spacer on each side of the mounting, then prise out the dust seals. Remove the wire circlips using a small electrical screwdriver to displace them. Draw out the spherical bearing using a bearing extractor, a drift or a drawbolt arrangement. Fit the new bearing using the Suzuki bearing installer, Part number 09924-84510 or a drawbolt arrangement. Retain the bearing using new wire circlips, ensuring that they seat fully. Apply molybdenum paste or grease to the spherical bearing and to the two new dust seals. Fit the dust seals and the headed spacers.

16 Suspension linkage: examination and renovation

1   The main suspension bellcrank ('cushion lever') is fitted with a pair of needle roller bearings fitted through the wider boss, plus a single spherical bearing in each of the remaining bosses. Each is sealed at each end by dust seals. If wear or damage is present in any of the bearings they should be removed and renewed, otherwise they should not be disturbed. The spherical bearings can be driven out of their bosses using a drift or a suitable drawbolt arrangement. The needle roller races can be inspected after the dust seals and the inner race have been removed. If the needle roller races are to be removed, use the Suzuki bearing puller (09923-73210) and slide hammer (09930-30102) or a similar puller arrangement to draw them out of the bellcrank bore.

2   The new needle roller races can be drawn into position using the Suzuki bearing installer set (09924-84510) or a drawbolt arrangement (see photograph). Apply grease to the spacer and dust seal lips before fitting. The same method is used to draw the new spherical bearings into position. Ensure that they are located centrally in their bores and apply some molybdenum paste or grease to the bearing and its dust seals. It is worth noting that each moving part in the suspension linkage is vulnerable to extensive wear if dirt or water find their way into the bearings. To prolong the life of the various bearings make sure that each one is well lubricated and that the dust seals are intact and fitted correctly.

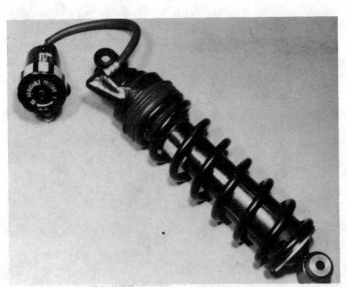

15.1 Suspension unit and adjuster are supplied as an assembly – do not attempt to separate them

16.1a Old sockets can be used as drifts to remove spherical bearings

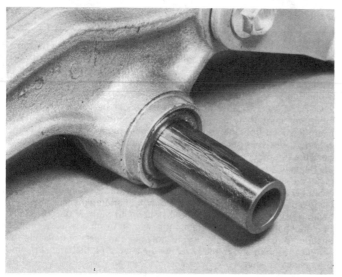

16.1b Centre bearing consists of inner sleeve ...

16.1c ... and two needle roller bearings

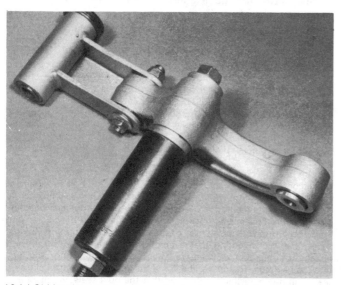

16.1d Old bearings can be removed using improvised drawbolt ...

16.2a ... and the new ones fitted in a similar fashion

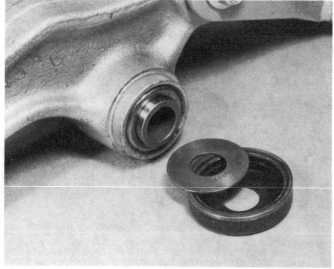

16.2b Do not forget to fit the plain washer and dust caps

16.2c Fit new seals on each side of spherical bearings ...

16.2d ... then place headed spacers in position

17 Stands: examination and maintenance

1   The centre stand is retained by two pivot bolts to lugs on the underside of the frame, each being secured by an R-pin passed through its end. A sleeve is fitted between each bolt and the stand pivots. It is good practice to remove the stand from time to time so that the pivots can be cleaned and greased. Examine the stand and the two pivots bolts for damage or cracking, and have any such damage repaired by welding before the stand collapses. If the bolts show signs of wear or distortion, renew them.
2   The side stand (prop stand) is secured by a shouldered pivot bolt to a lug on the left-hand side of the machine. This too should be removed periodically and checked for wear. If the pivot bolt has worn, make sure that the correct hardened bolt is used to replace it.
3   It is important to check the condition of both stand springs regularly, looking for indications of wear or developing cracks around the hooked ends. Bear in mind that if a spring fails while the machine is being ridden, the stand will drop onto the road. It is all too easy for this type of occurrence to result in a serious accident.

18 Footrests: examination and maintenance

1   The footrests are of the folding type, those fitted on the front being secured to the mounting brackets by clevis pins which are retained in turn by circlips, whilst the rear units are retained by bolts. If the machine is dropped, the footrests will normally fold up, and so are unlikely to become bent. If badly distorted in an accident it is usually preferable to renew a footrest complete.
2   The top surface is covered by a renewable rubber pad. This fits over a flat plate which is retained by two screws to the footrest. Renewal of the pad is self-explanatory once the two screws have been released and the pad and backing plate lifted away.

19 Brake pedal: examination and maintenance

The brake pedal is retained to its splined shaft by a pinch bolt. This should be kept tight to prevent movement of the pedal on the splines, and the subsequent wear of these areas. If the pedal is bent in an accident it may be possible to straighten slight damage by heating the pedal to a cherry red colour with a blowlamp and then hammering it straight. In most cases, however, it will be preferable to renew the pedal to preserve the appearance of the machine.

20 Instrument heads: removal and replacement

1   The speedometer and tachometer are fitted in an instrument panel mounted on the top yoke by two rubber-bushed bolts. The precise arrangement varies according to the model, the instrument heads either being separate, as in the case of the L models, or combined in a common housing. In the event of either instrument proving faulty, check first that the drive cable is in good condition as described below. Note that all models (except the L, ED, EE and EF versions) are equipped with an electronic tachometer, in which case check the wiring to the instrument, refering to Chapter 6 for details.
2   It is not practicable to repair a faulty instrument head, but before ordering a new unit check the local breakers (wreckers) yards for a good secondhand assembly. This is one area where a used part offers a substantial saving with little attendant risk if it fails at a later date.

21 Instrument drives: examination and renovation

1   In the case of the L, ED, EE and EF models, both the speedometer and tachometer are driven mechanically by flexible cables. These should always be checked first in the event of a fault, particularly where the instrument needle wavers a lot; this is usually due to a kinked cable.
2   The speedometer drive gearbox is located on the left-hand end of the front wheel spindle and can be inspected once the wheel has been removed. It is good practice to pack the gearbox with grease each time the wheel is detached.
3   On models fitted with a mechanically driven tachometer the drive is incorporated in the cylinder head cover and should require little attention. It is well lubricated by the oil feed to the camshafts and is unlikely to wear in use. In the event of damage to either drive unit, the affected parts must be renewed.

Chapter 5 Wheels, brakes and tyres

Refer to Chapter 7 for information relating to the 1986 to 1988 GS/GSX550 ES and GS550 L models

Contents

Specifications

UK GSX550 ESD, EE, ESE, EFE models

Tyre sizes

Front	100/90–16 54H
Rear	110/90–18 61H

Tyre pressures, psi (kg/cm²)

	Front	Rear
Normal riding – solo – all models	28 (2.00)	32 (2.25)
Normal riding – dual – all models	28 (2.00)	40 (2.80)

Minimum recommended tread depth

Front	1.6 mm (0.06 in)
Rear	2.0 mm (0.08 in)

Wheel rim runout

Axial (max)	2.0 mm (0.08 in)
Radial (max)	2.0 mm (0.08 in)

Wheel spindle runout

Front (max)	0.25 mm (0.01 in)
Rear (max)	0.25 mm (0.01 in)

Front brake

Type	Twin hydraulic disc brake
Disc thickness	5.0 ± 0.2 mm (0.20 ± 0.008 in)
Service limit	4.5 mm (0.18 in)
Disc runout (max)	0.30 mm (0.012 in)
Master cylinder bore	15.870 – 15.913 mm (0.6248 – 0.6265 in)
Master cylinder piston	15.827 – 15.854 mm (0.6231 – 0.6242 in)
Caliper bore	38.180 – 38.256 mm (1.5031 – 1.5061 in)
Caliper piston	38.098 – 38.148 mm (1.4999 – 1.5019 in)

Rear brake

Type	Single hydraulic disc
Disc thickness	6.7 ± 0.2 mm (0.26 ± 0.008 in)
Service limit	6.0 mm (0.24 in)
Disc runout (max)	0.30 mm (0.012 in)
Master cylinder bore	14.000 – 14.043 mm (0.5512 – 0.5529 in)
Master cylinder piston	13.957 – 13.984 mm (0.5495 – 0.5506 in)
Caliper bore	38.180 – 38.256 mm (1.5031 – 1.5061 in)
Caliper piston	38.098 – 38.148 mm (1.4999 – 1.5019 in)

Hydraulic fluid

Type	SAE J1703, DOT 3 or DOT 4 specification

Torque wrench settings

Component	kgf m	lbf ft
Front wheel spindle nut	3.6 – 5.2	26.0 – 37.6
Front wheel spindle clamp nut	1.5 – 2.5	10.8 – 18.1
Front master cylinder clamp bolt	0.5 – 0.8	3.6 – 5.8
Front caliper mounting bolt	2.5 – 4.0	18.1 – 28.9
Front caliper joining bolt	3.0 – 3.6	21.7 – 26.0
Brake hose union bolt	2.0 – 2.5	14.5 – 18.1
Caliper air bleed valve	0.7 – 0.9	5.1 – 6.5
Front brake anti-dive modulator to fork plunger housing bolt	0.6 – 0.8	4.3 – 5.8
Front disc mounting bolt	1.5 – 2.5	10.8 – 18.1
Rear caliper mounting bolt	1.5 – 2.5	10.8 – 18.1
Rear caliper joining bolt	2.8 – 3.2	20.3 – 16.6
Rear brake pedal pinch bolt	1.5 – 2.5	10.8 – 18.1
Rear brake torque arm nut	2.0 – 3.0	14.5 – 21.7
Rear master cylinder mounting bolt	1.5 – 2.5	10.8 – 18.1
Rear wheel spindle nut	5.0 – 8.0	36.2 – 57.9

US GS550 ED, ESD, ESE, ES3, LD, EF, ESF, LF models

Tyre sizes

Front	100/90-16 54H
Rear:	
ED, ESD, ESE, ES3, EF, ESF	110/90-18 61H
LD, LF	130/90-16 67H

Tyre pressures, psi (kg/cm²)

	Front	Rear
Solo:		
All models	28 (2.00)	32 (2.25)
Dual:		
ED, ESD, ESE, ES3, EF, ESF	28 (2.00)	40 (2.80)
LD, LF	28 (2.00)	36 (2.50)

Minimum recommended tread depth

Front	1.6 mm (0.06 in)
Rear	2.0 mm (0.08 in)

Wheel rim runout

Axial (max)	2.0 mm (0.08 in)
Radial (max)	2.0 mm (0.08 in)

Wheel spindle runout

Front (max)	0.25 mm (0.01 in)
Rear (max)	0.25 mm (0.01 in)

Front brake

Type:	
ED, ESD, ESE, ES3, EF, ESF	Twin hydraulic disc brake
LD, LF	Single hydraulic disc brake
Disc thickness	5.0 ± 0.2 mm (0.20 ± 0.008 in)
Service limit	4.5 mm (0.18 in)
Disc runout (max)	0.30 mm (0.012 in)
Master cylinder bore:	
ED, ESD, ESE, ES3, EF, ESF	15.870 – 15.913 mm (0.6248 – 0.6265 in)
LD, LF	12.700 – 12.743 mm (0.5000 – 0.5017 in)
Master cylinder piston:	
ED, ESD, ESE, ES3, EF, ESF	15.827 – 15.854 mm (0.6231 – 0.6242 in)
LD, LF	12.657 – 12.684 mm (0.4983 – 0.4994 in)
Caliper bore	38.180 – 38.256 mm (1.5031 – 1.5061 in)
Caliper piston	38.098 – 38.148 mm (1.4999 – 1.5019 in)

Rear brake

Type (ED, ESD, ESE, ES3, EF, ESF) .... Single hydraulic disc
Disc thickness .... 6.7 ± 0.2 mm (0.26 ± 0.008 in)
Service limit .... 6.0 mm (0.24 in)
Disc runout (max) .... 0.30 mm (0.012 in)
Master cylinder bore .... 14.000 – 14.043 mm (0.5512 – 0.5529 in)
Master cylinder piston .... 13.957 – 13.984 mm (0.5495 – 0.5506 in)
Caliper bore .... 38.180 – 38.256 mm (1.5031 – 1.5061 in)
Caliper piston .... 38.098 – 38.148 mm (1.4999 – 1.5019 in)

Type (LD, LF) .... Single leading shoe drum brake
Rear brake pedal free play .... 5.0 – 15.0 mm (0.2 – 0.6 in)
Rear brake pedal height .... 10 mm (0.4 in)
Brake drum internal diameter (service limit) .... 160.7 mm (6.33 in)
Brake lining thickness (service limit) .... 1.5 mm (0.06 in)

Hydraulic fluid

Type .... DOT 3 or DOT 4 specification

Torque wrench settings

Component	kgf m	lbf ft
Front wheel spindle nut	3.6 – 5.2	26.0 – 37.6
Front wheel spindle clamp nut	1.5 – 2.5	10.8 – 18.1
Front master cylinder clamp bolt	0.5 – 0.8	3.6 – 5.8
Front caliper mounting bolt	2.5 – 4.0	18.1 – 28.9
Front caliper joining bolt	3.0 – 3.6	21.7 – 26.0
Brake hose union bolt	2.0 – 2.5	14.5 – 18.1
Caliper air bleed valve	0.7 – 0.9	5.1 – 6.5
Front brake anti-dive modulator to fork plunger housing bolt	0.6 – 0.8	4.3 – 5.8
Front disc mounting bolt	1.5 – 2.5	10.8 – 18.1
Rear caliper mounting bolt	1.5 – 2.5	10.8 – 18.1
Rear caliper joining bolt	2.8 – 3.2	20.3 – 16.6
Rear brake pedal pinch bolt	1.5 – 2.5	10.8 – 18.1
Rear brake actuating lever bolt (LD, LF)	0.5 – 0.8	3.6 – 5.8
Rear brake torque arm nut	2.0 – 3.0	14.5 – 21.7
Rear master cylinder mounting bolt	1.5 – 2.5	10.8 – 18.1
Rear wheel spindle nut	5.0 – 8.0	36.2 – 57.9

Note: *At the time of writing no torque settings were available for the GS550 ESE and ES3 models.*

1 General description

The GSX/GS550 models are fitted with cast alloy wheels, the diameter and section varying according to model. Tyre sizes vary according to the wheel rim diameter and section, the majority of models using a 16 in front and 18 in rear tyre. The L version, in keeping with its 'custom' image, is equipped with a 16 in front and a fat 16 in rear tyre. The appropriate details of sizes and pressures for the various machines will be found in the Specifications at the front of this Chapter.

Braking on all models is by hydraulically-operated disc. A twin disc arrangement is fitted to the front wheel of all except the L models, which employ a single disc arrangement. All models except the L versions use a single rear disc brake, the L having a single leading shoe drum unit.

Some models feature an anti-dive arrangement designed to minimise the pitching effect encountered under heavy braking. It does this by utilising pressure in the front brake system to automatically stiffen the front fork damping effect. In the case of the 1985 US models, a revised arrangement is used which is not interconnected with the brake hydraulic system. Both systems allow a more compliant suspension arrangement than would otherwise be possible.

2 Wheels: examination and renovation

1 The wheels require little maintenance apart from regular cleaning. In the event of suspected impact damage, check the wheel for distortion by arranging it so that it is clear of the ground. Using a dial gauge mounted on the front fork or the swinging arm, as appropriate, check the axial (side-to-side) play and radial play (ovality). In each case this should not exceed 2.0 mm (0.08 in). If distorted beyond this amount the wheel must be renewed. Note that it cannot be repaired or trued.

2 Check for bearing wear by turning the wheel and by rocking it from side-to-side. Any 'grittiness' or unevenness in its movement, or any discernible free play in the bearing is indicative of the need for renewal. In the case of the rear wheel, take care not to confuse wheel bearing free play with movement in the swinging arm.

3 Give the whole wheel a close visual check for dents or cracks. Any cracking should be viewed with great suspicion, as it can lead to a sudden stress fracture under the high loadings experienced in normal use. If in any doubt, seek professional advice. Small nicks can be dressed out using a fine file or abrasive paper, and the resulting bare metal coated with one of the proprietary alloy wheel lacquers to prevent subsequent corrosion.

3 Front wheel: removal and installation

1 Place the machine on its centre stand, using a jack or an improvised stand to raise the wheel clear of the ground. Detach the brake caliper(s) by removing their two retaining bolts. Lift the caliper(s) clear of the disc and place a wooden wedge between the pads to prevent their accidental expulsion. Tie the caliper(s) clear of the forks to avoid placing strain on the hydraulic hose. Free the speedometer drive cable by unscrewing the knurled ring which secures it to the drive gearbox.

2 Straighten and remove the split pin which locks the wheel spindle nut and remove the nut. Slacken the clamp nuts then tap the wheel spindle part way out. Grasp the spindle end and withdraw it, supporting the wheel with one hand. The wheel can now be lowered clear of the forks and removed.

3 The wheel is installed by reversing the removal sequence. Grease the speedometer gearbox and ensure that it locates correctly against the fork lower leg as the wheel is offered up. Fit the wheel spindle and secure the nut to the prescribed torque figure. The pinch bolt or clamp half nuts can now be tightened. Refit the brake caliper(s) and check brake operation before using the machine.

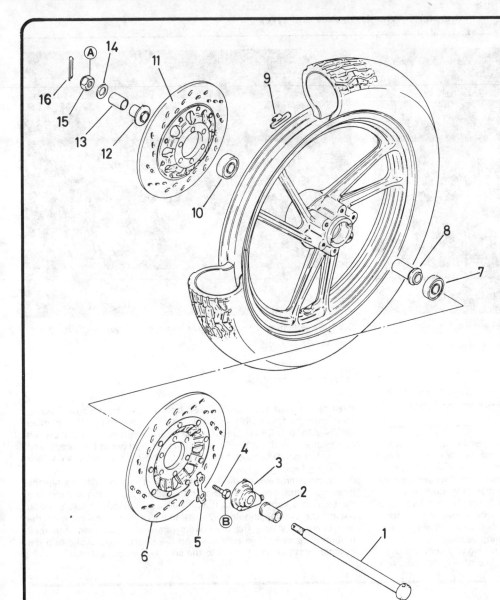

Fig. 5.1 Front wheel

1 Wheel spindle
2 Left-hand spacer – except L models
3 Speedometer gearbox
4 Bolt – 6 off
5 Lock washer – 3 off
6 Left-hand brake disc
7 Left-hand bearing
8 Spacer
9 Balance weight
10 Right-hand bearing
11 Right-hand brake disc – except
   L models
12 Bearing spacer
13 Right-hand spacer
14 Washer
15 Nut
16 Split pin

Torque settings
A 3.6 – 5.2 kgf m (26.0 – 37.5 lbf ft)
B 1.5 – 2.5 kgf m (11.0 – 18.0 lbf ft)
Note: no settings available for US
GS550 ESE and ES3 models

3.1a Remove the caliper mounting bolts and lift them clear of the discs

3.1b Unscrew speedometer drive cable at wheel end

3.2 Slacken clamp nuts and remove the wheel spindle

3.3 Note slots in hub to which speedometer drive gearbox is fitted

4 Front wheel bearings: renewal

1   Remove the wheel as described above. It is recommended that the brake discs are detached to avoid any risk of damage, though this is not essential if care is taken. If the discs are to be removed, note that they are handed and should be marked to ensure that they are refitted correctly. The tab washers which lock the mounting bolts must be renewed. Support the wheel on the workbench with the left-hand side uppermost. Using a long drift displace the spacer to one side, then drive the right-hand bearing out of the hub. Invert the wheel and remove the spacer, then drive out the remaining bearing.

2   Check the bearing by rotating it by hand, noting any unevenness or free play. Unless it operates smoothly and is free of play, the bearings must be renewed as a pair. The new bearings can be fitted by drawing them into the hub with the Suzuki bearing installer set, Part number 09924-84510 or 09941-34510 or an equivalent home-made drawbolt arrangement. Refer to the accompanying line drawing for details, and fit the left-hand bearing first. Position the spacer and then fit the remaining bearing.

3   As an alternative method, a large socket can be used to tap the bearings home. Ensure that the drift engages the outer race and that the bearing is kept square to the hub bore as it is tapped into position against the locating shoulder. Do not omit to fit the spacer between the two bearings. Where the discs were removed, clean them and their mounting flanges, then refit them on the correct side of the hub. Fit new tab washers and tighten to the specified torque setting.

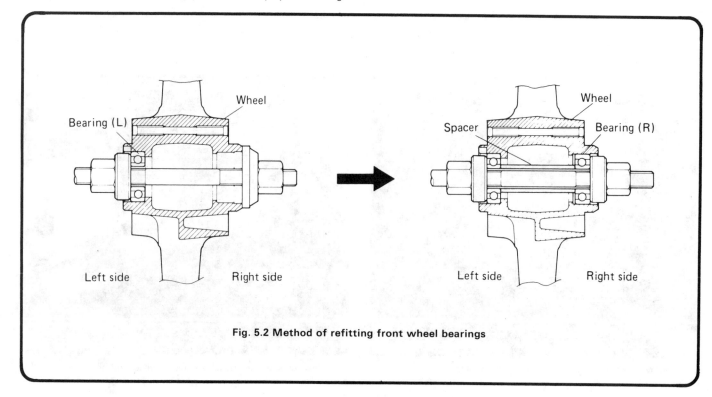

Fig. 5.2 Method of refitting front wheel bearings

Tyre removal: Deflate tyre and insert lever in close proximity to tyre valve

Use two levers to work bead over tyre rim

When first bead is clear, remove tyre as shown

Tyre fitting: Replace first bead over rim noting arrow indicating correct direction of rotation

Start second bead under the rim opposite the valve

Work bead under rim towards and each side of valve using lever if necessary

Use lever in final section

Air hose may be required for initial tyre inflation

5   Rear wheel: removal and installation

Disc brake models

1   Place the machine securely on its centre stand. To allow more manoeuvring space, release the two chainguard bolts and lift the guard away. Straighten and remove the split pin (where fitted) which retains the rear wheel spindle nut. Slacken and remove the nut, then withdraw the spindle, supporting the wheel as it comes free. Lower the wheel onto the ground and move it forwards slightly to allow the chain to be disengaged from the sprocket.

2   Note the position of the plain spacer at the left-hand side of the wheel and the headed spacer on the right-hand side; these may drop free as the wheel is removed and must be retrieved. The rear brake disc will by now be clear of the caliper, and care must be taken to avoid pressing the brake pedal accidentally. The caliper can be left in position.

3   When refitting the wheel, check that the cush drive hub is seated fully. If necessary, use soapy water to lubricate the rubbers, making installation easier. Position the wheel between the swinging arm ends and loop the drive chain around the sprocket. Lift the wheel into position and support it with a wooden block or similar. Ensure that the disc fits between the caliper halves and that the spacers are in position. Slide the wheel spindle through the swinging arm ends and the internal chain adjuster blocks, then fit the nut finger tight only. Set the chain adjuster bolts so that there is 20 – 30 mm (0.8 – 1.2 in) free play at the middle of the lower run of chain. Ensure that the wheel is pushed fully forward and that the alignment mark at each side is at the same position on the scale to ensure wheel alignment. Tighten the wheel spindle nut to the recommended torque setting, then tighten the two chain adjuster bolts to lock them.

Drum brake models

1   Place the machine securely on its centre stand. To allow more manoeuvring space, release the two chainguard bolts and lift the guard away. Straighten and remove the split pin which secures the brake torque arm nut, then remove the nut and displace the torque arm. Unscrew the adjuster nut from the end of the brake rod, freeing it from the brake arm. Fit the trunnion and nut onto the end of the rod for safe keeping.

2   Straighten and remove the split pin which retains the rear wheel spindle nut. Slacken and remove the nut, then withdraw the spindle, supporting the wheel as it comes free. Lower the wheel onto the ground and move it forwards slightly to allow the chain to be disengaged from the sprocket.

3   Note the position of the short plain spacer at the left-hand side of the wheel and the longer spacer on the right-hand side; these may drop free as the wheel is removed and must be retained. The brake backplate

assembly may drop free as the wheel is lowered clear of the fork ends; take care not to let it drop onto the floor.

4   When refitting the wheel, check that the cush drive hub is seated fully. If necessary, use soapy water to lubricate the rubbers, making installation easier. Position the wheel between the swinging arm ends and loop the drive chain around the sprocket. Lift the wheel into position and support it with a wooden block or similar. Check that the two spacers are in position. Slide the wheel spindle through the swinging arm ends and the internal chain adjuster blocks, then fit the nut finger tight only.

5   Set the chain adjuster bolts so that there is 20 – 30 mm (0.8 – 1.2 in) free play at the middle of the lower run of chain. Ensure that the wheel is pushed fully forward and that the alignment mark at each side is at the same position on the scale to ensure wheel alignment. Tighten the wheel spindle nut to the recommended torque setting, then tighten the two chain adjuster bolts to lock them.

6   Refit the torque arm and tighten the retaining nut firmly, back it off until one of the split pin holes aligns, then fit a new split pin. Refit the brake rod components, setting the adjuster nut to give 5 – 15 mm (0.2 – 0.6 in) free play at the pedal.

5.3a Position chain tension adjusters as shown, if they were removed

5.3b Note headed spacer between wheel and caliper

5.3c Note wheel alignment marks on side of swinging arm

5.3d Fit new cush drive rubbers if worn or damaged

Fig. 5.3 Rear wheel – except L models

1	Wheel spindle	15	Bolt – 6 off
2	Plate – 2 off	16	Spacer
3	Chain adjuster block – 2 off	17	Cush drive rubbers
4	E-clip – 2 off	18	Left-hand bearing
5	Adjusting bolt – 2 off	19	Spacer
6	End cover – 2 off	20	Balance weight
7	Bolt – where fitted	21	Right-hand bearing
8	Nut – 6 off	22	Brake disc
9	Lock washer – 3 off	23	Lock washer – 3 off
10	Sprocket	24	Bolt – 6 off
11	Spacer	25	Headed spacer
12	Oil seal	26	Caliper mounting bracket
13	Cush drive hub bearing	27	Washer
14	Cush drive hub	28	Nut
		29	Split pin

Torque settings
A 1.5 – 2.5 kgf m (11.0 – 18.0 lbf ft)
B 2.5 – 4.0 kgf m (18.0 – 29.0 lbf ft)
C 5.0 – 8.0 kgf m (36.0 – 58.0 lbf ft)
Note: no settings available for US GS550 ESE and ES3 models

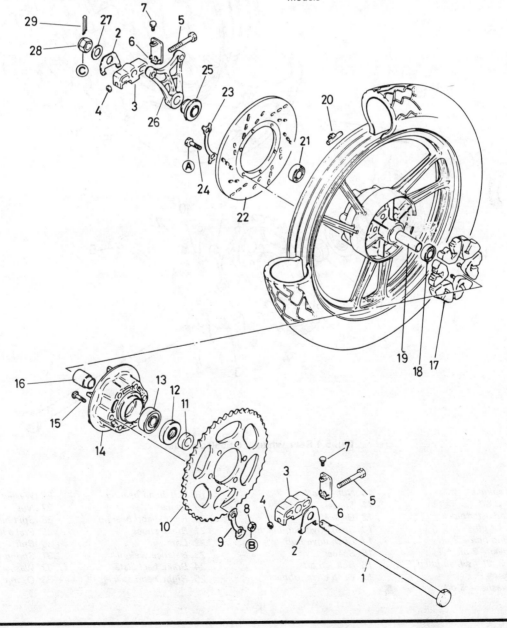

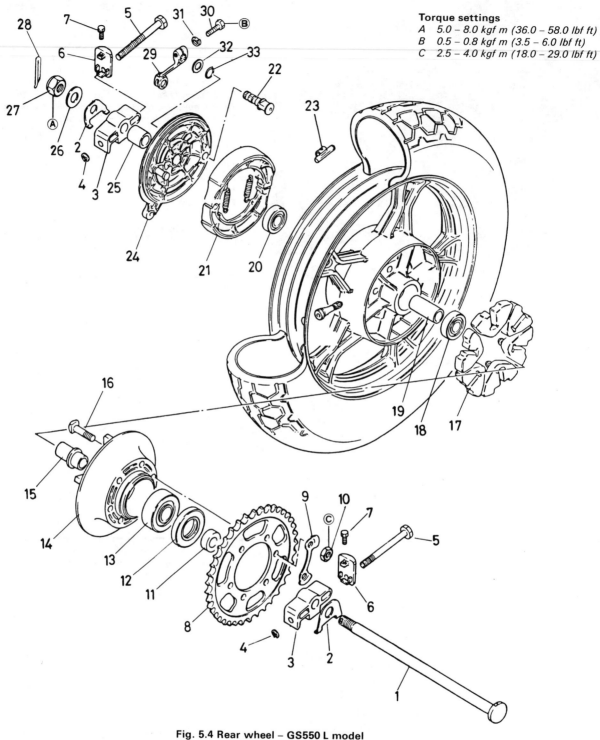

Torque settings
A 5.0 – 8.0 kgf m (36.0 – 58.0 lbf ft)
B 0.5 – 0.8 kgf m (3.5 – 6.0 lbf ft)
C 2.5 – 4.0 kgf m (18.0 – 29.0 lbf ft)

Fig. 5.4 Rear wheel – GS550 L model

1 Wheel spindle	10 Nut – 6 off	18 Left-hand bearing	26 Washer
2 Plate – 2 off	11 Spacer	19 Spacer	27 Nut
3 Chain adjuster block	12 Oil seal	20 Right-hand bearing	28 Split pin
4 E-clip – 2 off	13 Cush drive hub bearing	21 Brake shoes	29 Brake lever
5 Adjusting bolt – 2 off	14 Cush drive hub	22 Cam	30 Bolt
6 End cover – 2 off	15 Spacer	23 Balance weight	31 Spring washer
7 Bolt – 2 off – where fitted	16 Bolt – 6 off	24 Brake backplate	32 Washer
8 Sprocket	17 Cush drive rubbers	25 Right-hand spacer	33 O-ring
9 Lock washer – 3 off			

6   Rear wheel bearings: renewal

1   Remove the rear wheel as described above and pull off the cush drive hub and sprocket assembly. On drum brake models lift away the brake backplate assembly. On disc brake wheels it is preferable, though not essential, to remove the disc from the wheel. The bearing arrangement is generally similar to that described above for the front wheel, noting that the left-hand bearing should be removed last. When fitting the new bearings, note that the left-hand bearing should be fitted last, and that the part numbered edges should face outwards.

2   The cush drive/sprocket hub has its own bearing, and this can be driven out, together with the seal, from the inner face using a tubular drift or a suitably sized socket. When fitting the new bearing, grease it thoroughly, then tap it squarely into the recess. Fit a new seal where necessary, pressing it home against the bearing. When refitting the cush drive hub, do not omit the stepped spacer which fits between it and the wheel bearings.

6.1a Spacer fits between the two bearings

6.1b Fit the bearings with marked face outwards ...

6.1c ... and tap them home squarely

6.1d Headed spacer fits against the bearing as shown

6.2a Fit grease seal to cush drive hub ...

6.2b ... followed by the short spacer

6.2c Note stepped spacer which fits against inner face of bearing

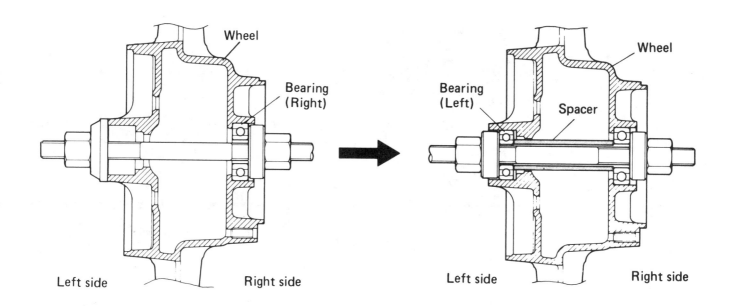

Fig. 5.5 Method of refitting rear wheel bearings

7 Brake pads: renewal

1   Brake pad wear can be checked with the caliper in position by prising off the plastic inspection cover. If either pad is worn down to the wear limit line, they should be renewed as a pair.

2   Pull off the R-clips at the outer ends of the pad support pins. Grasp the end of one pin with a pair of pliers and withdraw it. Lift away the two pad springs, then pull out the remaining pin. The pads are now free and can be withdrawn from the caliper, together with the backing shims. Wipe away residual brake dust using a rag moistened with alcohol or methylated spirit. On no account use an air line to remove the dust and take care not to inhale it.

3   Push the caliper pistons fully into the caliper to provide room for the new pads. Take care that the displaced fluid does not overflow from the reservoir. Fit the pads and their backing shim and slide one of the pins into place. Fit the pad springs, then slide the remaining pin into position, holding the spring ends down with a screwdriver. Replace the R-clips.

4   After new pads have been fitted, operate the lever or pedal repeatedly to allow the caliper to adjust to the new pad thickness, then check the level of the hydraulic fluid. For the first 100 miles or so, try to avoid heavy braking so that the pads can bed in properly. Excessively hard braking on new pads may cause glazing of the friction surface and impaired performance.

7.1 Prise off plastic cover to gain access to pads

7.2a Pad support pins are secured by R-pins (arrowed)

7.2b Depress spring ends, then pull out the pins with pliers

7.2c Pads and their backing shims can now be lifted away

8 Brake discs: examination and renovation

1   The condition of the brake discs can be checked with the wheel in place. Inspect the disc surface on both sides for scoring. Light scratching of the surface is inevitable and normal, but if excessive the braking performance will be reduced and renewal will be required. The thickness of the disc should be checked using a micrometer. If worn beyond the service limit of 4.5 mm (0.18 in) for the front disc(s) or 6.0 mm (0.24 in) in the case of the rear, or if wear is uneven, renew the discs.
2   Check the disc runout using a dial gauge mounted so that the probe bears on the outer edge of the disc. If runout is in excess of 0.3 mm (0.012 in) front or rear, renew the disc. Finally, check carefully for signs of cracking. This is not a common occurrence, but can be very dangerous if the disc breaks up when the machine is being used.
3   To remove the disc(s), remove the relevant wheel as described above. Where a twin front disc arrangement is fitted, note that the two discs are handed and must not be interchanged. To prevent this, mark them prior to removal. Straighten the locking tabs and remove the mounting bolts, then lift the discs away. When fitting the discs, clean off any dirt from them and the mounting boss to ensure that the disc

locates correctly. Fit new tab washers and tighten the mounting bolts evenly to the prescribed torque setting. Bend over the locking tabs to secure the mounting bolts. Finally, degrease the disc surface thoroughly before use.

9 Hydraulic system: general precautions

1   It is important that the precautions described below are observed when working on the system, bearing in mind the consequences of sudden failure on the road.
2   The hydraulic system must be kept free of air at all times. Any air bubbles, however small, will impair braking efficiency, possibly rendering the brake inoperative. If any part of the hydraulic system is disturbed, or if the brake feels 'spongy' in use, bleed the system as described in Section 15 of this Chapter.
3   Use only new hydraulic fluid conforming to SAE J1703 or DOT 3 specifications. The fluid will degrade in time, due to its hygroscopic nature. This tendency to absorb moisture will lower its boiling point, which in extreme cases can create air bubbles due to heat build-up under heavy braking. Do not keep old fluid which has been drained from the system.

4   Take great care not to spill fluid on paintwork or plastic surfaces, both of which will be damaged by it. Wash off any splashes promptly, and cover vulnerable areas before starting any dismantling work.
5   Always keep all internal hydraulic components clinically clean. Dust or dirt in the system will invariably get trapped by one of the seals, causing scoring and eventual leakage.

10 Hydraulic hoses: examination

1   The master cylinders and the brake calipers are connected by flexible hydraulic hoses, secured at each end by conventional banjo unions. The hoses must cope with considerable hydraulic pressure and also suspension movement. Although of tough construction, the hoses will deteriorate in time and should therefore be inspected closely, preferably whenever the pads are checked.

2   Look closely for signs of cracking or perishing of the outer casing, and renew the hose if it is in less than perfect condition. It is good practice to renew the hose as a precaution when the rest of the system is to be overhauled.
3   Before a hose can be renewed it will be necessary to drain the system. Remove the dust cap from the caliper bleed valve and fit a length of plastic tubing to it, placing the free end in a jar to catch the fluid. Open the bleed valve by about one turn, then operate the brake lever or pedal to 'pump' the fluid out.
4   Place a rag below the master cylinder union to catch any spilled fluid, then slacken and remove the union bolt. Repeat this sequence on the lower union, release the guide clips and remove the hose. The new hose can be refitted by reversing the removal sequence, noting that new sealing washers should be used. Fill and bleed the system as described in Section 15 and check that the brake works correctly before using the machine.

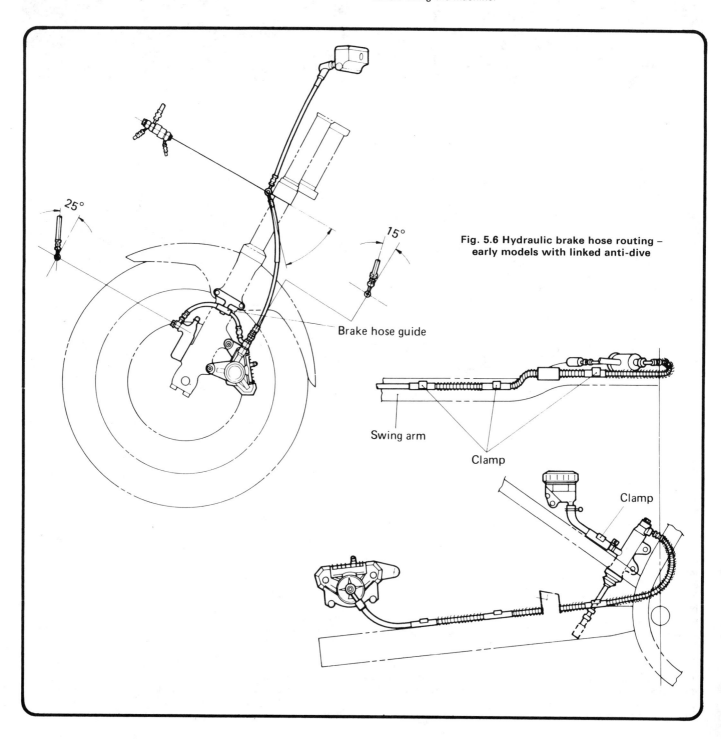

25°

15°

Fig. 5.6 Hydraulic brake hose routing –
early models with linked anti-dive

Brake hose guide

Swing arm

Clamp

Clamp

11 Front brake master cylinder: overhaul

1   Before starting any dismantling work it will be necessary to drain the hydraulic system as described in Section 10, paragraph 3 above. Remove the banjo union bolt to free the hydraulic hose from the master cylinder, taking care to avoid dripping fluid on the painted or plastic parts. Release the front brake switch from the underside of the master cylinder by removing the two retaining screws.

2   It is convenient to remove the front brake lever at this stage. Release the locknut, then remove the pivot bolt to free the lever. Unscrew the master cylinder clamp bolts and lift the unit away. Carefully clean the cylinder, then place it on the workbench to await dismantling.

3   Pull off the dust seal from the end of the body to expose the circlip which retains the piston assembly. Release the circlip, then displace the piston using compressed air via the hose union hole. In the absence of a compressed air supply a footpump or a bicycle tyre pump will suffice. To avoid spraying residual fluid around the workshop, wrap some rag around the piston bore. Clean the body and piston assembly, then measure the relevant dimensions using internal and external micrometers, comparing the readings obtained with those shown in the Specifications.

4   In the absence of measuring equipment, any assessment of the condition of the cylinder must be on the basis of careful scrutiny. In practice, the most likely cause of problems in the master cylinder is corrosion between the piston and cylinder surface. This can be largely avoided if the fluid is renewed as recommended every two years. Examine carefully the condition of the cylinder bore. This must show no sign of scoring or wear, and anything less than a perfect surface finish indicates the need for renewal. Note that if the bore is damaged, the cylinder should be renewed complete. If the cylinder is serviceable, check that the small relief port and the main feed port from the reservoir are clear. If necessary, the reservoir can be released after the securing screws have been removed.

5   The piston surface will not wear unless the seals are very badly worn and in this case the comparatively soft cylinder bore will invariably have suffered worse damage. The seals are best renewed as a precautionary measure, even if they appear unworn. If the seals are scored, worn or swollen they must be renewed. In an emergency the seals may be reused if in perfect condition, but remember that they will have worn to suit the bore surface and may be prone to leakage once disturbed.

6   When assembling the cylinder, soak the piston and seals in hydraulic fluid to provide lubrication. Slide the assembly into place and secure it with the circlip. The dust seal should be renewed, if damaged. Complete reassembly by reversing the dismantling sequence, using new sealing washers on the hose union, which should be tightened to the specified torque figure.

7   After assembly, remember that the system must be filled and bled as described in Section 15. Check that there are no leaks and that the brake works correctly before using the machine.

12 Front brake caliper: overhaul

1   Drain the hydraulic system as described in Section 10, paragraph 3 above, then detach the caliper unit by releasing the two caliper mounting bolts. Remove the pads and their backing shims as described in Section 7. Carefully clean the caliper prior to any dismantling work. Note that the caliper is of the twin piston type, and each half should be overhauled separately to avoid parts being interchanged between them.

2   Separate the two caliper halves by unscrewing the bolts which hold them together. As the caliper halves come apart, the small O-ring which seals the passage between them will drop free. This should be renewed each time the caliper halves are separated. Wrap each caliper half in clean cloth then displace the piston by applying compressed air via the hose union hole. Note that a certain amount of air will escape through the connecting passage, but there should still be enough pressure to displace the piston. Where the piston is stuck due to corrosion, first pull off the piston dust seal and carefully scrape away the corrosion, taking care to avoid marking the bore or piston surfaces. The piston can then be pulled out using internal circlip pliers or similar to grasp the inside surface.

3   Each caliper half contains two seals. The outer, convoluted, seal is a dust seal which excludes road and brake dust from the caliper. The importance of this is obvious, and it must be renewed if damaged in any way. The smaller inner seal contains the hydraulic fluid in the caliper. Its second and less obvious function is to control the position of the pads in relation to the disc when the brake is released. This is dependent on the elasticity of the seal, which is why a dragging brake can often be traced to a 'tired' seal. It is recommended, therefore, that both seals are renewed as a precautionary measure. Note that the piston seal can be worked out of its groove using a small electrical screwdriver, taking great care to avoid scratching the bore surface.

4   As in the case of the master cylinder, both the piston and the caliper body must be free from scoring, corrosion and visible wear. Should such damage be found, renewal will be necessary. Note that serious corrosion will often occur at the outer face of the piston where the dust seal has split.

5   The caliper is assembled by reversing the dismantling sequence, noting that every component must be spotlessly clean. Use hydraulic fluid to lubricate the seals and piston, and ensure that the dust seal locates correctly in the piston and body grooves. Refer to the accompanying line drawing for details of the relative positions of the various components, noting in particular the direction of the pad shim. Use new sealing washers on the hose union. Tighten all fasteners to the recommended torque setting.

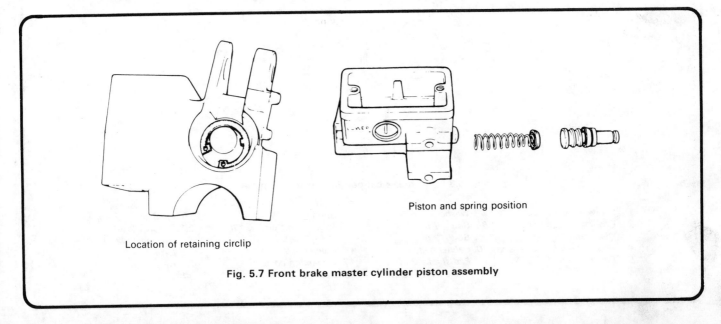

Location of retaining circlip   Piston and spring position

Fig. 5.7 Front brake master cylinder piston assembly

Torque settings
A   3.0 – 3.6 kgf m (21.5 – 26.0 lbf ft)
B   2.5 – 4.0 kgf m (18.0 – 29.0 lbf ft)
C   0.7 – 0.9 kgf m (5.0 – 6.0 lbf ft)
Note: *no settings available for US GS550 ESE and ES3 models*

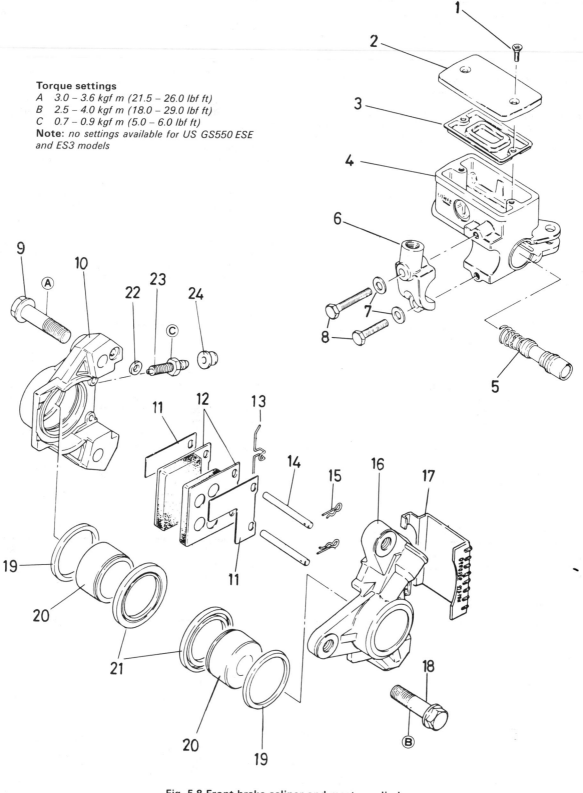

Fig. 5.8 Front brake caliper and master cylinder

1 Screw – 2 off	7 Washer – 2 off	13 Spring	19 Fluid seal – 2 off
2 Cover	8 Bolt – 2 off	14 Pad support pin – 2 off	20 Piston – 2 off
3 Diaphragm	9 Bolt – 2 off	15 R-clip – 2 off	21 Dust seal – 2 off
4 Master cylinder body	10 Caliper half	16 Caliper half	22 O-ring
5 Piston assembly	11 Pad shim – 2 off	17 Inspection cover	23 Bleed valve
6 Clamp	12 Brake pads – 2 off	18 Bolt – 2 off	24 Cap

13 Rear brake master cylinder: overhaul

1   Drain the rear brake hydraulic system as described in Section 10 above. Pull off the right-hand side panel to gain access to the master cylinder and reservoir. Disconnect the master cylinder pushrod from the operating arm inboard of the footrest bracket. The forked end of the pushrod is retained by a clevis pin which is secured in turn by a split pin. Straighten the split pin and remove it, then displace the clevis pin.

2   Remove the hose union bolt and lodge the hose clear of the master cylinder, taking care to avoid fluid spillages on the painted parts. Remove the reservoir mounting bolt and the two master cylinder mounting bolts. Lift away the master cylinder together with the reservoir. Unscrew the reservoir cap and drain any residual hydraulic fluid.

3   Release the clip which secures the reservoir hose to the cylinder and separate the two. Pull off the pushrod dust seal to expose the circlip. Remove the circlip and remove the pushrod assembly and the piston, followed by the primary cup and spring.

4   The master cylinder assembly should be examined in the same manner as described in Section 11 above for the front master cylinder. It is recommended that the seals are renewed as a matter of course whenever the cylinder is dismantled, soaking them in clean hydraulic

fluid prior to installation. When the cylinder has been refitted, refill and bleed the hydraulic system as described in Section 15 of this Chapter and check that the brake pedal and switch are adjusted correctly.

14 Rear brake caliper: overhaul

1   Drain the rear brake hydraulic system as described in Section 10 above, then remove the pads as described in Section 7. Disconnect the hydraulic hose taking care to avoid dripping residual fluid on the paintwork. Remove the split pin which secures the torque arm nut and remove the latter to free the torque arm. Remove the wheel spindle nut and displace the spindle sufficiently to allow the caliper to be lifted away.

2   Remove the two large Allen bolts and separate the caliper halves. Like the front caliper, the rear caliper is of the twin piston type, and each half should be dealt with separately to avoid interchanging the internal components. The general procedure from this point onwards is much the same as that described for the front caliper, and reference should be made to Section 12. It is recommended that the piston seals and the O-ring which seals the passage between the caliper halves are renewed as a matter of course.

13.1a Master cylinder pushrod is retained by a clevis pin

13.1b Note position of heavy return spring and smaller switch operating spring

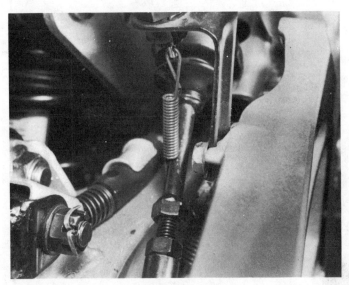

13.1c Switch spring fits behind pushrod as shown

13.2 Master cylinder is retained by two bolts (footrest plate removed for clarity)

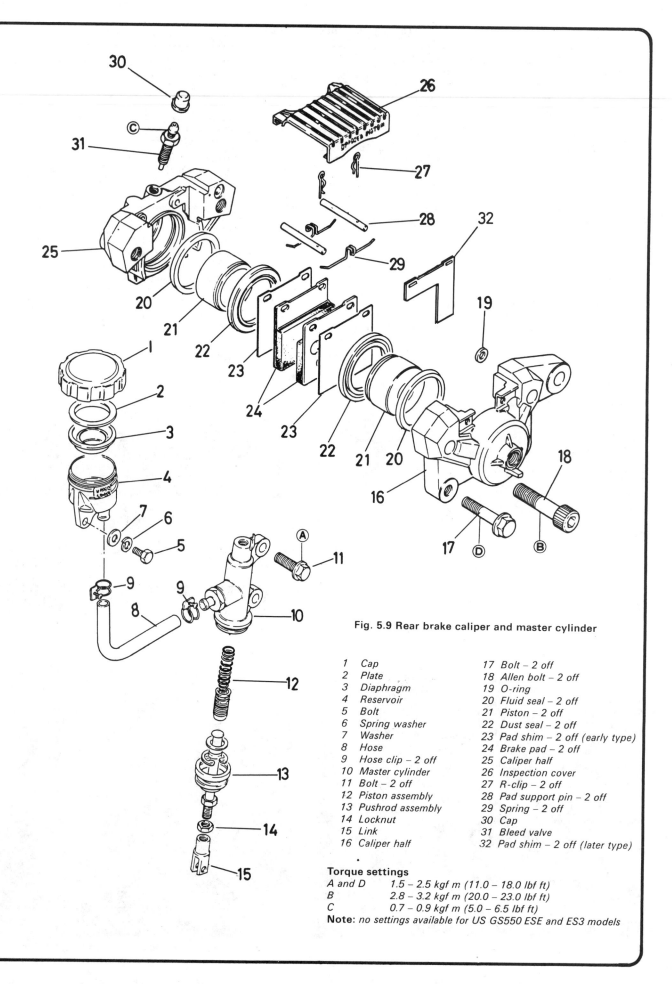

Fig. 5.9 Rear brake caliper and master cylinder

1	Cap	17	Bolt – 2 off
2	Plate	18	Allen bolt – 2 off
3	Diaphragm	19	O-ring
4	Reservoir	20	Fluid seal – 2 off
5	Bolt	21	Piston – 2 off
6	Spring washer	22	Dust seal – 2 off
7	Washer	23	Pad shim – 2 off (early type)
8	Hose	24	Brake pad – 2 off
9	Hose clip – 2 off	25	Caliper half
10	Master cylinder	26	Inspection cover
11	Bolt – 2 off	27	R-clip – 2 off
12	Piston assembly	28	Pad support pin – 2 off
13	Pushrod assembly	29	Spring – 2 off
14	Locknut	30	Cap
15	Link	31	Bleed valve
16	Caliper half	32	Pad shim – 2 off (later type)

Torque settings

A and D	1.5 – 2.5 kgf m (11.0 – 18.0 lbf ft)
B	2.8 – 3.2 kgf m (20.0 – 23.0 lbf ft)
C	0.7 – 0.9 kgf m (5.0 – 6.5 lbf ft)

Note: no settings available for US GS550 ESE and ES3 models

14.1 Release split pin, nut and torque arm bolt to free caliper

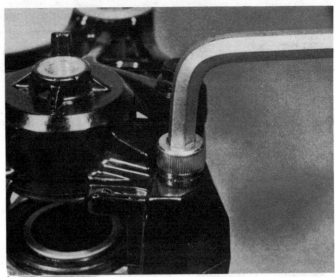

14.2a Rear caliper halves are held by two Allen bolts

14.2b Separate caliper halves, noting O-ring (arrowed)

14.2c Check for wear and corrosion, and renew piston seal

14.2d Piston should be free from scoring. Renew dust seal

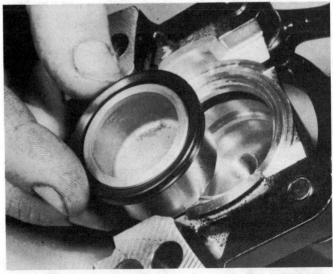

14.2e Fit seal to piston, lubricate with hydraulic fluid and install in caliper

14.2f Make sure that dust seal locates over lip in caliper body

15 Changing the hydraulic fluid and bleeding the system

1   This Section describes the procedure for changing the hydraulic fluid, an operation which should be carried out at approximately two year intervals to ensure that the system is kept clean and that the fluid does not become dangerously degraded. Where the system has already been drained during repair or overhaul work, or if it is suspected that air has entered the system, refer to the relevant parts of the procedure.

2   Obtain about two feet of small-bore plastic tubing of the type used for car screenwashers or in aquarium aeration systems. The tubing should fit snugly over the caliper bleed valve. Connect the tubing to the valve and place the free end in a glass jar or a similar receptacle. Open the bleed valve by 1/2 to 1 turn, then operate the brake lever repeatedly until all the fluid has been expelled.

Front brake

3   Remove the reservoir top and fill it to the upper level mark with new DOT 3 or SAE J1703 hydraulic fluid only. Where the system has been emptied it should first be primed by operating the lever until the fresh fluid starts to emerge through the plastic bleed tube. Take care that the reservoir is kept topped up throughout this stage, and also during the bleeding operation; even a small amount of air drawn in will necessitate starting again, so an assistant to monitor the fluid level would be invaluable. Where a twin disc system is fitted, deal with the left-hand caliper first, then the right-hand unit.

4   With the bleed valve closed, operate the brake lever until some resistance is felt. Now open the valve by about 1/2 a turn, whilst maintaining pressure on the lever. As soon as the lever stops moving, close the valve and then release the lever. Check the fluid level and top up as required. This sequence must be repeated until no further air bubbles can be seen emerging from the bleed tube.

5   When bleeding is complete, top up the reservoir and refit the top. Check that the brake feels firm when operated; there must be no sign of 'sponginess'. If the bleeding operation was carried out after poor braking had been noted, check the performance of the brake over the next few days. If any further deterioration is observed, the system must be leaking at some point and should be overhauled. Fluid leakage will be obvious, but note that air can be drawn past worn master cylinder seals without external signs.

Front brake: anti-dive models (not Posi-Damp)

6   Proceed as described above, noting that it is important that the system is bled in the correct sequence to avoid air pockets being trapped in the various components and connecting hoses. Start by bleeding the left-hand anti-dive unit, the left-hand caliper, the right-hand anti-dive unit and finally, the right-hand caliper. On occasion the process will have to be repeated several times to clear air pockets trapped in the anti-dive connecting hoses. In extreme cases it may help if the anti-dive modulator is released from the fork leg and held so that the air will flow up to the bleed valve.

Rear brake

7   The rear brake system can be dealt with in much the same way as has been described above, noting that the remarks concerning the bleeding sequence and anti-dive system do not apply.

16 Rear drum brake: examination and renovation

1   Remove the rear wheel as described earlier in this Chapter and lift away the brake backplate assembly. Clean out any dust from the drum using a rag moistened in petrol. **Do not** blow out the drum with compressed air, and take care to avoid inhaling the asbestos-based lining material. Examine the drum for wear or scoring. If it is badly scored or worn to 160.7 mm (6.33 in) or more, renewal will be necessary.

2   Examine the surface of the brake linings. If badly glazed or contaminated with oil or grease they should be renewed as a matter of course. Note that the source of any contamination should be investigated and rectified before proceeding further. The linings can be checked for wear by measuring them with a vernier caliper. If either is worn below the service limit of 1.5 mm (0.06 in) or less, they should be renewed as a pair. Note that the linings are bonded onto the shoes and cannot be supplied separately.

3   To remove the shoes, grasp them at the centre and "fold" them together. Once spring pressure has been released the shoes and springs can be lifted away. Before the shoes are disengaged from the springs, note the location of the spring ends.

4   Slacken and remove the pinch bolt which retains the brake arm to the splined end of the cam and lift it away. Displace the cam inwards and remove it. Clean the cam and its bore and check the condition of the O-ring which seals it. Renew the O-ring if necessary, and grease the cam before refitting it. Apply a light coating of grease to the operating end of the cam, then fit the shoes, taking care to avoid getting grease on the lining surfaces.

15.2 Use a length of tight fitting tubing over head of bleed nipple

17 Final drive chain: maintenance

1   To measure chain wear, remove the chainguard to expose the upper run of the chain. Taking great care to avoid trapped fingers, slowly rotate the rear wheel and check for loose or damaged rollers, pins or side plates. Damage of this type will necessitate chain renewal, so further examination will be pointless. Check both sprockets for damaged or hooked teeth. If serious wear or damage is found, renew the chain and both sprockets as a set. Measure the distance between 21 pins of the chain, taking the measurement in several places. If this exceeds the service limit of 323.8 mm (12.75 in), renew the chain. The chain is of the 'endless' type, and renewal requires the removal of the rear wheel and swinging arm assembly. The correct replacement chain is DAIDO DID50HDL or TAKASAGO RK50SMO.

2   Chain adjustment is correct when there is 20 – 30 mm (0.8 – 1.2 in) free play at the centre of the lower run, measured with the machine on its centre stand. Chains rarely wear evenly, so it is important to rotate the wheel until the tightest point is found.

5   If adjustment is required, slacken the brake torque arm nut, remove the split pin from the wheel spindle nut and slacken it. Turn each adjuster bolt by an equal amount to obtain the required tension. Check that the alignment marks on each adjuster are in the same relative position to ensure wheel alignment. Tighten the wheel spindle nut and torque arm nut to their respective torque settings, then tighten the adjuster bolts to lock them. Remember to fit a new split pin to secure the spindle and torque arm nuts.

6   Regular cleaning and lubrication will prolong the life of the chain. Wash off any road dirt with paraffin (kerosene) only, then lubricate the cleaned chain with gear oil. On no account use an aerosol lubricant unless of a type specifically designed for use with O-ring chains. Ordinary types of aerosol lubricant will rot and destroy the O-rings.

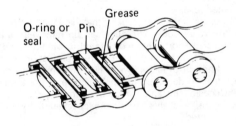

Fig. 5.10 Sectioned view of the sealed final drive chain

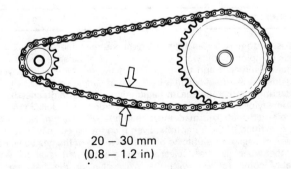

20 – 30 mm
(0.8 – 1.2 in)

Fig. 5.11 Measuring final drive chain free play

18 Tyres: removal and refitting

1   It is strongly recommended that should a repair to a tubeless tyre be necessary, the wheel is removed from the machine and taken to a tyre fitting specialist who is willing to do the job or taken to an official dealer. This is because the force required to break the seal between the wheel rim and tyre bead is considerable and considered to be beyond the capabilities of an individual working with normal tyre removing tools. Any abortive attempt to break the rim to bead seal may also cause damage to the wheel rim, resulting in an expensive wheel replacement. If, however, a suitable bead releasing tool is available, and experience has already been gained in its use, tyre removal and refitting can be accomplished as follows.

2   Remove the wheel from the machine by following the instructions for wheel removal as described in the relevant Section of this Chapter. Deflate the tyre by removing the valve insert and when it is fully deflated, push the bead of the tyre away from the wheel rim on both sides so that the bead enters the centre well of the rim. As noted, this operation will almost certainly require the use of a bead releasing tool.

3   Insert a tyre lever close to the valve and lever the edge of the tyre over the outside of the wheel rim. Very little force should be necessary; if resistance is encountered it is probably due to the fact that the tyre beads have not entered the well of the wheel rim all the way round the tyre. Should the initial problem persist, lubrication of the tyre bead and the inside edge and lip of the rim will facilitate removal. Use a recommended lubricant, a diluted solution of washing-up liquid or french chalk. Lubrication is usually recommended as an aid to tyre fitting but its use is equally desirable during removal. The risk of lever damage to wheel rims can be minimised by the use of proprietary plastic rim protectors placed over the rim flange at the point where the tyre levers are inserted. Suitable rim protectors may be fabricated very easily from short lengths (4 – 6 inches) of thick-walled nylon petrol pipe which have been split down one side using a sharp knife. The use of rim protectors should be adopted whenever levers are used and, therefore, when the risk of damage is likely.

4   Once the tyre has been edged over the wheel rim, it is easy to work around the wheel rim so that the tyre is completely free on one side.

5   Working from the other side of the wheel, ease the other edge of the tyre over the outside of the wheel rim, which is furthest away. Continue to work around the rim until the tyre is freed completely from the rim.

6   Refer to the following Section for details relating to puncture repair and the renewal of tyres. See also the remarks relating to the tyre valves in Section 20.

7   Refitting of the tyre is virtually a reversal of removal procedure. If the tyre has a balance mark (usually a spot of coloured paint), as on the tyres fitted as original equipment, this must be positioned alongside the valve. Similarly, any arrow indicating direction of rotation must face the right way.

8   Starting at the point furthest from the valve, push the tyre bead over the edge of the wheel rim until it is located in the central well. Continue to work around the tyre in this fashion until the whole of one side of the tyre is on the rim. It may be necessary to use a tyre lever during the final stages. Here again, the use of a lubricant will aid fitting. It is recommended strongly that when refitting the tyre only a recommended lubricant is used because such lubricants also have sealing properties. Do not be over generous in the application of lubricant or tyre creep may occur.

9   Fitting the upper bead is similar to fitting the lower bead. Start by pushing the bead over the rim and into the well at a point diametrically opposite the tyre valve. Continue working round the tyre, each side of the starting point, ensuring that the bead opposite the working area is always in the well. Apply lubricant as necessary. Avoid using tyre levers unless absolutely essential, to help reduce damage to the soft wheel rim. The use of the levers should be required only when the final portion of bead is to be pushed over the rim.

10   Lubricate the tyre beads again prior to inflating the tyre, and check that the wheel rim is evenly positioned in relation to the tyre beads. Inflation of the tyre may well prove impossible without the use of a high pressure air hose. The tyre will retain air completely only when the beads are firmly against the rim edges at all points and it may be found when using a foot pump that air escapes at the same rate as it is pumped in. This problem may also be encountered when using an air hose on new tyres which have been compressed in storage and by virtue of their profile hold the beads away from the rim edges. To overcome this difficulty, a tourniquet may be placed around the circumference of the tyre, over the central area of the tread. The compression of the tread in this area will cause the beads to be pushed outwards in the desired direction. The type of tourniquet most widely used consists of a length of hose closed at both ends with a suitable clamp fitted to enable both ends to be connected. An ordinary tyre valve is fitted at one end of the tube so that after the hose has been

secured around the tyre it may be inflated, giving a constricting effect. Another possible method of seating beads to obtain initial inflation is to press the tyre into the angle between a wall and the floor. With the airline attached to the valve additional pressure is then applied to the tyre by the hand and shin, as shown in the accompanying illustration. The application of pressure at four points around the tyre's circumference whilst simultaneously applying the airhose will often effect an initial seal between the tyre beads and wheel rim, thus allowing inflation to occur.

11 Having successfully accomplished inflation, increase the pressure to 40 psi and check that the tyre is evenly disposed on the wheel rim. This may be judged by checking that the thin positioning line found on each tyre wall is equidistant from the rim around the total circumference of the tyre. If this is not the case, deflate the tyre, apply additional lubrication and reinflate. Minor adjustments to the tyre position may be made by bouncing the wheel on the ground.

12 Always run the tyre at the recommended pressures and never under or over-inflate. The correct pressures for various weights and configurations are given in the Specifications Section of this Chapter.

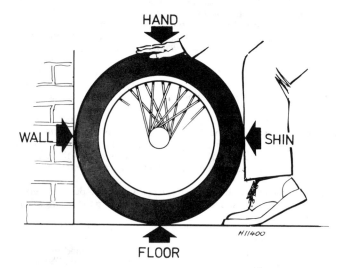

Fig. 5.12 Method of seating the beads on tubeless tyres

19 Puncture repair and tyre renewal

1 The primary advantage of the tubeless tyre is its ability to accept penetration by sharp objects such as nails etc without loss of air. Even if loss of air is experienced, because there is no inner tube to rupture, in normal conditions a sudden blow-out is avoided. If a puncture of the tyre occurs, the tyre should be removed for inspection for damage before any attempt is made at remedial action. The temporary repair of a punctured tyre by inserting a plug from the outside should not be attempted. Although this type of temporary repair is used widely on cars, the manufacturers strongly recommend that no such repair is carried out on a motorcycle tyre. Not only does the tyre have a thinner carcass, which does not give sufficient support to the plug, the consequences of a sudden deflation are often sufficiently serious that the risk of such an occurrence should be avoided at all costs.

3 The tyre should be inspected both inside and out for damage to the carcass. Unfortunately the inner lining of the tyre – which takes the place of the inner tube – may easily obscure any damage and some experience is required in making a correct assessment of the tyre condition.

4 There are two main types of tyre repair which are considered safe for adoption in repairing tubeless motorcycle tyres. The first type of repair consists of inserting a mushroom-headed plug into the hole from

the inside of the tyre. The hole is prepared for insertion of the plug by reaming and the applications of an adhesive. The second repair is carried out by buffing the inner lining in the damaged area and applying a cold or vulcanised patch. Because both inspection and repair, if they are to be carried out safely, require experience in this type of work, it is recommended that the tyre be placed in the hands of a repairer with the necessary skills, rather than repaired in the home workshop.

5 In the event of an emergency, the only recommended 'get-you-home' repair is to fit a standard inner tube of the correct size. If this course of action is adopted, care should be taken to ensure that the cause of the puncture has been removed before the inner tube is fitted. It will be found that the valve hole in the rim is considerably larger than the diameter of the inner tube valve stem. To prevent the ingress of road dirt, and to help support the valve, a spacer should be fitted over the valve.

6 In the event of the unavailability of tubeless tyres, ordinary tubed tyres may be fitted to these wheel rims. Use tyres of an equivalent type and grade to ensure their suitability. It is recommended that the advice of the tyre manufacturer or a reputable supplier is sought to ensure that a compatible replacement tyre is fitted.

20 Tyre valves: description and renewal

1 It will be appreciated from the preceding Sections that the adoption of tubeless tyres has made it necessary to modify the valve arrangement, as there is no longer an inner tube which can carry the valve core. The problem has been overcome by fitting a separate tyre valve which passes through a close-fitting hole in the rim, and which is secured by a nut and locknut. The valve is fitted from the rim well, and it follows that the valve can be removed and replaced only when the tyre has been removed from the rim. Leakage of air from around the valve body is likely to occur only if the sealing seat fails or if the nut and locknut become loose.

2 The valve core is of the same type as that used with tubed tyres, and screws into the valve body. The core can be removed with a small slotted tool which is normally incorporated in plunger type pressure gauges. Some valve dust caps incorporate a projection for removing valve cores. Although tubeless tyre valves seldom give trouble, it is possible for a leak to develop if a small particle of grit lodges on the sealing face. Occasionally, an elusive slow puncture can be traced to a leaking valve core, and this should be checked before a genuine puncture is suspected.

3 The valve dust caps are a significant part of the tyre valve assembly. Not only do they prevent the ingress of road dirt in the valve, but also act as a secondary seal which will reduce the risk of sudden deflation if a valve core should fail.

21 Wheel balancing

1 It is customary on all high performance machines to balance the wheels complete with tyre and tube. The out of balance forces which exist are eliminated and the handling of the machine is improved in consequence. A wheel which is badly out of balance produces through the steering a most unpleasant hammering effect at high speeds.

2 Some tyres have a balance mark on the sidewall, usually in the form of a coloured spot. This mark must be in line with the tyre valve, when the tyre is fitted to the inner tube. Even then the wheel may require the addition of balance weights, to offset the weight of the tyre valve itself.

3 If the wheel is raised clear of the ground and is spun, it will probably come to rest with the tyre valve or the heaviest part downward and will always come to rest in the same position. Balance weights must be added to a point diametrically opposite this heavy spot until the wheel will come to rest in ANY position after it is spun.

4 If juddering is noticed, consult a Suzuki Service Agent for advice on the correct choice of balance weights, noting that the type used on spoked wheels cannot be used on cast alloy wheels, and vice versa. For obvious reasons, ensure that the weights are fitted securely.

Chapter 6 Electrical system

Contents

Specifications

UK GSX550 ESD, EE, ESE, EFE models

Battery
Type	YB10L-B
Voltage	12 volts
Capacity	43.2 kC (12 Ah)/10HR
Nominal electrolyte specific gravity (SG)	1.2800 @ 20°C (68°F)

Alternator
Type	3-phase
No-load voltage	More than 75Vac @ 5000 rpm
Regulated voltage	13.5 – 15.5V @ 5000 rpm

Starter motor
Brush length (min)	9.0 mm (0.40 in)
Commutator undercut (min)	0.2 mm (0.008 in)

Starter relay
Resistance	Approx 3 – 4 ohms

Fuses
Headlamp	10A
Turn signal	10A
Ignition	10A
Main	15A
Power source	10A

Bulb wattages (all rated at 12V)

Headlamp	60/55W
Parking (city) lamp	4W
Tail/brake lamp	5/21W
Turn signal lamp	21W
Speedometer lamp	3.4W
Tachometer lamp	3.4W
Turn signal warning lamp	3.4W
High beam warning lamp	1.7W
Neutral indicator lamp	3.4W
Oil pressure lamp	3.4W
Side stand warning lamp	3.4W
Number (licence) plate lamp	5W
Gear position indicator	1.12W

US GS550 ED, ESD, ESE, ES3, LD, EF, ESF, LF models

Battery

Type	YB10L-B
Voltage	12 volts
Capacity	43.2 kC (12 Ah)/10HR
Nominal electrolyte specific gravity (SG)	1.2800 @ 20°C (68°F)

Alternator

Type	3-phase
No-load voltage	More than 75Vac @ 5000 rpm
Regulated voltage	13.5 – 15.5V @ 5000 rpm

Starter motor

Brush length (min)	9.0 mm (0.40 in)
Commutator undercut (min)	0.2 mm (0.008 in)

Starter relay

Resistance	Approx 3 – 4 ohms

Fuses

Headlamp	10A
Turn signal	10A
Ignition	10A
Main	15A
Power source	10A

Bulb wattage (all rated at 12V)

Headlamp	60/55W
Position lamp:	
LD	4W
LF	3.4W
Tail/brake lamp	8/23W (3/32 cp)
Turn signal lamp	23W (32 cp)
Speedometer lamp:	
ED, ESD, ESE, ES3, EF, ESF	3.4W
LD, LF	1.7W
Tachometer lamp:	
ED, ESD, ESE, ES3, EF, ESF	3.4W
LD, LF	1.7W
Turn signal warning lamp	3.4W
High beam warning lamp	1.7W
Neutral indicator lamp	3.4W
Oil pressure lamp	3.4W
Side stand warning lamp	3.4W
Licence plate lamp	8W (4 cp)
Gear position indicator	1.12W

1 General description

The electrical system is supplied by a crankshaft-mounted alternator, the rotor being retained on the tapered end of the crankshaft and the stator windings being housed inside the left-hand outer cover. The alternating current (ac) from the alternator is fed to a combined electronic regulator/rectifier unit, where it is converted to direct current (dc) and the system voltage limited to a nominal 12 volts before being passed to the battery and the electrical circuit of the machine. A 12 volt lead-acid battery provides a store of electrical power for starting and lighting, and to ensure a stable supply of power to the system, irrespective of engine speed.

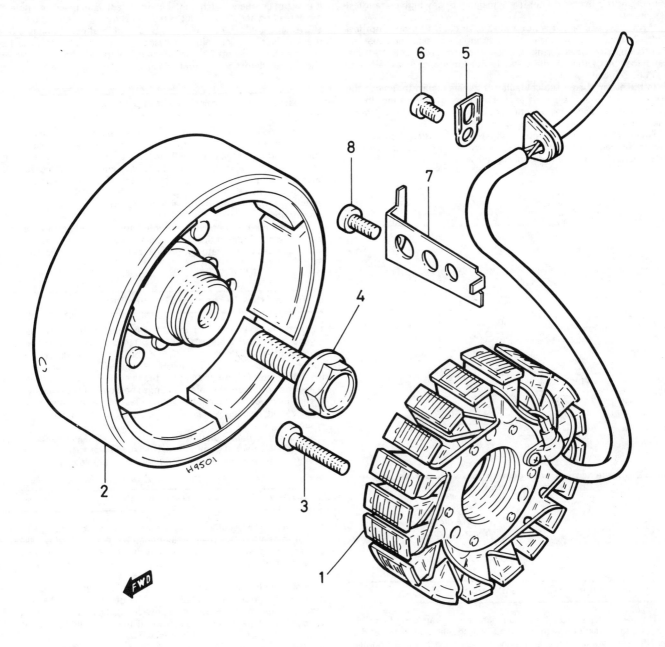

Fig. 6.1 Alternator

1	Stator	3	Screw – 3 off	5	Clamp	7	Clamp
2	Rotor	4	Bolt	6	Screw	8	Screw

2 Testing the electrical system: general

1   Many of the tests described in this Chapter require that a circuit or component is checked for continuity. This is accomplished by testing whether or not conductivity exists between the two terminals under test. In many instances it is not essential that a specific resistance is present, and in this case a simple dry battery and bulb can be connected as shown in the acompanying line drawing to provide a cheap and effective tester.

2   Where it is necessary to measure a specific voltage or resistance, a multimeter will be required. An inexpensive instrument is quite adequate for this type of work, and these can be obtained from many electrical or electronics suppliers as well as from most good motorcycle dealers. The purchase of a basic multimeter is strongly recommended and will prove an invaluable tool. Suzuki Service Agents can provide a suitable meter as Part number 09900-25002.

3   Care must be taken with all electrical tests, but particularly where the rectifier is involved. On no account must this be shorted or subjected to high currents or it will be destroyed in a fraction of a

second. For this reason do not use a 'megger' or any high current test instrument.

4   Where test equipment is not available, or the owner does not feel confident about a particular test, it is strongly recommended that the work is entrusted to a Suzuki Service Agent or an electrical expert. Remember that although the tests are not unduly complex, a single error could prove costly.

5   In the event of an electrical fault it is generally best to remove the seat, fuel tank and side panels as a preliminary to any testing. In the case of the headlamp/instrument panel area, removal of the fairing, where fitted, will improve access considerably.

6   Finally, always check the obvious first. Most faults can be traced to loose or broken leads or connectors, or switch defects, and checking these first may avoid a lot of unnecessary work.

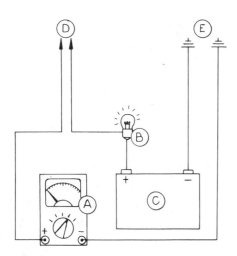

Fig. 6.2 Simple testing arrangement showing dry battery and bulb circuit and multimeter circuit

A   Multimeter   D   Positive probe
B   Bulb   E   Negative probe
C   Battery

3   Wiring and connectors: examination

1   The wiring used throughout the machine is colour-coded and will be found to correspond with the colour wiring diagrams at the end of this Chapter. Where multi-pin connectors are used these are handed and thus cannot be connected wrongly.

2   Inspect the wiring for signs of breakage or damage to the outer covering which might indicate an open or short circuit. On rare occasions a wire may be trapped or crushed, leaving the outer cover intact but the inner core partially or completely broken. This can cause mysterious intermittent faults, as can poor connections or water in connector blocks. A wiring run is easily checked using the meter set on the resistance scale as a continuity tester. Note that the machine's battery should be disconnected to avoid any risk of damage to the meter.

4   Testing the charging output

1   Before making this test note that it is important that the battery is known to be sound and fully charged. A faulty or discharged battery will give misleading results.

2   Remove the seat to gain access to the battery terminals. Set the meter to the 0 – 20 volts dc range (or a higher range where necessary) and connect the positive probe to the battery (+) terminal and the negative probe to the battery (−) terminal. Start the engine and allow

it to warm up, then switch on the lights, select main beam and note the meter reading at 5000 rpm. If the reading shown is below 13.5 volts, or above 15.5 volts, there is likely to be a fault in either the alternator or the regulator/rectifier unit. If necessary, check the alternator no-load performance (Section 5), the alternator stator windings (Section 6) and the regulator/rectifier unit (Section 7).

5   Testing the alternator no-load performance

1   Trace the alternator wiring back to the three bullet connectors and separate them. Set the meter to a range capable of handling at least 80 volts ac (note that the meter will probably be damaged if a lower range or any dc range is selected). Start the engine and measure the alternator output between successive pairs of output leads, a total of three tests. The relevant connections are shown in the accompanying line drawing. Note that the polarity of the probes is unimportant when measuring ac output.

2   In each case, the above test should show a reading of at least 75 volts ac at 5000 rpm. If one or more pairs of leads show a lower or zero reading, check the stator windings as described in the following Section.

6   Testing the alternator stator windings

1   If the no-load test had indicated a fault in the stator, stop the engine and set the meter to the resistance range. Using the same pattern of tests described above, check for continuity between successive pairs of leads. The exact resistance figure is not supplied by the manufacturer, but it is still possible to check for failure. If the stator is in good condition, the three readings should be approximately equal. A zero reading or a reading of infinite resistance indicates a short or open circuit respectively and will require the renewal of the stator assembly.

2   Check that the insulation between each set of windings and the stator core is intact. If continuity exists between any lead and the core, a short circuit has occurred and renewal will be necessary.

7   Testing the regulator/rectifier unit

1   The regulator/rectifier unit is mounted beneath the seat, just to the rear of the battery, and can be identified by its finned alloy casing. If checks on the system have indicated that the alternator is operating correctly and charging faults persist, check the unit as described below.

2   Trace the leads back from the regulator/rectifier unit and separate them at the multi-pin connector. Set the multimeter to the ohms x1 scale, then measure the resistance between the various pairs of leads as indicated in the accompanying table. If the unit fails to produce the appropriate values, it should be renewed.

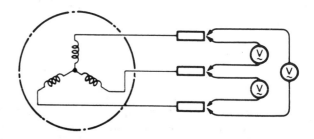

Fig. 6.3 Alternator output test

6.2 Stator assembly is retained inside cover by three screws

7.1 Regulator/rectifier is mounted behind the battery

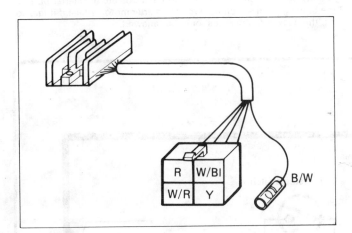

	⊕ Probe of tester				
		R	W/Bl	W/R	Y	B/W
⊖ Probe of tester	R		OFF	OFF	OFF	OFF
	W/Bl	4-10Ω		OFF	OFF	OFF
	W/R	4-10Ω	OFF		OFF	OFF
	Y	4-10Ω	OFF	OFF		OFF
	B/W	30-80Ω	4-10Ω	4-10Ω	4-10Ω	

Fig. 6.4 Regulator/rectifier test table

8 Battery: examination and maintenance

1 The battery is housed in a tray below the seat and may be reached once the seat has been removed. Most normal maintenance operations can be carried out with the battery in position. If the battery is removed for charging or testing, note that the breather hose must be pulled out as the battery is lifted away. When refitting the battery, check that the hose is routed correctly. The relevant routing information will be found on the lid of the air filter casing.

2 The transparent plastic case of the battery permits the upper and lower levels of the electrolyte to be observed without disturbing the battery by removing the side cover. Maintenance is normally limited to keeping the electrolyte level between the prescribed upper and lower limits and making sure that the vent tube is not blocked. The lead plates and their separators are also visible through the transparent

case, a further guide to the general condition of the battery. If electrolyte level drops rapidly, suspect over-charging and check the system.

3 Unless acid is split, as may occur if the machine falls over, the electrolyte should always be topped up with distilled water to restore the correct level. If acid is spilt onto any part of the machine, it should be neutralised with an alkali such as washing soda or baking powder and washed away with plenty of water, otherwise serious corrosion will occur. Top up with sulphuric acid of the correct specific gravity (1.260 to 1.280) only when spillage has occurred. Check that the vent pipe is well clear of the frame or any of the other cycle parts.

4 It is seldom practicable to repair a cracked battery case because the acid present in the joint will prevent the formation of an effective seal. It is always best to renew a cracked battery, especially in view of the corrosion which will be caused if the acid continues to leak.

5 If the machine is not used for a period of time, it is advisable to

remove the battery and give it a 'refresher' charge every six weeks or so from a battery charger. The battery will require recharging when the specific gravity falls below 1.260 (at 20°C – 68°F). The hydrometer reading should be taken at the top of the meniscus with the hydrometer vertical. If the battery is left discharged for too long, the plates will sulphate. This is a grey deposit which will appear on the surface of the plates, and will inhibit recharging. If there is sediment on the bottom of the battery case, which touches the plates, the battery needs to be renewed. Prior to charging the battery, note the correct charging rate. If charging from an external source with the battery on the machine, disconnect the leads, or the rectifier will be damaged.

6   Note that when moving or charging the battery, it is essential that the following basic safety precautions are taken:

(a)   Before charging check that the battery vent is clear or, where no vent is fitted, remove the combined vent/filler caps. If this precaution is not taken the gas pressure generated during charging may be sufficient to burst the battery case, with disastrous consequences.

(b)   Never expose a battery on charge to naked flames or sparks. The gas given off by the battery is highly explosive.

(c)   If charging the battery in an enclosed area, ensure that the area is well ventilated.

(d)   Always take great care to protect yourself against accidental spillage of the sulphuric acid contained within the battery. Eyeshields should be worn at all times. If the eyes become contaminated with acid they must be flushed with fresh water immediately and examined by a doctor as soon as possible. Similar attention should be given to a spillage of acid on the skin.

Note also that although, should an emergency arise, it is possible to charge the battery at a more rapid rate than that recommended, this will shorten the life of the battery and should therefore be avoided if at all possible.

7   Occasionally, check the condition of the battery terminals to ensure that corrosion is not taking place, and that the electrical connections are tight. If corrosion has occurred, it should be cleaned away by scraping with a knife and then using emery cloth to remove the final traces. Remake the electrical connections whilst the joint is still clean, then smear the assembly with petroleum jelly (NOT grease) to prevent recurrence of the corrosion. Badly corroded connections can have a high electrical resistance and may give the impression of complete battery failure.

9   Starter circuit and relay: preliminary checks

1   In the event of a starter malfunction, always check first that the battery is fully charged. A partly discharged battery may provide enough power for the lighting circuit, but not the very heavy current required to crank the engine. This can be checked by switching the lights on and operating the starter button. If the starter relay clicks and the lights dim or extinguish, a flat battery is indicated.

2   If the relay has failed it will not emit the characteristic click as the contacts close. To check its operation, remove the right-hand side panel. The relay is easily identified by its heavy duty starter motor lead, which should be disconnected from the relay terminal. Connect a 12 volt bulb between the starter lead terminal and a convenient earth (ground) point. Switch on the ignition and operate the starter button. If the bulb lights, the fault lies with the starter motor, whilst if it fails to light, the relay is faulty and should be renewed.

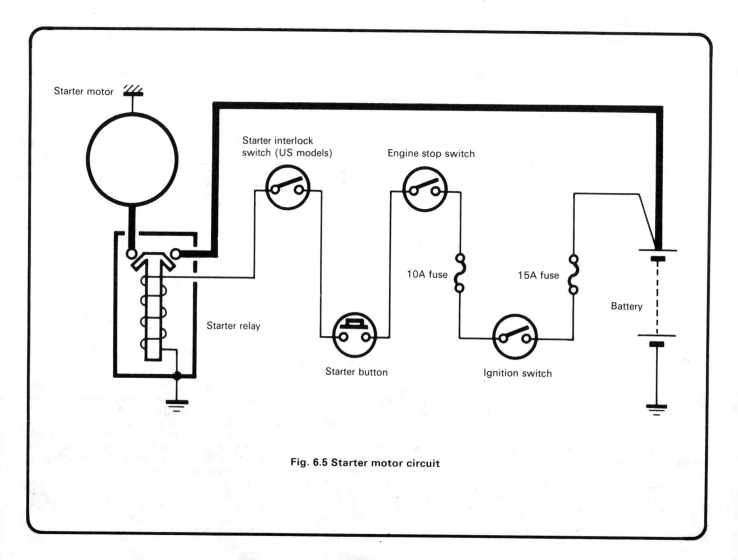

Fig. 6.5 Starter motor circuit

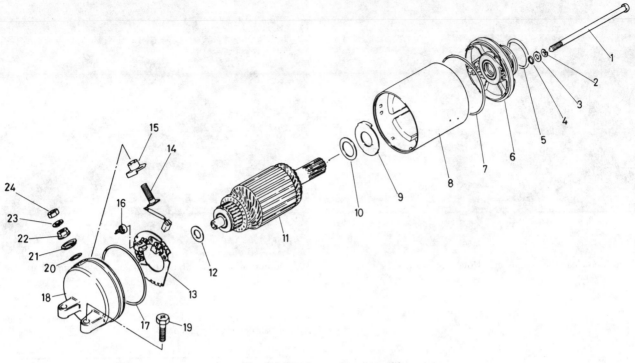

Fig. 6.6 Starter motor assembly

1	Screw – 2 off	7	O-ring	13	Brush plate	19	Bolt – 2 off
2	Spring washer – 2 off	8	Housing	14	Brush	20	O-ring
3	Washer – 2 off	9	Shim	15	Holder	21	Bush
4	O-ring – 2 off	10	Shim	16	Spring – 2 off	22	Nut
5	O-ring	11	Armature	17	O-ring	23	Spring washer
6	End cover	12	Shim	18	End cover	24	Nut

10 Starter motor: removal and overhaul

Note: The design of the engine is such that the starter motor cannot be removed from its recess unless the cam chain tensioner unit has first been detached from the cylinder block. The mechanism is held by two bolts and is easily removed. When refitting it, however, it is necessary to follow the correct procedure to ensure that the chain is tensioned automatically. See Chapter 1, Section 39, paragraph 10 onwards for details.

1 Remove the starter motor cover and disconnect the starter cable, having first checked that the ignition is switched off. Remove the two bolts which retain the starter motor, pull the motor to the right to disengage it, then lift it clear of its recess.

2 Release the two long screws which retain the motor end covers and lift away the brush assembly. Measure the length of the brushes, renewing them if they have worn below the minimum length of 9 mm (0.35 in).

3 Inspect the commutator segments on which the brushes bear. If badly burnt or scored, the only alternative to renewal is to have the commutator skimmed and the segments re-cut by a vehicle electrical specialist. The minimum undercut is 0.2 mm (0.008 in). A dirty commutator can be restored by carefully cleaning it with fine (400 grit) emery paper.

4 The armature windings may be checked by testing between each commutator segment and the armature core with a multimeter set on the resistance scale. If any segment is shorted to the core, the armature must be renewed. Check that there is conductivity between each pair of segments, any open circuit indicating the need for renewal.

5 When assembling the motor, ensure that the brushes are fitted in their respective holders. Fit the brush plate over the commutator, and check that it aligns properly when the end cover is fitted. The brush plate and the end cover have locating notches to ensure alignment. Apply a thread locking compound to the two retaining screws and tighten them securely.

10.2 Check brush length using vernier caliper

10.3 Check and clean the commutator. Note plain washer

10.5 Do not omit washer on right-hand end of armature shaft

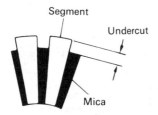

Fig. 6.7 Commutator undercut measurement

11 Headlamp: adjustment

E models
1   The rectangular headlamp unit is housed in the handlebar fairing moulding. This is in turn secured to the steering head and forms a backing for the instrument panel. The housing is fixed in relation to the forks, and to provide horizontal and vertical alignment two separate adjustment screws are located in the edge of the rim; the lower screw controls vertical alignment and the upper screw controls horizontal alignment.

L models
2   A round headlamp unit is fitted to brackets on each fork leg. Vertical alignment is adjusted by slackening the two mounting bolts and turning the assembly to the desired position. Horizontal alignment is controlled by a screw in the rim edge.

ES and EF models
3   A rectangular unit is housed inside the fairing. Adjustment is controlled by two knobs which can be accessed from the inside of the fairing. This arrangement permits adjustments to be made whilst riding.

All models
5   The horizontal alignment should be set so that the beam shines straight ahead on main beam. The correct position is best found on an experimental basis during a night-time ride. Vertical alignment must comply with local laws, and these may vary from state to state in the US. In the UK, lighting regulations require that the headlamp is adjusted so that the light will not dazzle a person standing at a distance of not less than 25 feet from the machine and on the same plane, and whose eye level is not less than 3 ft 6 inches from the ground.

Adjustment should be made with the rider seated normally, plus any regular passenger or luggage.

12 Headlamp: bulb renewal

1   In the case of the unfaired machines, remove the screws which pass through the front edge of the headlamp housing and lift the headlamp assembly clear of its recess. Pull off the rubber dust seal from the back of the reflector unit and unplug the wiring connector. On machines equipped with a front parking (city) lamp, pull the bulbholder out of its rubber collar.
2   On the machines equipped with a fairing it is possible to reach the bulbholder from inside the fairing without disturbing the headlamp unit. Start by unplugging the wiring connector, then pull off the rubber dust seal.
3   The headlamp bulb is retained by a ring which can be released by twisting it anti-clockwise. Lift away the ring and spring, then lift out the bulb, holding it by the metal base only. On no account should the bulb envelope be touched. If this is done accidentally, wipe off any finger marks carefully, using a paper tissue moistened with methylated spirit or alcohol. Where a parking lamp is fitted, its bulb can be removed from the bulbholder by turning it anti-clockwise.

13 Tail/brake lamp: bulb renewal

1   The design of the tail lamp assembly varies according to the model, but in each case access to bulbs is gained after removing the lens, this being retained by two or more screws. The lamp contains a twin filament stop/tail bulb and in the case of the E and ES models, a separate number (licence) plate bulb. In each case the bulbs are of the bayonet fitting type and are removed by pushing them inwards slightly and twisting anti-clockwise. The twin filament types have offset pins to ensure that they are fitted correctly. It is important to replace bulbs with items of the same wattage, and the metal parts of the bulbholder should be checked for corrosion.

14 Turn signal lamps: bulb renewal

Release the screws which retain the lens and lift it away. Remove the bulb by pushing it inwards slightly and twisting anti-clockwise. In certain areas the front turn signal lamps double as running lamps, in which case twin filament bulbs are fitted. These have offset pins to ensure that they are fitted correctly. Check that the rubber seal is sound before refitting the lens.

11.3 Headlamp adjusters (arrowed) as fitted to half and full fairing models

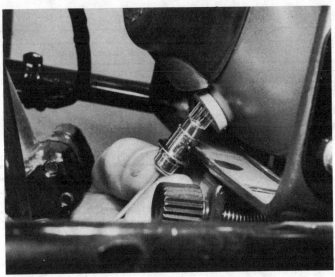

12.1 Parking (city) lamp is a push fit in back of headlamp

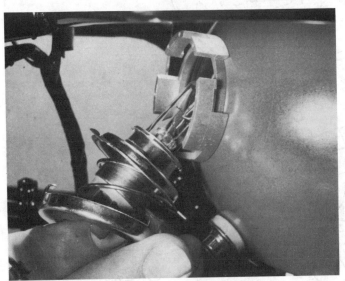

12.3 Headlamp bulb is retained by bayonet-fitting ring

13.1 Separate stop/tail and number (licence) plate bulbs are fitted

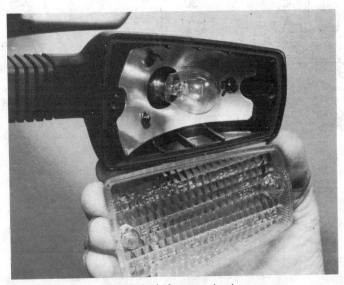

14.1 Turn signal bulb is reached after removing lens

15 Instrument panel: examination – all except L models

1 The instrument panel assembly houses the speedometer, tachometer, fuel gauge and the various warning and instrument illumination lamps. Access to the panel can be gained after removing the fairing, releasing the instrument panel wiring connectors and speedometer drive cable and removing the two mounting nuts. Once detached, remove the bottom cover, then release the screws which secure the top of the panel to the base. Note that to change bulbs, other than those of the check panel, it will be necessary to remove the bottom cover only.

2 The accompanying circuit diagram shows the instrument panel wiring connections in detail, and should be used in conjunction with the main wiring diagram to locate any fault in the panel. A multimeter can be used as a continuity tester to trace a suspected break in the wiring or a blown bulb, without having to remove the instrument panel from the machine.

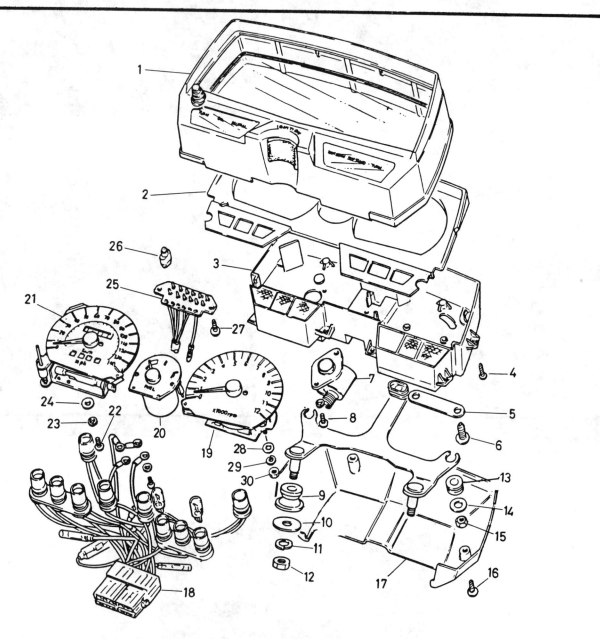

Fig. 6.8 Instrument console – all E, ES and EF models

1 Top cover	
2 Panel	
3 Housing	
4 Screw	
5 Retaining plate	
6 Screw	
7 Speedometer cable terminal – where fitted	
8 Screw – 2 off	16 Screw – 4 off
9 Grommet – 2 off	17 Bottom cover
10 Washer – 2 off	18 Wiring
11 Spring washer – 2 off	19 Tachometer
12 Nut – 2 off	20 Fuel gauge
13 Grommet – 2 off	21 Speedometer
14 Washer – 3 off	22 Screw – 4 off
15 Nut – 3 off	23 Spring washer – 4 off
24 Washer – 4 off	
25 Gear position indicator	
26 Bulb	
27 Screw – 2 off	
28 Washer – 2 off	
29 Spring washer – 2 off	
30 Nut – 2 off	

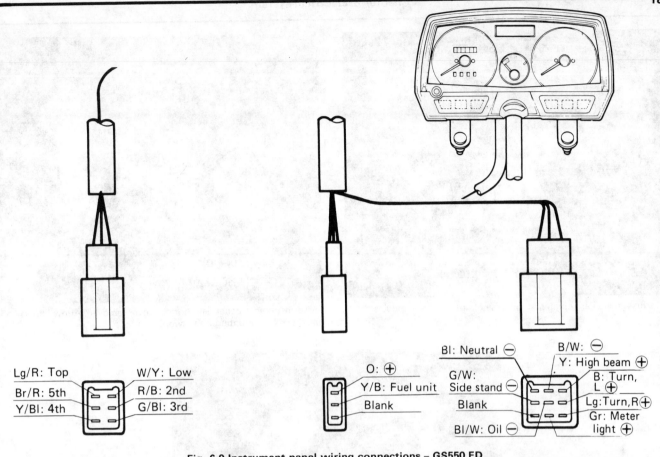

Fig. 6.9 Instrument panel wiring connections – GS550 ED

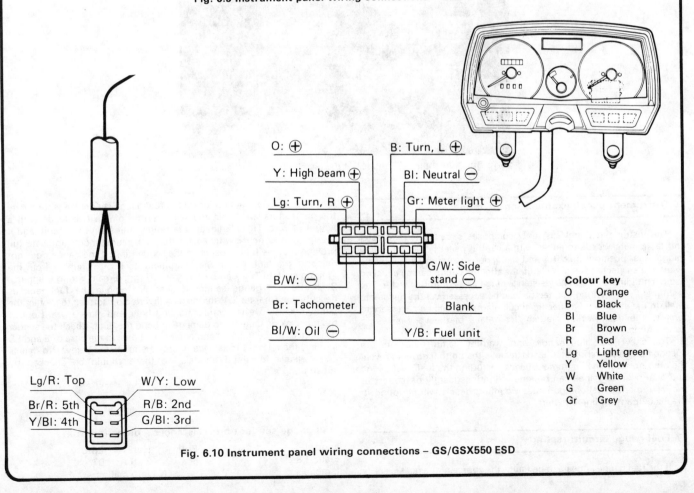

Fig. 6.10 Instrument panel wiring connections – GS/GSX550 ESD

15.1a Instruments are combined into a single panel (not L models)

15.1b Instrument panel with bottom cover removed. Arrow shows panel bracket mounting bolt (two fitted)

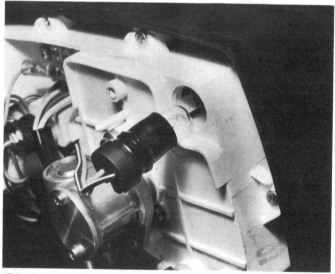

15.1c Bulbs are a push-fit in back of the panel

16 Instrument panel: examination – L models

1   The instrument panel assembly comprises separate speedometer and tachometer heads together with a central panel housing the fuel gauge, gear position indicator and the various warning lamps. In the event of a suspected electrical fault, the affected circuit can be checked using a multimeter set on its resistance range as a continuity tester. The instrument panel wiring connectors can be accessed via the headlamp shell. In the absence of a specific circuit diagram it will be necessary to refer to the main wiring diagram for details of the various wiring connections.

2   To renew the illumination and warning lamp bulbs in the speedometer and tachometer heads, remove the bottom cover to reveal the bulb holders. The instrument heads, including the fuel level gauge and gear position panel, can be renewed independently of the rest of the instrument panel components. Mounting details will be found in the accompanying line drawing.

17 Fuel gauge circuit: testing

1   If the fuel gauge appears to be faulty, the source of the fault is easily traced. Open the seat and locate the fuel gauge sender leads. Separate the connectors, then join the harness side of the two leads with a length of wire. This eliminates the sender unit from the circuit, and if the ignition is now switched on the fuel gauge should indicate full proving that the fault must lie in the sender unit. If the gauge does not respond, the fault lies in the instrument itself or its supply from the ignition switch. This can be checked using the main wiring diagram.

2   If the fuel gauge sender is suspect, remove the fuel tank as described in Chapter 2. With the tank inverted on soft rag to protect the paintwork, remove the sender holding bolts and manoeuvre it out of the tank, taking care not to damage or bend the float. Check the sender resistances at the full, half and empty positions. In the case of E and ES models, the relevant resistance figures are indicated below. No details are available for the L models, so these should be checked by substituting a new unit.

Fuel gauge sender unit resistances – ohms (approx)

Model	Full	Half	Empty
E and ES	6	32.5	97
L models		No information	

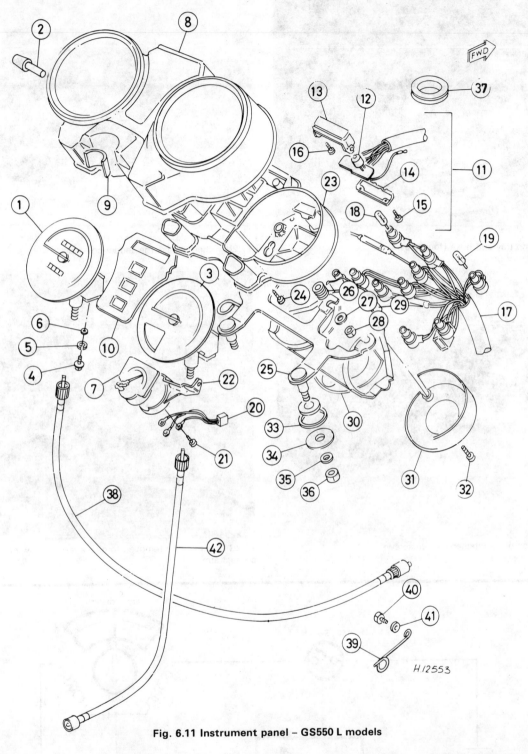

Fig. 6.11 Instrument panel – GS550 L models

H.12553

1 Speedometer
2 Reset knob
3 Tachometer
4 Screw – 4 off
5 Spring washer – 4 off
6 Washer – 4 off
7 Fuel gauge
8 Top cover
9 Shield
10 Warning lamp lens
11 Gear position indicator
assembly

12 Bulb – 6 off
13 Display panel
14 Cover
15 Screw – 2 off
16 Screw – 2 off
17 Warning lamp wiring
18 Bulb – 5 off
19 Bulb – 5 off
20 Fuel gauge wiring
21 Screw – 3 off
22 Fuel gauge housing

23 Instrument housing
24 Screw – 4 off
25 Mounting bracket
26 Grommet – 4 off
27 Washer – 2 off
28 Nut – 2 off
29 Bottom cover
30 Speedometer bottom cover
31 Tachometer bottom cover
32 Screw – 4 off
33 Grommet – 2 off

34 Washer – 2 off
35 Spring washer – 2 off
36 Nut – 2 off
37 Gear position indicator wiring
grommet
38 Speedometer cable
39 Cable guide
40 Bolt
41 Washer
42 Tachometer cable

17.2a Remove drip tray and hose (four screws) ...

17.2b ... then release the sender cover plate

17.2c Sender assembly is retained by two screws

17.2d Cover can be removed to check resistance windings and contact arm

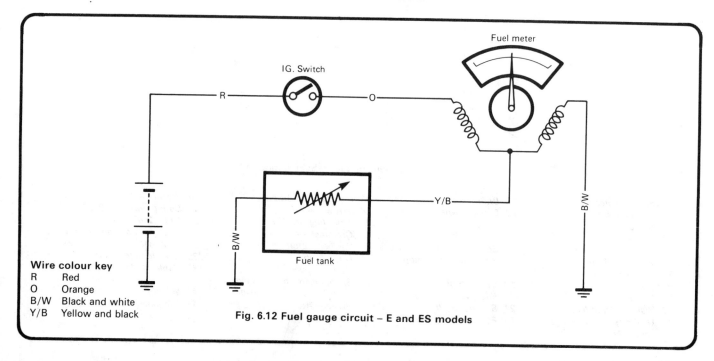

Wire colour key

R   Red
O   Orange
B/W   Black and white
Y/B   Yellow and black

IG. Switch

Fuel meter

Fuel tank

Fig. 6.12 Fuel gauge circuit – E and ES models

18 Turn signal relay: examination and renewal

1   The turn signal relay is retained in a resilient mounting behind the left-hand side panel. If the unit is functioning normally, a series of audible clicks will be heard as the lamps flash. It should be noted that the most likely cause of problems with the turn signal system is a failed bulb or a break in the wiring. In such cases, there is usually one click, after which the remaining lamp on that side of the machine will flash rapidly and weakly. It follows that the bulbs and wiring should be checked before turning attention to the relay.

2   If the system is inoperative on both sides, check the supply to the relay. If a faulty relay is indicated, it is best checked by substitution. Note that if one side of the system operates the relay can be assumed to be serviceable and the fault must lie in the lamps, switch and wiring on that side.

19 Warning lamp switches: testing

1   Each machine is fitted with various switches which control the warning and indicator lamps in the instrument panel. In the event of a failure not attributable to the bulb or wiring, check the relevant switch using a multimeter or a continuity tester. If the switch fails to show an open circuit in one direction and a closed circuit in the other, it should be renewed. Further details on the various switches are given below.

Gear position indicator switch
2   Trace the wiring back from the gear position switch and separate the connector. Refer to the wiring diagram and check each lead in turn whilst selecting the relevant gear. In each case, the lead should be earthed when its gear is selected and isolated in all other positions. If the switch is operating normally, check and renew any blown bulbs.

Oil pressure switch
3   Disconnect the oil pressure switch lead and connect the meter probes between its terminal and earth (ground). With the engine off, continuity should be indicated. If the engine is now started, the meter should indicate isolation as the switch responds to rising pressure. If the switch does not operate as described above, it must be renewed. If the switch operates normally, check the warning lamp bulb and the associated wiring.

Side stand switch
4   Trace and disconnect the leads from the side stand switch and test for continuity when the stand is down. If the stand is now retracted,

the meter should indicate isolation. If required, the switch can be adjusted by altering its position using the adjuster nuts on the body.

20 Handlebar switches: maintenance and testing

1   Generally speaking, the switch clusters can be expected to give little trouble despite their necessarily complicated construction. The switches take the form of two halves which are clamped around the handlebar ends, the right-hand unit doubling as the housing for the throttle twistgrip. The assemblies are in a somewhat exposed position and occasionally the ingress of water may cause short circuits. This can be resolved by separating the switch halves and spraying the switches with a water dispersal fluid such as WD40. To prevent recurrent problems, pack the switch halves with silicone grease.

2   In the event of more serious malfunctions, trace the switch wiring back to its connectors and check for continuity using a multimeter set on the resistance range. The switch contacts and wiring colours are shown in the wiring diagrams at the end of this Chapter. It is difficult to repair a faulty switch, but worth trying before ordering a new assembly. Note that it is well worth checking the local breakers (wreckers) for a used switch cluster before resorting to a new unit.

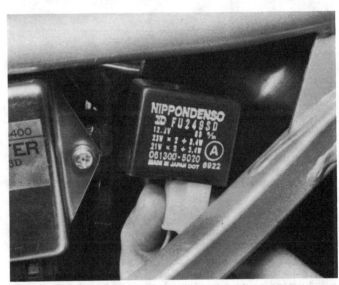

18.1 Turn signal relay is fitted to rear of ignition unit

19.4 Side stand switch is fitted to bracket on frame

20.1a The right-hand and ...

20.1b ... left-hand handlebar switch clusters ...

20.1c ... can be separated for inspection and lubrication

21 Ignition switch: removal and replacement

The combined ignition and lighting master switch is bolted to the underside of the upper yoke and may be removed after the instrument panel has been detached to gain access to the retaining bolts. Trace back the switch wiring to the connector and separate it before lifting the switch away. It is not possible to repair or dismantle a defective switch because of its sealed construction; a new unit must be fitted.

22 Brake lamp switches: location and maintenance

1   The front brake lamp switch takes the form of a small sealed unit retained by two screws to the underside of the right-hand handlebar switch assembly. In the event of a fault, try soaking the switch with WD40 or similar. If this fails to resolve the problem, the switch must be renewed. A certain amount of adjustment is possible if the retaining screws are slackened and the switch body moved to the required position.
2   The rear brake switch is located next to the rear master cylinder (near the brake pedal, L models). The switch is of the plunger type and is operated by a spring from the brake arm. The switch is adjusted by moving the body in relation to the mounting bracket. Slacken the switch body locknut and turn the nuts in the required direction until the desired setting is achieved, holding the switch body to prevent it from turning.
3   Both switches should be adjusted so that the brake lamp comes on just before the brake begins to operate. If either switch malfunctions, it must be renewed.

23 Fuses: location

1   The fuses are housed in a moulded plastic box behind the right-hand side panel, the function and rating of each fuse being clearly marked. The fuses are of the blade type and are encapsulated in plastic. The plastic bodies are colour coded to indicate their rating. Spare fuses are provided in the fuse box, and these should always be replaced, if used.
2   Before renewing a blown fuse, check for any obvious fault or short

circuit in the associated wiring, particularly if any one fuse has failed more than once.
3   The fuse box incorporates an accessory terminal. Note that the terminal has a 10 amp fuse, and any accessory connected to it must be within this rating.

24 Horn(s): location and examination

Depending on the model, a single or twin horn arrangement is fitted and is retained on a flexible steel bracket to the front of the frame. If the horn fails or operates feebly, it can be adjusted using the small screw provided after the locknut has been slackened. The screw should be set to give the best consistent note. If adjustment fails to restore the horn, it must be renewed; it is not possible to dismantle it for repair.

22.2 Rear brake switch can be adjusted

23.1 Spare fuse is housed in fuse box cover

24.1 Horn is bolted to bracket above the oil cooler

Cable and wire routing diagrams overleaf

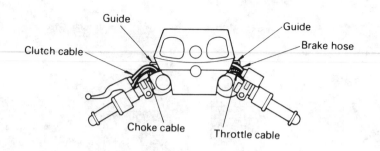

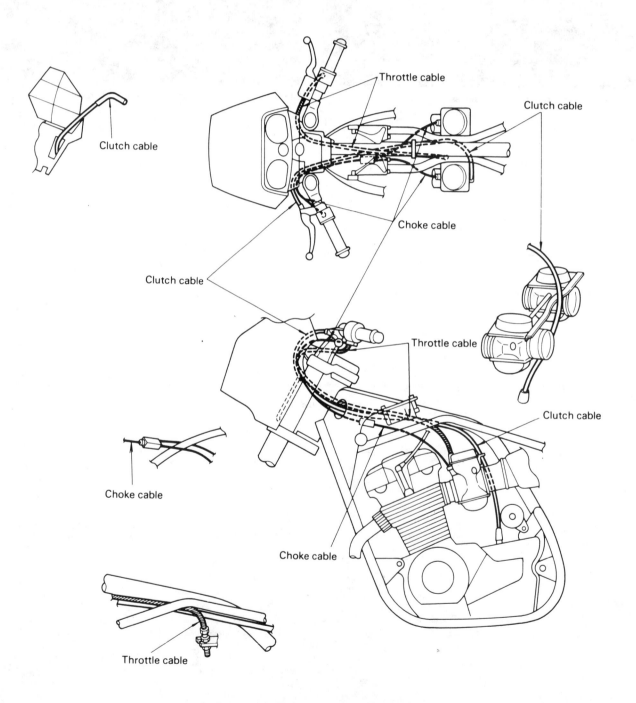

Correct routing of control cables – typical

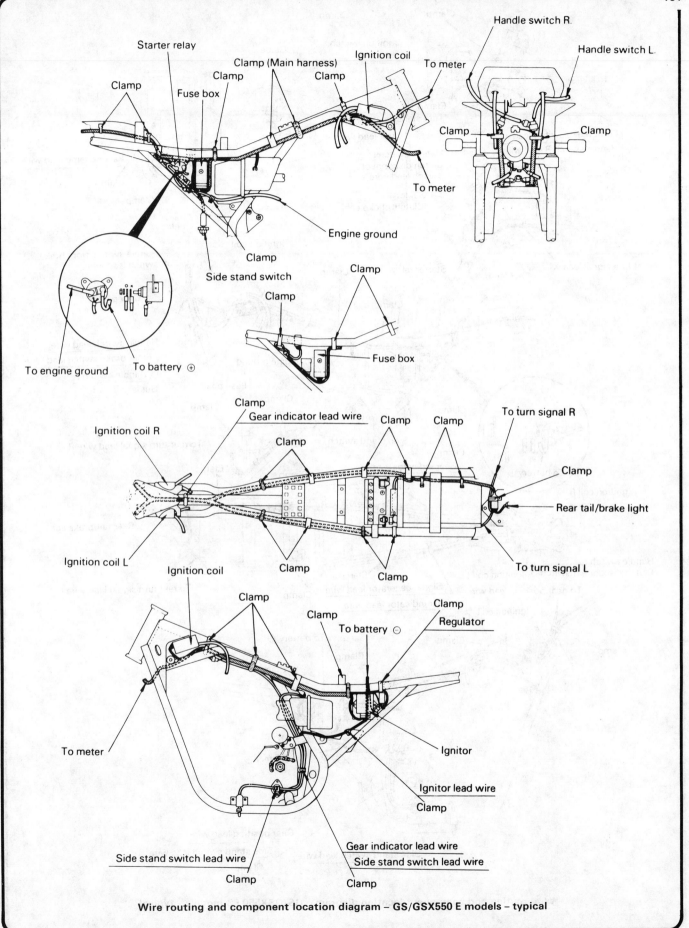

Wire routing and component location diagram – GS/GSX550 E models – typical

192

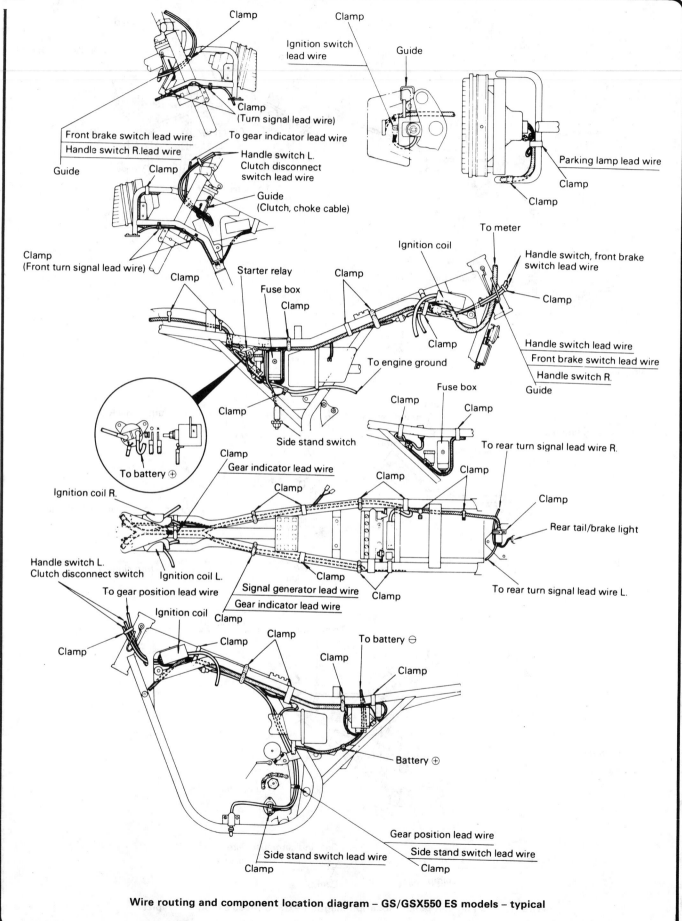

Clamp

Clamp

Ignition switch
lead wire

Guide

Front brake switch lead wire

Handle switch R.lead wire

Guide

Clamp

Clamp
(Turn signal lead wire)

To gear indicator lead wire

Handle switch L.
Clutch disconnect
switch lead wire

Guide
(Clutch, choke cable)

Parking lamp lead wire

Clamp

Clamp

To meter

Ignition coil

Handle switch, front brake
switch lead wire

Clamp

Clamp
(Front turn signal lead wire)

Clamp

Starter relay

Fuse box

Clamp

Clamp

Clamp

Handle switch lead wire

Front brake switch lead wire

Handle switch R.

Guide

To engine ground

To battery ⊕

Clamp

Side stand switch

Clamp

Gear indicator lead wire

Ignition coil R.

Clamp

Clamp

Clamp

Fuse box

Clamp

To rear turn signal lead wire R.

Clamp

Rear tail/brake light

Handle switch L.
Clutch disconnect switch

Ignition coil L.

To gear position lead wire

Ignition coil

Clamp

Clamp

Clamp

Clamp

Signal generator lead wire

Gear indicator lead wire

Clamp

To rear turn signal lead wire L.

Clamp

Clamp

To battery ⊖

Clamp

Clamp

Battery ⊕

Gear position lead wire

Side stand switch lead wire

Side stand switch lead wire

Clamp

Clamp

Wire routing and component location diagram – GS/GSX550 ES models – typical

Chapter 7 The 1986 to 1988
GS/GSX550 ES and GS550 L models

Contents

Specifications

Note: *specifications are only given where they differ from those in the preceding chapters. If the information required is not shown in this section refer back to the GSX550 ESE information for the UK models and the GS550 ESF or LF information for US models.*

Model dimensions and weights – US GS550 LG model

Overall length	2125 mm (83.6 in)
Overall width	825 mm (32.5 in)
Overall height	1155 mm (45.5 in)
Wheelbase	1440 mm (56.7 in)
Dry weight:	
49-state model	189 kg (416.7 lb)
California model	190 kg (418.9 lb)

Specifications relating to Chapter 1

Engine – UK models

Compression pressure	10 – 15 kg cm² (142 – 214 psi)

Engine – US models

Piston ring free end gap:	
Top	About 8.0 mm (0.31 in)
Service limit	6.4 mm (0.25 in)
Second	About 8.5 mm (0.33 in)
Service limit	6.8 mm (0.27 in)
Piston ring installed end gap:	
Top	0.10 – 0.25 mm (0.004 – 0.010 in)
Second	0.10 – 0.30 mm (0.004 – 0.012 in)
Service limit	0.7 mm (0.03 in)

Specifications relating to Chapter 2

Carburettor – UK models

Identity number	43580
Jet needle clip position	4th groove from top
Throttle valve	110
Pilot screw	Preset (2 turns out)
Pilot air jet	135

Carburettor – US models

Identity number:

GS550 ESG 49-state model	43660
GS550 ESG California model	43650
GS550 LG 49-state model	43630
GS550 LG California model	43640
Starter jet	100

Specifications relating to Chapter 4

Front forks – UK GSX550 ESG, ESH

Oil quantity (per leg)	317 cc (11.2 Imp fl oz)
Cap bolt torque setting	2.0 – 3.0 kgf m (14.5 – 21.7 lbf ft)

Front forks – GS550 LG

Stroke	140 mm (5.5 in)
Oil level	181 mm (7.1 in)
Oil grade	SAE 10W fork oil
Oil quantity (per leg)	248 cc (8.4 US fl oz)
Fork spring free length (service limit)	449 mm (17.7 in)
Front wheel spindle pinch bolt torque setting	1.5 – 2.5 kgf m (10.8 – 18.1 lbf ft)

Specifications relating to Chapter 5

Tyre sizes – GS550 LG

Front	100/90-19 57H

Torque wrench settings – GS550 LG model

Front wheel spindle pinch bolt	1.5 – 2.5 kgf m (10.8 – 18.1 lbf ft)

1 Introduction

The first six chapters of this manual cover the GS/GSX550 models from their introduction in 1983 up until 1986 when the G suffix models were introduced. All later models, namely the UK GSX550 ESG, ESH and the US GS550 ESG, LG, are covered in this supplementary chapter. Throughout the manual all models are identified by their Suzuki production code, rather than the year of manufacture. If not known, the correct code can be ascertained from the machine's frame number, details of which will be found on page 5 of the manual for earlier models and at the end of this section for later models.

Note that in the case of later UK GSX550 E (handlebar-faired) and GSX550 EFE (fully-faired) models, reference should be made to chapters 1 to 6 for all information because both models remained unchanged since their introduction in 1984 until their discontinuation in 1988.

Apart from detail changes to colour and graphics the models covered in this chapter differ in very few respects from their predecessors. When working on one of these models refer first to this chapter to check if a revised procedure or specification is given. If the information required is not found the task will be unchanged from that given in the appropriate part of chapters 1 to 6.

To assist owners in identifying their machines the following table gives the full model codes, initial frame numbers and the approximate dates of import; note that the latter may not necessarily coincide with the machine's date of registration.

UK models	Initial frame no.	Dates of import	
GSX550 ESG	GN71D-112893	Mar '86 – Jan '88	
GSX550 ESH	GN71D-115583	Jan '88 – Dec '88	

US models	Initial frame no.	Dates of import	Model year
GS550 ESG	JS1GN74A G2100001	Nov '85 – 1986	1986
GS550 LG	JS1GN72L G2100001	Nov '85 – 1986	1986

2 Routine maintenance: service intervals – UK models

For GSX550 ESG and ESH models the following engine and chassis maintenance schedule should be followed instead of that given on page 26 of this manual. The reference number to the right of the task relates to the appropriate text in the Routine Maintenance section of the manual.

	Sec no.
Initial two months (600 mi/1000 km)	
Engine fastener check	3, 12
Valve clearances check	4
Fuel pipe inspection	7
Engine oil and filter renewal	8
Idle speed check	7
Clutch adjustment check	11
Drive chain check	13
Brake check	14, 15
Tyre check	17
Steering check	18
Chassis fasteners check	20
Every 600 mi (1000 km)	
Drive chain clean and lubrication	13
Every 2000 mi (3000 km)	
Air filter clean	1
Yearly, or every 4000 mi (6000 km)	
Battery check	2
Engine fasteners check	3, 12
Valve clearances check	4
Spark plugs clean	6
Fuel pipe check	7
Engine oil and filter renewal	8
Idle speed check	7
Brake check	14, 15
Tyre check	17
Steering check	18
Chassis fastener check	20
Two yearly, or every 7500 mi (12 000 km)	
Air filter element renewal	1
Spark plug renewal	6
Front fork oil renewal	19
Two yearly	
Brake fluid renewal	16
Four yearly	
Fuel pipe renewal	7
Brake hose renewal	15

3 Evaporative emission control system: general – California models

1 Although different in design, the evaporative emission control systems fitted to the ESG and LG models operate in exactly the same way as the earlier system described in Chapter 2, Section 16.

2 Other than performing a check of the system hoses at the recommended interval of every 4000 miles (6000 km) there is no maintenance required. The manufacturer does, however, recommend that the hoses are renewed every four years.

3 The charcoal canister is located in the compartment at the rear of the seat and its vapour and purge hoses are tied to the frame tubes at various intervals along their length. Ensure that the hoses are not trapped at any point and that they are well secured, yet not compressed, by the clamps provided.

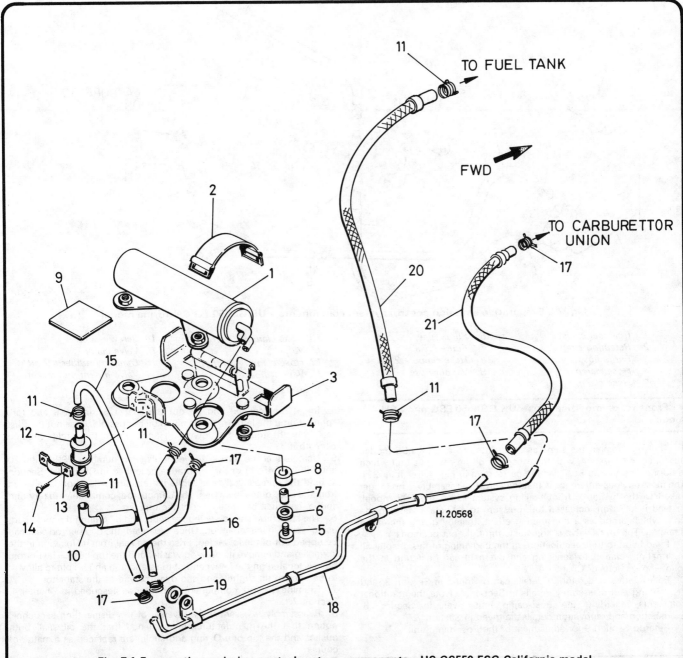

TO FUEL TANK

FWD

TO CARBURETTOR UNION

H.20568

Fig. 7.1 Evaporative emission control system components – US GS550 ESG California model

1 Charcoal canister	7 Spacer – 3 off	12 Valve	17 Hose clamp – 4 off
2 Retaining strap	8 Grommet – 3 off	13 Valve clamp	18 Vapour and purge pipes
3 Mounting bracket	9 Damping rubber – 3 off	14 Screw – 2 off	19 Washer
4 Nut – 3 off	10 Vapour hose	15 Vapour hose	20 Vapour hose
5 Bolt – 3 off	11 Hose clamp – 6 off	16 Purge hose	21 Purge hose
6 Washer – 3 off			

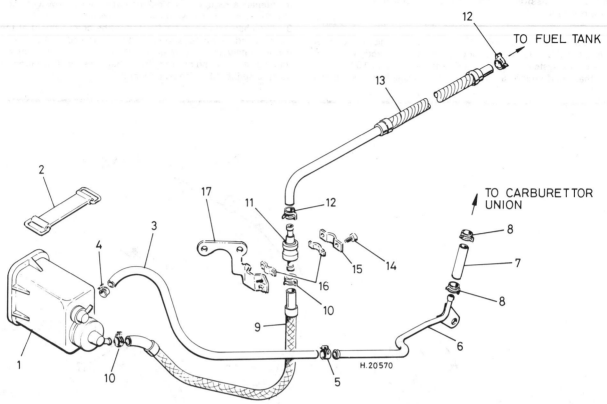

Fig. 7.2 Evaporative emission control system components – US GS550 LG California model

1 *Charcoal canister*	6 *Purge pipe*	10 *Hose clamp – 2 off*	14 *Screw – 2 off*
2 *Retaining strap*	7 *Purge hose*	11 *Valve*	15 *Valve clamp*
3 *Purge hose*	8 *Hose clamp – 2 off*	12 *Hose clamp – 2 off*	16 *Damping rubber – 2 off*
4 *Hose clamp*	9 *Vapour hose*	13 *Vapour hose*	17 *Valve mounting bracket*
5 *Hose clamp*			

4 Front forks: modifications – UK GSX550 ESG and ESH models

1 The forks remain the same as those fitted to the UK ESE model, described in Chapter 4, with the exception of the anti-dive unit which is now of the Suzuki Posi-damp type (shown in Fig. 4.7 as item 37). The most obvious difference is that the anti-dive assembly is no longer linked to the hydraulic front braking system as on the ESE model. Instead it relies on increased fork pressure to activate a valve in the unit, which produces a constricting effect, thereby giving increased damping. The unit's valve is adjustable through four positions.

2 In addition to the specifications at the beginning of this chapter all information relating to servicing and overhaul can be found in the following sections of Chapter 4:

3 Fork removal and refitting details can be found in Section 3, and dismantling and reassembly details in Section 4. Note the additional comments regarding the Posi-damp unit given in Section 6. Examination and renovation details are given in Section 7.

4 Refer to Section 9 for adjustment of the Posi-damp unit.

5 Front forks: dismantling and reassembly – GS550 LG model

1 Remove the front wheel as described in Section 6 of this chapter.

2 Remove the fork legs from the machine as described in Chapter 4, Section 3.

3 Dealing with each fork separately, prise out the dust cap from the top of the stanchion. The top plug is retained by a wire circlip and is removed by depressing the plug, against spring pressure, while the circlip is removed; note that the plug may be expelled forcibly when the pressure is released.

4 Invert the fork leg and tip out the spacer, spring seat and fork spring. Pump the leg to expel as much oil as possible. Prise out the dust seal from the top of the lower leg and remove the circlip situated beneath it.

5 Using either the Suzuki service tools (Part numbers 09940–34520 and 09940–34561) or the alternative described in Chapter 4, Section 4, hold the damper rod head while its retaining Allen bolt is released from the base of the lower leg. The damper rod, complete with rebound spring, can then be tipped out of the fork leg.

6 The stanchion and lower leg are separated by pulling the two apart, using a slide-hammer action. Once separated, the damper rod seat can be tipped out of the lower leg. Prise the oil seal from its location in the lower leg and remove its backing washer and the top bush. The bottom bush is located on the lower end of the stanchion and is split to allow it to be opened up slightly and slid over the end of the stanchion.

7 Examine the fork components for wear as described in Chapter 4, Section 7.

8 Reassembly is essentially a reversal of the dismantling sequence, noting that the manufacturer recommends that the oil seal, both bushes and the top bolt O-ring and circlip are replaced as a matter of course.

9 The bottom bush can be fitted to the stanchion by hand, taking care not to scratch the Teflon coating of the bush. Assemble the damper rod and rebound spring and position fully into the stanchion. Smear the stanchion with fresh fork oil and fit the damper rod seat to the end of the rod protruding from the stanchion. Using the holding tool to prevent the damper rod being pushed back up the stanchion, insert the stanchion into the lower leg. Ensure that the threads of the damper rod Allen bolt are clean and dry before applying a thread locking compound to its threaded portion, and fit the Allen bolt and its sealing washer to the lower leg, tightening to the specified torque setting.

10 Press the top bush into its housing in the lower leg, followed by the backing washer and oil seal; use a piece of tubing which bears on the

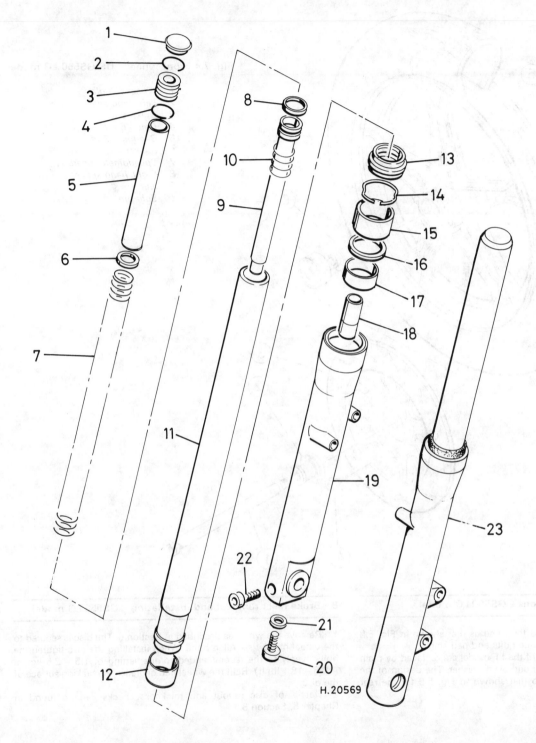

**Fig. 7.3 Front forks –
US GS550 LG model**

1 Dust cap
2 Circlip
3 Top plug
4 O-ring
5 Spacer
6 Spring seat
7 Fork spring
8 Damper rod piston ring
9 Damper rod
10 Rebound spring
11 Stanchion
12 Bottom bush
13 Dust seal
14 Circlip
15 Oil seal
16 Backing washer
17 Top bush
18 Damper rod seat
19 Right-hand lower leg
20 Allen bolt
21 Sealing washer
22 Wheel spindle pinch bolt
23 Left-hand fork leg

H.20569

seal's hard outer edge to drift the seal into position. Secure the assembly with the circlip and fit the dust seal.
11 If removed, replace the oil drain plug and fill the fork with the specified quantity and type of oil. Holding the leg upright measure the fork oil level using a dipstick marked at the correct distance from the top of the stanchion. Fit the fork spring with its closer-pitched coils uppermost and tapered section towards the bottom, then install the spring seat and spacer. Finally refit the top plug, depressing it to permit the fitting of a new retaining circlip. Ensure that the circlip is correctly seated in its groove before refitting the dust cap.

6 Front wheel: removal and refitting – GS550 LG model

1 Although component layout differs slightly from the LF model described in Chapter 5, Section 3, note that the removal and installation procedure is unchanged. Due to the fitting of modified front forks the wheel spindle is now secured to the right-hand leg by a pinch bolt, rather than the clamp used on all other models.
2 The GS550 LG front wheel assembly is shown in the accompanying illustration.

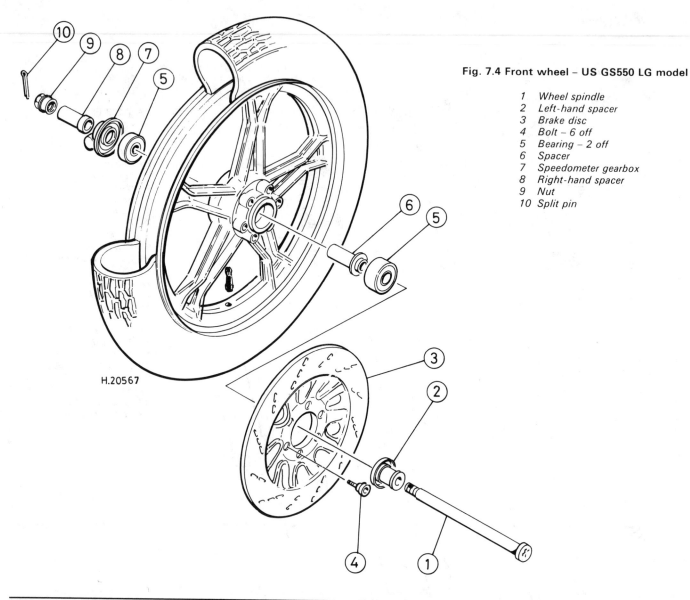

H.20567

Fig. 7.4 Front wheel – US GS550 LG model

1 Wheel spindle
2 Left-hand spacer
3 Brake disc
4 Bolt – 6 off
5 Bearing – 2 off
6 Spacer
7 Speedometer gearbox
8 Right-hand spacer
9 Nut
10 Split pin

7 Brake caliper: modifications – GS550 LG model

1 The caliper assembly remains the same as that shown in Fig. 5.8 with the exception of the mounting bolts and pad shims.
2 The flanged mounting bolts of the LF model are replaced by plain bolts fitted with a spring washer and plain washer. The design of the brake pad shim has changed to that shown in Fig. 5.9 for the rear caliper assembly.

8 Brake disc: removal and installation – GS550 LG model

1 Remove the wheel as described in Section 6. The disc is secured to the wheel hub by six Allen bolts. When installing the disc tighten the bolts evenly to the recommended torque setting of 1.5 – 2.5 kgf m (10.8 – 18.1 lbf ft). Refit the wheel and degrease the braking surface of the disc.
2 Details of disc runout and thickness checks can be found in Chapter 5, Section 8.

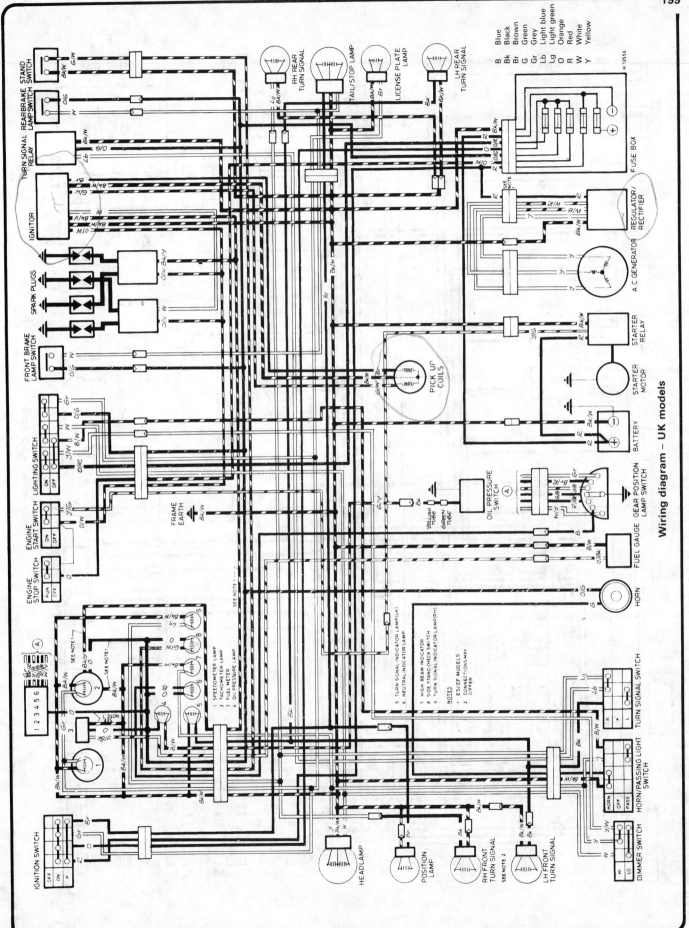

Wiring diagram – UK models

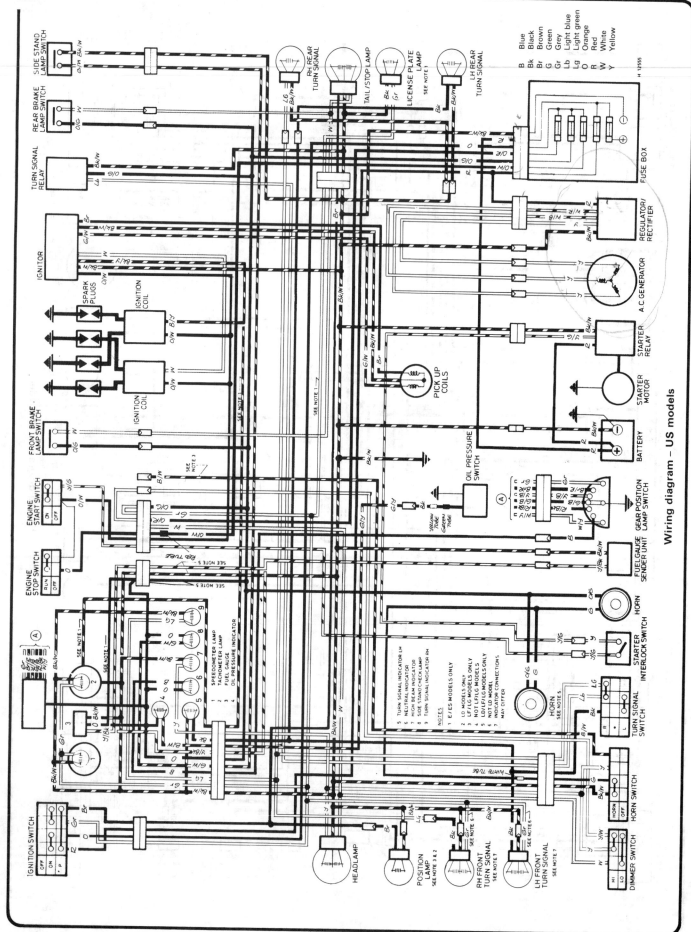

Wiring diagram – US models

Conversion factors

Length (distance)
Inches (in)	X	25.4	= Millimetres (mm)	X	0.0394	= Inches (in)
Feet (ft)	X	0.305	= Metres (m)	X	3.281	= Feet (ft)
Miles	X	1.609	= Kilometres (km)	X	0.621	= Miles

Volume (capacity)
Cubic inches (cu in; in³)	X	16.387	= Cubic centimetres (cc; cm³)	X	0.061	= Cubic inches (cu in; in³)
Imperial pints (Imp pt)	X	0.568	= Litres (l)	X	1.76	= Imperial pints (Imp pt)
Imperial quarts (Imp qt)	X	1.137	= Litres (l)	X	0.88	= Imperial quarts (Imp qt)
Imperial quarts (Imp qt)	X	1.201	= US quarts (US qt)	X	0.833	= Imperial quarts (Imp qt)
US quarts (US qt)	X	0.946	= Litres (l)	X	1.057	= US quarts (US qt)
Imperial gallons (Imp gal)	X	4.546	= Litres (l)	X	0.22	= Imperial gallons (Imp gal)
Imperial gallons (Imp gal)	X	1.201	= US gallons (US gal)	X	0.833	= Imperial gallons (Imp gal)
US gallons (US gal)	X	3.785	= Litres (l)	X	0.264	= US gallons (US gal)

Mass (weight)
Ounces (oz)	X	28.35	= Grams (g)	X	0.035	= Ounces (oz)
Pounds (lb)	X	0.454	= Kilograms (kg)	X	2.205	= Pounds (lb)

Force
Ounces-force (ozf; oz)	X	0.278	= Newtons (N)	X	3.6	= Ounces-force (ozf; oz)
Pounds-force (lbf; lb)	X	4.448	= Newtons (N)	X	0.225	= Pounds-force (lbf; lb)
Newtons (N)	X	0.1	= Kilograms-force (kgf; kg)	X	9.81	= Newtons (N)

Pressure
Pounds-force per square inch (psi; lbf/in²; lb/in²)	X	0.070	= Kilograms-force per square centimetre (kgf/cm²; kg/cm²)	X	14.223	= Pounds-force per square inch (psi; lbf/in²; lb/in²)
Pounds-force per square inch (psi; lbf/in²; lb/in²)	X	0.068	= Atmospheres (atm)	X	14.696	= Pounds-force per square inch (psi; lbf/in²; lb/in²)
Pounds-force per square inch (psi; lbf/in²; lb/in²)	X	0.069	= Bars	X	14.5	= Pounds-force per square inch (psi; lbf/in²; lb/in²)
Pounds-force per square inch (psi; lbf/in²; lb/in²)	X	6.895	= Kilopascals (kPa)	X	0.145	= Pounds-force per square inch (psi; lbf/in²; lb/in²)
Kilopascals (kPa)	X	0.01	= Kilograms-force per square centimetre (kgf/cm²; kg/cm²)	X	98.1	= Kilopascals (kPa)
Millibar (mbar)	X	100	= Pascals (Pa)	X	0.01	= Millibar (mbar)
Millibar (mbar)	X	0.0145	= Pounds-force per square inch (psi; lbf/in²; lb/in²)	X	68.947	= Millibar (mbar)
Millibar (mbar)	X	0.75	= Millimetres of mercury (mmHg)	X	1.333	= Millibar (mbar)
Millibar (mbar)	X	0.401	= Inches of water (inH₂O)	X	2.491	= Millibar (mbar)
Millimetres of mercury (mmHg)	X	0.535	= Inches of water (inH₂O)	X	1.868	= Millimetres of mercury (mmHg)
Inches of water (inH₂O)	X	0.036	= Pounds-force per square inch (psi; lbf/in²; lb/in²)	X	27.68	= Inches of water (inH₂O)

Torque (moment of force)
Pounds-force inches (lbf in; lb in)	X	1.152	= Kilograms-force centimetre (kgf cm; kg cm)	X	0.868	= Pounds-force inches (lbf in; lb in)
Pounds-force inches (lbf in; lb in)	X	0.113	= Newton metres (Nm)	X	8.85	= Pounds-force inches (lbf in; lb in)
Pounds-force inches (lbf in; lb in)	X	0.083	= Pounds-force feet (lbf ft; lb ft)	X	12	= Pounds-force inches (lbf in; lb in)
Pounds-force feet (lbf ft; lb ft)	X	0.138	= Kilograms-force metres (kgf m; kg m)	X	7.233	= Pounds-force feet (lbf ft; lb ft)
Pounds-force feet (lbf ft; lb ft)	X	1.356	= Newton metres (Nm)	X	0.738	= Pounds-force feet (lbf ft; lb ft)
Newton metres (Nm)	X	0.102	= Kilograms-force metres (kgf m; kg m)	X	9.804	= Newton metres (Nm)

Power
Horsepower (hp)	X	745.7	= Watts (W)	X	0.0013	= Horsepower (hp)

Velocity (speed)
Miles per hour (miles/hr; mph)	X	1.609	= Kilometres per hour (km/hr; kph)	X	0.621	= Miles per hour (miles/hr; mph)

Fuel consumption*
Miles per gallon, Imperial (mpg)	X	0.354	= Kilometres per litre (km/l)	X	2.825	= Miles per gallon, Imperial (mpg)
Miles per gallon, US (mpg)	X	0.425	= Kilometres per litre (km/l)	X	2.352	= Miles per gallon, US (mpg)

Temperature
Degrees Fahrenheit = (°C x 1.8) + 32   Degrees Celsius (Degrees Centigrade; °C) = (°F - 32) x 0.56

*It is common practice to convert from miles per gallon (mpg) to litres/100 kilometres (l/100km),
where mpg (Imperial) x l/100 km = 282 and mpg (US) x l/100 km = 235

English/American terminology

Because this book has been written in England, British English component names, phrases and spellings have been used throughout. American English usage is quite often different and whereas normally no confusion should occur, a list of equivalent terminology is given below.

English	American	English	American
Air filter	Air cleaner	Number plate	License plate
Alignment (headlamp)	Aim	Output or layshaft	Countershaft
Allen screw/key	Socket screw/wrench	Panniers	Side cases
Anticlockwise	Counterclockwise	Paraffin	Kerosene
Bottom/top gear	Low/high gear	Petrol	Gasoline
Bottom/top yoke	Bottom/top triple clamp	Petrol/fuel tank	Gas tank
Bush	Bushing	Pinking	Pinging
Carburettor	Carburetor	Rear suspension unit	Rear shock absorber
Catch	Latch	Rocker cover	Valve cover
Circlip	Snap ring	Selector	Shifter
Clutch drum	Clutch housing	Self-locking pliers	Vise-grips
Dip switch	Dimmer switch	Side or parking lamp	Parking or auxiliary light
Disulphide	Disulfide	Side or prop stand	Kick stand
Dynamo	DC generator	Silencer	Muffler
Earth	Ground	Spanner	Wrench
End float	End play	Split pin	Cotter pin
Engineer's blue	Machinist's dye	Stanchion	Tube
Exhaust pipe	Header	Sulphuric	Sulfuric
Fault diagnosis	Trouble shooting	Sump	Oil pan
Float chamber	Float bowl	Swinging arm	Swingarm
Footrest	Footpeg	Tab washer	Lock washer
Fuel/petrol tap	Petcock	Top box	Trunk
Gaiter	Boot	Torch	Flashlight
Gearbox	Transmission	Two/four stroke	Two/four cycle
Gearchange	Shift	Tyre	Tire
Gudgeon pin	Wrist/piston pin	Valve collar	Valve retainer
Indicator	Turn signal	Valve collets	Valve cotters
Inlet	Intake	Vice	Vise
Input shaft or mainshaft	Mainshaft	Wheel spindle	Axle
Kickstart	Kickstarter	White spirit	Stoddard solvent
Lower leg	Slider	Windscreen	Windshield
Mudguard	Fender		

Index